"Russ Harris is an open, centered, and engaged teacher of acceptance and commitment therapy (ACT), and, in *ACT Made Simple*, he succeeds in delivering a transparent account of a complex and powerful treatment. I recommend this book to mental health and medical providers and to their teachers."

—Patricia J. Robinson, Ph.D., coauthor of *Behavioral Consultation and Primary Care* and *The Mindfulness and Acceptance Workbook for Depression*

"*ACT Made Simple* is simply the most accessible book written to date for therapists interested in learning ACT. Russ Harris explains ACT concepts in a style that is both engaging and straightforward. His advice on overcoming therapy roadblocks is invaluable and will be useful to both novice and experienced ACT practitioners."

—Jason B. Luoma, Ph.D., psychologist at Portland Psychotherapy Clinic, Research, and Training Center

"Perhaps the most elegant, easily digestible book on using the principles of mindfulness and acceptance to improve your own life and the lives of others. Inside are a litany of creative exercises and strategies that are ready for immediate use. But none of the benefits would be possible without the supportive, entertaining voice of Russ Harris. There is something new to be learned with each reading."

—Todd B. Kashdan, Ph.D., professor of psychology at George Mason University and author of *Curious? Discover the Missing Ingredient to a Fulfilling Life*

"ACT aims to increase psychological flexibility. Learn from this book and you'll be *doing* ACT rather than just talking about doing ACT. And you'll be doing it with greater flexibility."

—Hank Robb, Ph.D., ABPP

"Let's face it: psychological concerns are complex. If modern behavior therapy is to rise to the occasion of reducing human suffering, it will require a similarly intricate and comprehensive approach. ACT attempts to provide a multifaceted treatment model to address these complexities, and *ACT Made Simple* has risen to the occasion by reducing the difficulties in understanding the unique ACT approach. Harris's expressive style is matchless. Comprehensive scientific and clinical literature rarely reads this well. This is a clear, understandable introduction to a powerful intervention approach. Many practitioners who are new to ACT will want to start with *ACT Made Simple*."

—Daniel J. Moran, Ph.D., BCBA, coauthor of *ACT in Practice*

"This much-needed book is a must for mental health clinicians interested in learning ACT. True to his physician roots, Harris has taken a very practical approach to understanding ACT. He does a wonderful job of taking complicated ACT concepts and making them easy to understand. His writing is full of wit, self-disclosure, and down-to-earth communication. Readers of this book will finish it with a much better understanding of core ACT principles and interventions."

—Kirk D. Strosahl, Ph.D., coauthor of *The Mindfulness and Acceptance Workbook for Depression*

"For newcomers to ACT, there is no better place to start than with this book. Russ Harris masterfully makes ACT come alive with an accessible writing style and illustrative examples of its application in alleviating a wide range of types of human suffering. Practical tips and homework assignments throughout will actively engage you to go beyond merely reading about ACT and begin to apply it to your own life and in your work with clients. For those who may have been holding out for *ACT for Dummies*, the wait is over. This book is for you!"

—Robert Zettle, Ph.D., professor of psychology at Wichita State University and author of *ACT for Depression*

"For those of you who train or supervise nurses, physicians, social workers, or other professionals unfamiliar with psychological lingo, *ACT Made Simple* is a must. Russ Harris has succeeded in the challenge of translating difficult psychological concepts embedded in ACT into plain, colorful, diverse language that anyone working clinically will understand. Each section is simply organized, easy to follow, and user-friendly. Harris has included highly useful sections of practical tips and common pitfalls that even the trained ACT therapist will find useful. I highly recommend *ACT Made Simple* as a primer for ACT training."

—JoAnne Dahl, Ph.D., author of *The Art and Science of Valuing in Psychotherapy*

"*ACT Made Simple* is just that. Dr. Harris has, once again, written a very accessible book that should be read by all clinicians wanting to learn, engage or otherwise implement ACT in their practice. This book is a must for ACT readers. My thanks to Dr. Harris for making ACT so user-friendly and understandable."

—Robyn D. Walser, Ph.D., author of *The Mindful Couple*

ACT
made simple

**An Easy-to-Read Primer
on Acceptance and
Commitment Therapy**

RUSS HARRIS

New Harbinger Publications, Inc.

Distributed in Canada by Raincoast Books

Copyright © 2009 by Russ Harris
New Harbinger Publications, Inc.
5674 Shattuck Avenue
Oakland, CA 94609
www.newharbinger.com

Acquired by Catharine Sutker; Cover design by Amy Shoup;
Edited by Carole Honeychurch; Text design by Tracy Carlson

Library of Congress Cataloging-in-Publication Data

Harris, Russ, 1938-
   ACT made simple : an easy-to-read primer on acceptance and commitment therapy / Russ Harris ; foreword by Steven C. Hayes.
      p. cm.
   Includes bibliographical references and index.
   ISBN-13: 978-1-57224-705-5 (pbk. : alk. paper)
   ISBN-10: 1-57224-705-3 (pbk. : alk. paper) 1. Acceptance and commitment therapy. I. Title.
   RC489.A32H37 2009
   616.89'1425--dc22

                                    2009023487

13 12 11

15 14 13 12 11 10 9 8 7

Dedication

To my brother Genghis: for all your love, support, inspiration, and encouragement over the years; for pushing me when I needed pushing; for anchoring me when I needed stability; for showing me the way when I got lost; and for bringing so much light, love, and laughter into my life.

Foreword

Acceptance and commitment therapy (ACT) is oddly counterintuitive. The mind fights it. Even experienced ACT therapists and successful ACT clients can connect with something in the work, move forward, and then weeks later suddenly find that the vitality is gone from that connection because they have subtly reformulated it mentally into something more "normal" but also much less useful.

ACT is not about training the normal mode of the mind. It is about getting out of your mind and into your life. Minds don't like that agenda.

This very phenomenon partially explains why ACT is a new therapy for most clinicians, even though it was developed almost thirty years ago.

We deliberately spent a long time working out the underlying processes and theory in hopes that these would serve as a guide when we lost our way. We could say, in precise behavioral language, what was meant by "mind." We could research, in precise behavioral experiments, how defusion altered the impact of cognition or how acceptance changed the role of emotion.

This strategy did indeed help keep the work focused, but it greatly delayed thorough presentations of the work. (The first book on ACT was completed only ten years ago, nearly twenty years after ACT began.) It also made early ACT writings very complex. Clients have a hard time shifting from a problem-solving mode into a mindful appreciation mode. The underlying theory explains why and what to do about it—and we were ready with these detailed geek-science explanations even if at times they were virtually unreadable to those not versed in behavior analysis.

Fortunately, the heart of the work shone through for some at least. Creative clinicians and authors, including the author of this beautiful new book, began to find simpler and clearer ways to help others connect with the work. The advent of ACT self-help books accelerated that process even further as authors learned how to write in ways that people can understand.

Now the ACT literature is vast, with scores of books and hundreds of articles. Clinicians need a place to begin to explore that territory. My prediction is that they have just found it.

Russ Harris is brilliant in his ability to sniff out needless complexity and present complex clinical ideas in an accessible way. *ACT Made Simple* is ACT. Unquestionably. This book rings with a clear note on every page. Russ has put in the years to understand the work deeply (even the geek science underlying relational frame theory) and learn to apply and extend it with integrity. In this book, he has brought his considerable talents to bear on the clear presentation and formulation of the ACT model, and he has brought his clinical creativity to new methods and new ways of getting to the heart of these issues with clients.

That is a great combination and a significant contribution. Particularly if you are new to the work, this book will do a masterful job of opening up the ACT model for you to explore. It is just as the title says: *ACT Made Simple*.

—Steven C. Hayes, Ph.D.
University of Nevada

Acknowledgments

First, a humongous thank you to my wife, Carmel, for all her love and support; for putting up with my obsessive-compulsive writing disorder; for encouraging me to keep writing during all those dark patches where I thought I was writing nothing but crap; and for being my "sounding board" and actively helping me to develop my ideas.

Thanks also to all those friends and colleagues who read early drafts and gave me invaluable feedback: Julian McNally, Georg Eifert, Hank Robb, and Ros Lethbridge.

As usual, I'd like to dump a zillion truckloads of gratitude on Steve Hayes, the originator of ACT—and that gratitude also extends to Kelly Wilson, Kirk Strosahl, Robyn Walser, and Hank Robb, all huge sources of inspiration for me. I also am very thankful to the entire ACT community, which is very supportive and inspirational; many ideas within these pages have arisen from discussions on the worldwide ACT Listserv.

Next I'd like to thank my agent, Sammie Justesen, for all her good work; and a heap of thanks to the entire team at New Harbinger—including Jess Beebe, Catherine Sutker, and Matt McKay—for all the hard work, care, and attention they have invested in this book.

Editors are the unsung heroes of successful books, and so I'd like to sing my thanks to the heroic efforts of my editor, Jean Blomquist, who truly had her work cut out for her in knocking this book into shape.

And finally I want to thank my son, Max. While he is far too young to help me with the book directly, he has helped enormously in a more indirect manner, simply by being in my life and filling it with so much love.

What's It All About?

Life is spelt H.A.S.S.L.E.—Albert Ellis

Life is difficult.—M. Scott Peck

Life is suffering.—Buddha

Shit happens!—Anonymous

WHY, WHY, WHY?

Why is it so hard to be happy? Why is life so difficult? Why do humans suffer so much? And what can we realistically do about it? Acceptance and commitment therapy (ACT) has some profound and life-changing answers to these questions. This book aims to take the complex theory and practice of ACT and make it accessible and enjoyable. If, like me, you've got a bookcase full of mostly unfinished academic textbooks, you'll appreciate the fact that ACT is engaging and playful. I've deliberately kept technical jargon to an absolute minimum and opted for everyday language wherever possible. I hope to make ACT accessible to the broadest possible range of professionals—from coaches, counselors, and mental health nurses, to social workers, psychologists, psychiatrists, and all health professionals.

SO WHAT IS ACT?

We officially say ACT as the word "act" and not as the initials A-C-T. There's a good reason for this. At its core, ACT is a behavioral therapy: it's about taking action. But it's not about just any old action. First, it's about values-guided action. There's a big existential component to this model: What do you want to stand for in life? What really matters, deep in your heart? What do you want to be remembered for at your funeral? ACT gets you in touch with what really matters in the big picture: your heart's deepest desires for whom you want to be and what you want to do during your brief time on this planet. You then use these core values to guide, motivate, and inspire behavioral change. Second, it's about "mindful" action: action that you take consciously, with full awareness—open to your experience and fully engaged in whatever you're doing.

ACT gets its name from one of its core messages: accept what is out of your personal control, and commit to taking action that enriches your life. The aim of ACT is to help us create a rich, full, and meaningful life, while accepting the pain that life inevitably brings. ACT does this by

- teaching us psychological skills to handle painful thoughts and feelings effectively, in such a way that they have much less impact and influence—these are known as *mindfulness skills*; and

- helping us to clarify what's truly important and meaningful to us—that is, clarify our values—and use that knowledge to guide, inspire, and motivate us to set goals and take action that enriches our life.

ACT rests on an underlying theory of human language and cognition called relational frame theory (RFT), a theory that now has over one hundred and fifty published peer-reviewed articles supporting its principles. We won't cover RFT in this book because it's quite technical and takes a fair bit of work to understand, whereas the aim of this book is to welcome you into ACT, simplify the main concepts, and get you off to a quick start.

The good news is you can be an effective ACT therapist without knowing anything about RFT. If ACT is like driving your car, RFT is like knowing how the engine works: you can be an excellent driver while knowing absolutely nothing about the mechanics. (Having said that, many ACT therapists say that when they understand RFT, it improves their clinical effectiveness. Therefore, if you're interested, appendix 2 will tell you where to go for more information.)

WHO IS THIS BOOK FOR?

I've aimed this book primarily at newcomers to ACT who want a quick and simple introduction to the model. It will also be useful for more experienced practitioners who want a quick refresher course: an ACT primer, if you like. I've designed it to complement other ACT textbooks that offer more theory or more in-depth discussions of the ACT processes and their clinical applications. I'll mention some of these textbooks as we go along and others in the resources section (appendix 2) at the end.

HOW TO USE THIS BOOK

If you're brand-new to ACT, I strongly recommend you read this entire book from cover to cover *before* you start using any of it. This is because the six core processes of ACT are all interdependent, so unless you have a good sense of the entire model and the way these different strands interweave, you may well get confused and head off in the wrong direction.

And, of course, reading it is not enough; you'll also need to actively practice the exercises as you go. After all, you can't learn to drive merely by reading about it; you have to actually get in a car, put your hands on the wheel, and take it for a spin. When you're ready to start using ACT with your clients, you can either use this book to loosely guide you, or you might prefer to use a protocol-based ACT textbook that will coach you along in detail, session-by-session.

First off, in chapters 1 through 3, we're going to zip through an overview of the model and the theory underlying it. Then in chapters 4 and 5, we'll cover the basics of getting started, including how to do experiential therapy, obtain informed consent, and structure your ongoing sessions. In chapters 6 through 12, we'll go step-by-step through the six core processes of ACT and how to apply them to a wide range of clinical issues. The emphasis in each chapter will be on simplicity and practicality so you can start using this approach straight away. (But please keep in mind: newcomers should first read the whole book, cover to cover, before applying it.)

In the last section of the book, chapters 13 through 15, we'll cover a wide range of important topics including common therapist pitfalls, overcoming barriers to change, enhancing the client-therapist relationship, dancing around the six core processes, embodying ACT in everyday life, mixing and matching ACT with other models, and where to go next on your journey as an ACT therapist.

From chapter 5 onward, you'll find these "practical tip" text boxes popping up:

Practical Tip In these sections, you'll find practical tips to help your clinical practice and common pitfalls to watch out for.

YOUR ROLE IN ALL THIS

I heard a great saying recently: "Be yourself: everyone else is already taken." Your role in learning and practicing ACT is to be yourself. I wasted a lot of time and effort in my early ACT work trying to do ACT word-for-word as written in the textbooks. And then, after I saw Steve Hayes and Kelly

Wilson—two of the founders of ACT—in action, I tried very hard to copy their unique styles of doing therapy. This didn't work very well for me. It all went much better when I allowed myself to be me and developed my own style and my own way of speaking, a manner that felt natural and also suited the clients I work with. I'm sure you'll find the same.

So as you go through this book, use your creativity. Feel free to adapt, modify, and reinvent the tools and techniques within these pages (provided you're remaining true to the ACT model) to suit your own personal style. Wherever I present metaphors, scripts, worksheets, or exercises, change the words to fit your way of speaking. And if you have better or different metaphors that accomplish the same ends, then please use yours rather than the ones in this book. There's enormous room for creativity and innovation within the ACT model, so please do take every advantage of it.

GETTING STARTED

Few people come to ACT and dive in head first. You, like most, may start off by dipping a toe in the water. Next, you put a whole foot in. Then a knee. Then an entire leg. Now you find yourself in this odd position, with one leg in the water and one leg out. And generally you stay there for quite a while, half in, half out, not quite sure if ACT is for you. Finally, one day, you take the plunge. And when you do so, you discover the water is warm, welcoming, and invigorating; you feel liberated, buoyant, and resourceful; and you want to spend a lot more time in it. Once this happens, there's generally no going back to your old way of working. (So if this hasn't already happened to you, I hope it will by the end of this book.)

One reason for this initial uncertainty about ACT is that it challenges conventional wisdom and overturns the ground rules of most Western psychology. For example, most models of therapy are extremely focused on symptom reduction. Their assumption is that clients need to reduce their symptoms before they can lead a better life. ACT takes a radically different stance. ACT assumes that (a) quality of life is primarily dependent upon mindful, values-guided action, and (b) this is possible regardless of how many symptoms you have—provided that you respond to your symptoms with mindfulness.

To put it another way, mindful, values-congruent living is the desired outcome in ACT, not symptom reduction. So although ACT typically reduces symptoms, this is never the goal. (By the way, as "values-congruent living" is a bit of a mouthful, for the most of the book I'll shorten it to "valued living." Sorry, I know it's not great English.)

Thus in ACT, when we teach a client mindfulness skills, the aim is *not* to reduce his symptoms but to fundamentally *change his relationship with his symptoms* so that they no longer hold him back from valued living. The fact that his symptoms reduce is considered a "bonus" rather than the main point of therapy.

Of course, we don't say to our clients, "We're not going to try to reduce your symptoms!" Why not? Because (a) this would set up all sorts of unnecessary therapeutic barriers, and (b) we know that symptom reduction is extremely likely. (Even though we never aim for it, in almost every trial and study ever done on ACT, there is significant symptom reduction—although sometimes it occurs more slowly than in other models.)

So what this means is, if you come to ACT from models that are very focused on trying to reduce symptoms, it's truly a massive paradigm shift. Fortunately most people—therapists and clients alike—find it a liberating one. However, because ACT is so different from most other psychological approaches, many practitioners initially feel awkward, anxious, vulnerable, confused, or inadequate. I certainly did. (And I still do at times!) The good news is ACT gives you the means to effectively handle those perfectly natural feelings. And the more you practice ACT on yourself to enrich and enhance your own life and to resolve your own painful issues, the more effective you'll be in applying it with your clients. (How's that for a bonus?) So, enough of the preamble: let's get started!

CHAPTER 1

ACT in a Nutshell

WHAT IS A "MIND"?

This is too hard. I can't do this. Why isn't this working? It all seemed so easy when I read it in the textbook. I wish there was a real therapist here to tell me what to do. Maybe I'm not cut out for this sort of work. I'm so dumb. Maybe I should refer this client to someone else who knows what they're doing.

Does your mind ever say things like this to you? Mine certainly does. And so does the mind of every therapist I've ever known. Now take a moment to reflect on what else your mind does that's unhelpful. For example, does it ever compare you harshly to others, or criticize your efforts, or tell you that you can't do the things you want to do? Does it ever dredge up unpleasant memories from the past? Does it find fault with your life as it is today and conjure up alternative lives where you'd be ever so much happier? Does it ever drag you into scary scenarios about the future and warn you about all the possible things that might go wrong? If so, it sounds as if you have a normal human mind. You see, in ACT, we start from the assumption that the normal psychological processes of a normal human mind readily become destructive, and sooner or later, they create psychological suffering for all of us. And ACT speculates that the root of this suffering is human language itself.

Language and the Mind

Human language is a highly complex system of symbols that includes words, images, sounds, facial expressions, and physical gestures. Humans use language in two domains: public and private. The public use of language includes speaking, talking, miming, gesturing, writing, painting, sculpting, singing, dancing, acting, and so on. The private use of language includes thinking, imagining, daydreaming, planning, visualizing, analyzing, worrying, fantasizing, and so on. (A commonly used term for the private use of language is *cognition*.)

Now clearly the mind is not a "thing" or an "object." We use the word "mind" to describe incredibly complex set of interactive cognitive processes, such as analyzing, comparing, evaluating, planning, remembering, visualizing, and so on. And all of these complex processes rely on the sophisticated system of symbols we call human language. Thus in ACT, when we use the word "mind," we're using it as a metaphor for "human language."

Your Mind Is Not Your Friend—or Your Enemy

ACT regards the mind as a double-edged sword. It's very useful for all sorts of purposes, but if we don't learn how to handle it effectively, it will hurt us. On the bright side, language helps us make maps and models of the world; predict and plan for the future; share knowledge; learn from the past; imagine things that have never existed and go on to create them; develop rules that guide our behavior effectively and help us to thrive as a community; communicate with people who are far away; and learn from people who are no longer alive.

The dark side of language is that we use it to lie, manipulate, and deceive; to spread libel, slander, and ignorance; to incite hatred, prejudice, and violence; to make weapons of mass destruction and industries of mass pollution; to dwell on and "relive" painful events from the past; to scare ourselves by imagining unpleasant futures; to compare, judge, criticize, and condemn both ourselves and others; and to create rules for ourselves that can often be life constricting or destructive. Because language is both a blessing and a curse, we often say in ACT, "Your mind is not your friend—and it's not your enemy either." So now that we know what a "mind" is, let's turn to a very important question.

WHAT IS THE AIM OF ACT?

The aim of ACT, in lay terms, is to create a rich, full, and meaningful life while accepting the pain that inevitably goes with it. Later this chapter, we'll look at a more technical definition of ACT, but first take a moment to consider this question: why does life inevitably involve pain?

Clearly there are many, many reasons. We'll all experience frustration, disappointment, rejection, loss, and failure. We'll all experience illness, injury, and aging. We'll all face our own death and the death of our loved ones. On top of that, many basic human emotions—normal feelings that each and every one of us will repeatedly experience throughout our lives—are inherently painful: fear, sadness, guilt, anger, shock, and disgust, to name but a few.

And as if all that were not enough, we each have a mind that can conjure up pain at any moment. Thanks to human language, wherever we go, whatever we do, we can experience pain instantly. In any moment, we can relive a painful memory or get lost in a fearful prediction of the future. Or we can get caught up in unfavorable comparisons ("Her job is better than mine") or negative self-judgments ("I'm too fat," "I'm not smart enough," and so on).

Thanks to human language, we can even experience pain on the happiest days of our lives. For example, suppose it's Susan's wedding day, and all of her friends and family are gathered together to honor her joyful new union. She is blissfully happy. But then she has the thought *I wish my father were here*—and she remembers how he committed suicide when she was only sixteen years old. Now, on one of the happiest days of her life, she's in pain.

And we're all in the same boat as Susan. No matter how good our quality of life, no matter how privileged our situation, all we need do is remember a time when something bad happened, or imagine a future where something bad happens, or judge ourselves harshly, or compare our life to someone else's that seems better, and instantly we're hurting.

Thus, thanks to the sophistication of the mind, even the most privileged of human lives inevitably involves significant pain. Unfortunately, typical human beings commonly handle their pain ineffectively. All too often when we experience painful thoughts, feelings, and sensations, we respond in ways that are self-defeating or self-destructive in the long run. Because of this, one major element of ACT is teaching people how to handle pain more effectively through the use of mindfulness skills.

WHAT IS MINDFULNESS?

"Mindfulness" is an ancient concept, found in a wide range of ancient spiritual and religious traditions, including Buddhism, Taoism, Hinduism, Judaism, Islam, and Christianity. Western psychology has only recently started to recognize the many benefits of developing mindfulness skills. If you read a few books on the subject, you'll find "mindfulness" defined in a variety of different ways, but they all basically boil down to this:

Mindfulness means paying attention with flexibility, openness, and curiosity.

This simple definition tells us three important things. First, mindfulness is an *awareness* process, not a *thinking* process. It involves bringing awareness or paying attention to your experience in this moment as opposed to being "caught up" in your thoughts. Second, mindfulness involves a particular attitude: one of openness and curiosity. Even if your experience in this moment is difficult, painful, or unpleasant, you can be open to it and curious about it instead of running from it or fighting with it. Third, mindfulness involves flexibility of attention: the ability to consciously direct, broaden, or focus your attention on different aspects of your experience.

We can use mindfulness to "wake up," connect with ourselves, and appreciate the fullness of each moment of life. We can use it to improve our self-knowledge—to learn more about how we feel and think and react. We can use it to connect deeply and intimately with the people we care about, including ourselves. And we can use it to consciously influence our own behavior and increase our range of responses to the world we live in. It is the art of living consciously—a profound way to enhance psychological resilience and increase life satisfaction.

Of course there's a lot more to ACT than just mindfulness. It's also about valued living: taking action, on an ongoing basis, that is guided by and aligned with core values. Indeed, we teach mindfulness skills in ACT with the express purpose of facilitating valued action: to help people live by their values. In other words, the outcome we aim for in ACT is mindful, valued living. This will become clearer in the next section, where we look at the six core processes of ACT.

THE SIX CORE THERAPEUTIC PROCESSES OF ACT

The six core therapeutic processes in ACT are contacting the present moment, defusion, acceptance, self-as-context, values, and committed action. Before we go through them one by one, take a look at the diagram in figure 1.1, which is light-heartedly known as the ACT "hexaflex." (This diagram differs from the standard version you'll find in most ACT textbooks in that underneath each technical term I've written a short catchphrase to help you remember what it means.)

Let's take a look now at each of the six core processes of ACT.

Contacting the Present Moment (*Be Here Now*)

Contacting the present moment means being psychologically present: consciously connecting with and engaging in whatever is happening in this moment. Humans find it very hard to stay present. Like other humans, we know how easy it is to get caught up in our thoughts and lose touch with the world around us. We may spend a lot of time absorbed in thoughts about the past or the future. Or instead of being fully conscious of our experience, we may operate on automatic pilot, merely "going through the motions." Contacting the present moment means flexibly bringing our awareness to either the physical world around us or the psychological world within us, or to both simultaneously. It also means consciously paying attention to our here-and-now experience instead of drifting off into our thoughts or operating on "automatic pilot."

Defusion (*Watch Your Thinking*)

Defusion means learning to "step back" and separate or detach from our thoughts, images, and memories. (The full term is "cognitive defusion," but usually we just call it "defusion.") Instead of getting caught up in our thoughts or being pushed around by them, we let them come and go as if they were just cars driving past outside our house. We step back and watch our thinking instead of getting tangled up in it. We see our thoughts for what they are—nothing more or less than words or pictures. We hold them lightly instead of clutching them tightly.

Acceptance (*Open Up*)

Acceptance means opening up and making room for painful feelings, sensations, urges, and emotions. We drop the struggle with them, give them some breathing space, and allow them to be as

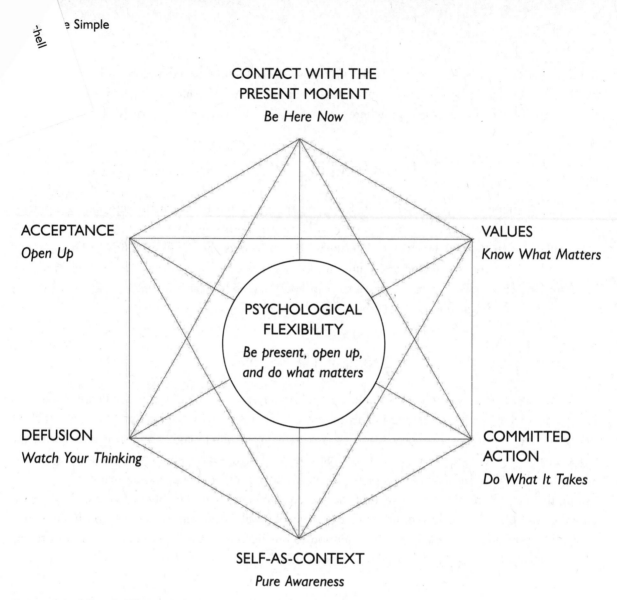

CONTACT WITH THE
PRESENT MOMENT
Be Here Now

ACCEPTANCE
Open Up

VALUES
Know What Matters

PSYCHOLOGICAL
FLEXIBILITY
*Be present, open up,
and do what matters*

DEFUSION
Watch Your Thinking

COMMITTED
ACTION
Do What It Takes

SELF-AS-CONTEXT
Pure Awareness

Figure 1.1 **The ACT Hexaflex**

they are. Instead of fighting them, resisting them, running from them, or getting overwhelmed by them, we open up to them and let them be. (Note: This doesn't mean liking them or wanting them. It simply means making room for them!)

Self-as-Context (*Pure Awareness*)

In everyday language, we talk about the "mind" without recognizing that there are two distinct elements to it: the thinking self and the observing self. We're all very familiar with the thinking self:

that part of us which is always thinking—generating thoughts, beliefs, memories, judgments, fantasies, plans, and so on. But most people are unfamiliar with the observing self: the aspect of us that is aware of whatever we're thinking, feeling, sensing, or doing in any moment. Another term for it is "pure awareness." In ACT, the technical term is *self-as-context*. For example, as you go through life, your body changes, your thoughts change, your feelings change, your roles change, but the "you" that's able to notice or observe all those things never changes. It's the same "you" that's been there your whole life. With clients, we generally refer to it as "the observing self" rather than use the technical term "self-as-context."

Values (*Know What Matters*)

how to accomplish this step.

Deep in your heart, what do you want your life to be about? What do you want to stand for? What you want to do with your brief time on this planet? What truly matters to you in the big picture? *Values* are desired qualities of ongoing action. In other words, they describe how we want to behave on an ongoing basis. Clarifying values is an essential step in creating a meaningful life. In ACT, we often refer to values as "chosen life directions." We commonly compare values to a compass because they give us direction and guide our ongoing journey.

Committed Action (*Do What It Takes*)

Committed action means taking effective action, guided by our values. It's all well and good to know our values, but it's only via ongoing values-congruent action that life becomes rich, full, and meaningful. In other words, we won't have much of a journey if we simply stare at the compass; our journey only happens when we move our arms and legs in our chosen direction. Values-guided action gives rise to a wide range of thoughts and feelings, both pleasant and unpleasant, both pleasurable and painful. So committed action means "doing what it takes" to live by our values even if that brings up pain and discomfort. Any and all traditional behavioral interventions—such as goal setting, exposure, behavioral activation, and skills training—can be used in this part of the model. And any skill that enhances and enriches life—from negotiation to time management, from assertiveness to problem solving, from self-soothing to crisis coping—can be taught under this section of the hexaflex (provided that it's in the service of valued living and *not* in the service of experiential avoidance, which we'll talk about in chapter 2).

Psychological Flexibility: A Six-Faceted Diamond

Keep in mind that the six core processes of ACT aren't separate processes. Although we talk about them that way for pragmatic purposes—to help therapists and clients learn and apply the ACT model—it's more useful to think of them as six facets of one diamond. And the diamond itself is psychological flexibility.

Psychological flexibility is the ability to be in the present moment with full awareness and openness to our experience, and to take action guided by our values. Put more simply, it's the ability to "be present, open up, and do what matters." Technically speaking, the primary aim of ACT is to increase psychological flexibility. The greater our ability to be fully conscious, to be open to our experience, and to act on our values, the greater our quality of life because we can respond far more effectively to the problems and challenges life inevitably brings. Furthermore, through engaging fully in our life and allowing our values to guide us, we develop a sense of meaning and purpose, and we experience a sense of vitality. We use the word "vitality" a lot in ACT, and it's important to recognize that *vitality* is not a feeling; it is a sense of being fully alive and embracing the here and now, regardless of how we may be feeling in this moment. We can even experience vitality on our deathbed or during extreme grief because "There is as much living in a moment of pain as in a moment of joy" (Strosahl, 2004, p. 43).

THE ACT TRIFLEX

The six core processes can be "lumped together" into three functional units, as in figure 1.2 below. Both defusion and acceptance are about separating from thoughts and feelings, seeing them for what they truly are, making room for them, and allowing them to come and go of their own accord. In other words: "Opening up."

Self-as-context (aka the observing self) and contacting the present moment both involve making contact with verbal and nonverbal aspects of your here-and-now experience. In other words: "Being present."

Values and committed action involve the effective use of language to facilitate life-enhancing action. In other words: "Doing what matters."

Thus psychological flexibility is the ability to "be present, open up, and do what matters."

THE ACT ACRONYM

There's a simple acronym that encapsulates the entire model, and it's often useful to share this with clients. The acronym is—surprise, surprise!—ACT:

A = Accept your thoughts and feelings, and be present.

C = Choose a valued direction.

T = Take action.

(And on that note, I should mention that throughout this book, I use the phrase "thoughts and feelings" as a form of shorthand. By "thoughts," I mean all manner of cognitions, including memories and images, and the term "feelings" includes emotions, sensations, and urges.)

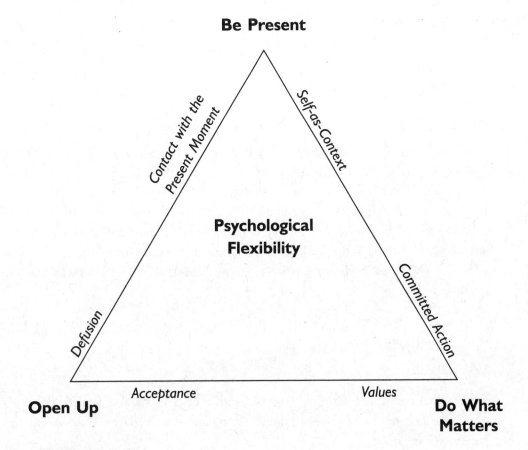

Figure 1.2 **The ACT Triflex**

THE ACT IN A NUTSHELL METAPHOR

The following transcript describes a physical metaphor that I originally put together to quickly summarize the ACT model to clients. (Many ACT textbooks caution against didactically explaining the model to clients: the danger is we can get bogged down in long-winded explanations, or the client will intellectualize the model. However, there are situations in which it's useful to metaphorically—as opposed to didactically—explain the model, and we can adapt the ACT in a Nutshell Metaphor in many ways. Indeed, as you read through the book, you'll notice how we can use and modify pieces of it for multiple purposes, especially work with defusion and acceptance. The transcript that follows takes place toward the end of a first session, as part of informed consent. (To get a better sense of how this exercise is done, you can watch a free You Tube video of the exercise on www.act madesimple.com/free _ resources). There are five sections to it, which I've numbered for future reference.

SECTION 1

Therapist: It's hard to explain what ACT is about simply by describing it, and it probably wouldn't make much sense even if I tried. So would it be okay if I showed you what it's about by using a metaphor?

Client: Sure.

Therapist: Great. (*The therapist picks up a clipboard or a large hardback book and shows it to the client.*) I want you to imagine that this clipboard represents all the difficult thoughts and feelings and memories that you have been struggling with for so long. And I'd like you to take hold of it and grip it as tightly as you can so that I can't pull it away from you. (*Client grips it tightly.*) Now I'd like you to hold it up in front of your face so you can't see me anymore—and bring it up so close to your face that it's almost touching your nose. (*The client holds the clipboard directly in front of her face, blocking her view of both the therapist and the surrounding room.*)

Therapist: Now what's it like trying to have a conversation with me while you're all caught up in your thoughts and feelings?

Client: Very difficult.

Therapist: Do you feel connected with me, engaged with me? Are you able to read the expressions on my face? If I were doing a song-and-dance routine now, would you be able to see it?

Client: (*chuckling*) No.

Therapist: And what's your view of the room like, while you're all caught up in this stuff?

Client: I can't see anything except the clipboard.

Therapist: So while you're completely absorbed in all this stuff, you're missing out on a lot. You're disconnected from the world around you, and you're disconnected from me. Notice, too, that while you're holding on tightly to this stuff, you can't do the things that make your life work. Check it out—grip the clipboard as tightly as you possibly can. (*The client tightens her grip.*) Now if I asked you to cuddle a baby, or hug the person you love, or drive a car, or cook dinner, or type on a computer while you're holding on tightly to this, could you do it?

Client: No.

Therapist: So while you're all caught up in this stuff, not only do you lose contact with the world around you and disconnect from your relationships, but also you become incapable of doing the things that make your life work.

Client: (*nodding*) Okay.

SECTION 2

Therapist:	Is it alright if I just drag my chair across so I'm sitting beside you? There's something else I want to demonstrate here.
Client:	Sure.
Therapist:	(*pulls his chair alongside that of the client*) Could I have the clipboard back for a moment? (*Therapist takes the clipboard back.*) Can I just check—you don't have any neck or shoulder problems do you?
Client:	No.
Therapist:	Okay. I'm just checking because this involves a bit of physical exertion. What I'd like you to do is place both your hands flat on one side of the clipboard here, and I'm going to put my hands on the other side, and I'd like you to push the clipboard away from you. Push firmly, but don't push so hard you knock me over. (*As the client tries to push the clipboard away, the therapist pushes back. The harder the client pushes, the more the therapist leans into it.*) And just keep pushing. You hate this stuff, right? You hate these thoughts and feelings. So push as hard as you can—try to make them go away. (*The therapist maintains the struggle so that the client keeps pushing while the therapist pushes back.*) So here you are, trying very hard to push away all these painful thoughts and feelings. You've been doing this for years, and are they going anywhere? Sure, you're keeping them at arm's length, but what's the cost to you? How does it feel in your shoulders?
Client:	(*chuckling*) Not too bad actually. It's a good workout.
Therapist:	(*pushing harder*) Okay, this is fine for now, we've only been going a few seconds, but how will you be feeling after a whole day of this?
Client:	I'd be pretty tired.
Therapist:	(*still pushing the clipboard back and forth with the client*) And if I asked you now to type on a computer, or drive a car, or cuddle a baby, or hug somebody you love while you're doing this, could you do it?
Client:	No.
Therapist:	And what's it like trying to have a conversation with me while you're doing this?
Client:	Very distracting.
Therapist:	Do you feel a bit closed in or cut off?
Client:	Yes.

SECTION 3

The therapist now stops resisting. He eases off the pressure, and takes the clipboard back.

Therapist: Okay, now let's try something else. Is it okay if I just place the clipboard on your lap, and we just let it sit there? (*Client nods. The therapist places the clipboard on the client's lap.*) Now isn't that a lot less effort? How are your shoulders now?

Client: A lot better.

Therapist drags his chair back across the room.

Therapist: Notice that you are now free to invest your energy in doing something constructive. If I asked you now to cook a meal, or play the piano, or cuddle a baby, or hug somebody you love—now you could do it, right?

Client: (*chuckling*) Yes.

Therapist: And what's it like to have a conversation with me now as opposed to doing this (*mimes pushing the clipboard away*) or this (*mimes holding the clipboard up in front of his face*)?

Client: Easier.

Therapist: Do you feel more engaged with me? Can you read my face now?

Client: Yes.

Therapist: Notice, too, you now have a clear view of the room around you. You can take it all in. If I started doing a song-and-dance routine, you'd be able to see it.

Client: (*smiles*) Yes. (*She gestures down at the clipboard.*) But it's still here. I don't want it.

SECTION 4

Therapist: Absolutely. It's still there. And of course you don't want it; who would all these painful thoughts and feelings? But notice, now this stuff is having much less impact on you. Now I'm sure in the ideal world you'd like to do this. (*Therapist mimes throwing the clipboard on the floor.*) But here's the thing: you've been trying to do that for years. Let's do a brief recap. You've tried drugs, alcohol, self-help books, therapy, withdrawing from the world, lying in bed, avoiding challenging situations, beating yourself up, blaming your parents, distracting yourself, rehashing the past, trying to figure out why you're like this, being busy, doing self-development courses, and lots of other things too, I'm willing to bet. So no one can call you lazy! You've clearly put a lot of time, effort, and money into trying to get rid of these thoughts and feelings. And yet, despite all that effort, they're still showing up. They're still here today. (*The therapist points to the clipboard in the client's lap.*) Some of these things you do make this stuff go away for a short while, but it soon comes back again, doesn't it? And isn't it the case that this is now bigger and heavier than it was all those years ago when you first started struggling with this stuff? There are more painful feelings, thoughts, and memories here than there were five years ago, right?

Client: Yes.

Therapist: So even though this is what every instinct in your body tells you to do (*mimes throwing the clipboard onto the floor*), that strategy clearly isn't having the effects you want. It's really just making things worse. So we don't want to do more of what doesn't work, right?

Client: I guess not.

SECTION 5

Therapist: So here's what ACT is all about. We're going to learn some skills called mindfulness skills that will enable you to handle painful thoughts and feelings far more effectively—in such a way that they have much less impact and influence over you. So instead of doing this (*picks up clipboard and holds it in front of his face*) or this (*mimes pushing clipboard away*), you can do this (*drops the clipboard into his lap and lets go of it.*) And notice, this not only allows you to be connected with the world around you and to engage in what you're doing, but it also frees you up to take effective action. When you're no longer struggling with this stuff, or absorbed in it, or holding on to it, you are free. (*The therapist holds his arms up in a gesture of freedom.*) So now you can put your energy into doing the things that improve your quality of life—like hugging people you love or riding your bike or playing the guitar. (*The therapist mimes these activities.*) How does that sound to you?

Client: (*smiling*) Okay.

Obviously it doesn't always go that smoothly—when does therapy *ever* go as smoothly as in the textbooks?—but hopefully this metaphor gives you a sense of what ACT is all about: creating a rich and meaningful life while accepting the pain that goes with it. It also demonstrates that we teach mindfulness skills not as some spiritual pathway to enlightenment but in order to facilitate effective action. (Unfortunately, we don't have the space here to describe some of the ways clients may occasionally object to this metaphor, and how we can respond effectively to those objections. However you can download a description of these objections and responses at: www.actmadesimple .com/nutshell _ metaphor _ objections _ and _ responses)

Dissecting the Metaphor

ACT speculates that there are two core psychological processes—"cognitive fusion" and "experiential avoidance"—that are responsible for most psychological suffering. Section 1 of the transcript is a metaphor for *cognitive fusion*: getting caught up or entangled in our thoughts, or holding on to them tightly. Section 2 is a metaphor for *experiential avoidance*: the ongoing struggle to avoid, suppress, or get rid of unwanted thoughts, feelings, memories, and other "private experiences." (A *private experience* means any experience you have that no one else can know about unless you tell them: emotions, sensations, memories, thoughts, and so on.) N.B. You don't want to turn this exercise into a strength test or a pushing competition. If you suspect your client may push aggressively against the clipboard, then preempt him. Say, "When I ask you to push, please don't push too hard. Don't try to push me over, just push gently!" Also, modify your own counterpressure; after a few seconds you could ease off and just leave the clipboard resting gently in midair, gently sandwiched in between your hands and the client's hands.

Section 3 is a metaphor for acceptance, defusion, and contacting the present moment. Instead of the term "acceptance," we often talk about "dropping the struggle," "sitting with the feeling," "letting it be," "making room for it," or "willingness to have it." You can see how these terms nicely fit the physical metaphor of letting the clipboard sit on the client's lap. Instead of the term "defusion," we often talk about "letting go" or "stepping back" or "distancing," "separating," "disentangling," or "dropping the story"—and again, as the client separates from the clipboard and lets go of it, the metaphor ties in well with such ways of talking.

Section 4 highlights the ineffectiveness and the costs of experiential avoidance; in ACT, this process is referred to as *creative hopelessness* or *confronting the agenda*. Why such odd names? Because we're trying to create a sense of hopelessness in the client's agenda of controlling her thoughts and feelings. This paves the way for the alternate agenda of mindfulness and acceptance, which is the very opposite of control.

Finally, section 5 highlights the link between mindfulness, values, and committed action. Presenting the entire ACT in a Nutshell Metaphor as an exercise generally takes no more than about five minutes.

What's Next?

In the next chapter, we'll look at cognitive fusion and experiential avoidance in more detail and see how they readily lead to six core pathological processes that are the "flip sides" of the six core therapeutic processes. But before reading on, why not try the ACT in a Nutshell Exercise on a friend or colleague to see if you can summarize what ACT is about? First, I recommend that you act it out loud a couple of times: run through each step with an imaginary client, as if you're an actor rehearsing for a play. Then give it a go for real.

I suspect you may be somewhat reluctant to do this; you may be thinking it's silly, or unimportant, or just not your style. However, even if you never do this with a real client, running through the metaphor in this way will be a valuable learning experience. Not only will it help you to grasp the model, it'll also help you enormously if you ever want to explain it to curious friends, colleagues, relatives, or guests at your next dinner party. So even though you're probably feeling reluctant, why not give it a go? You may be pleasantly surprised at the results.

CHAPTER 2

Stuck, Not Broken

WHERE THERE'S PAIN, THERE'S LIFE

The ACT model is inherently optimistic. ACT assumes that even in the midst of tremendous pain and suffering, there's an opportunity to find meaning, purpose, and vitality. We can find awe-inspiring examples of this in books such as *Man's Search for Meaning* by Victor Frankl (1959), which chronicles Frankl's experiences as an inmate in the Auschwitz concentration camp, or *Long Walk to Freedom*, the autobiography of Nelson Mandela. In ACT, we're not aiming to merely reduce human suffering; we're also aiming to help people learn and grow as a result of their suffering, and to use their pain as a springboard into creating rich and meaningful lives. This optimistic attitude is evident in the ACT saying: "Our clients are not broken, they are just stuck." And what is it that gets ordinary people so stuck that they end up depressed, addicted, isolated, phobic, or suicidal? Two *normal* processes of the *normal* human mind: cognitive fusion and experiential avoidance.

COGNITIVE FUSION

Why the term "fusion"? Well, think of two sheets of metal fused together. If you couldn't use the term "fused," how would you describe them? Welded? Melded? Bonded? Joined? Attached? Stuck? All these terms point to the same idea: no separation. In a state of cognitive fusion, we're inseparable from our thoughts: we're welded to them, bonded to them, so caught up in them that we aren't even aware that we are thinking. Thus *defusion* means separating, detaching, or distancing from our thoughts: taking a step back and seeing them for what they are: nothing more or less than words and pictures.

Cognitive fusion basically means that our thoughts dominate our behavior. Thus in ACT, we may talk with clients of being "pushed around by your thoughts" or "allowing thoughts to tell you what to do," or we may talk of thoughts as bullies, or we may compare the mind to a fascist dictator, or we may ask, "What happens when you let that thought run your life?" Similarly, when our thoughts dominate our attention, we often talk about being "hooked," "entangled," "caught up," or "carried off" by them. (A quick reminder: when we use the terms "thinking," "thoughts," "cognition," and "mind" in ACT, we use them all as metaphors for "human language," which includes beliefs, assumptions, thoughts, attitudes, memories, images, words, gestures, fantasies, and some aspects of emotions.)

Human beings dwell in two different worlds. At birth, we dwell only in the "world of direct experience," the world as we know it directly through the five senses: the world that we can see, hear, touch, taste, and smell. But as we grow older, we learn to think, and as that ability grows, we start to spend more and more time in a second world, the "world of language." Fusion means we're stuck in the world of language: we're so caught up in all those words and pictures running through our head that we lose contact with the world of direct experience. Mindfulness is like a shuttle between these two worlds: it transports us from the world of language into the world of direct experience.

Hands As Thoughts Metaphor

Imagine for a moment that your hands are your thoughts. When you reach the end of this paragraph, I'd like you to put this book down and hold your hands together, palms open, as if they're the pages of an open book. Then I'd like you to slowly and steadily raise your hands up toward your face. Keep going until they're covering your eyes. Then take a few seconds to look at the world around you through the gaps in between your fingers and notice how this affects your view of the world. Please do this exercise now, before reading on.

* * *

So what would it be like going around all day with your hands covering your eyes in this manner? How much would it limit you? How much would you miss out on? How would it reduce your ability to respond to the world around you? This is like fusion: we become so caught up in our thoughts that we lose contact with many aspects of our here-and-now experience, and our thoughts have such a huge influence over our behavior that our ability to act effectively is significantly reduced.

Now once again, when you reach the end of this paragraph, I'd like you to cover your eyes with your hands, but this time, lower them from your face very, very slowly. As the distance between your hands and your face increases, notice how much easier it is to connect with the world around you. Please do this now before reading on.

* * *

What you just did is like defusion. How much easier is it to take effective action without your hands covering your eyes? How much more information can you take in? How much more connected are you with the world around you?

This metaphor (Harris, 2009), which you can use with clients to explain fusion and defusion, demonstrates the purposes of defusion: to engage fully in our experience and facilitate effective action. People often feel better when they defuse from painful thoughts and memories, but in ACT we consider this a bonus or by-product; it's not the intention or goal. (Remember, we're not trying to reduce or eliminate our symptoms. We're trying to fundamentally transform our relationship with painful thoughts and feelings so we no longer perceive them as "symptoms.") Thus defusion is not some clever tool to control feelings: it's a means to become present and take effective action. We need to make this clear to our clients, because if they start using defusion techniques to try and control their feelings, they'll soon be disappointed.

We facilitate defusion through experiential exercises. If we try to explain it conceptually before doing it experientially, we'll probably get bogged down in all sorts of time-wasting intellectual discussions. However, after we've taken clients experientially through defusion, we may then like to explain it didactically, as below.

Simple Summary of Fusion vs. Defusion

In a state of fusion, a thought can seem like

- the absolute truth;

- a command you have to obey or a rule you have to follow;

- a threat you need to get rid of as soon as possible;

- something that's happening right here and now even though it's about the past or the future;

- something very important that requires all your attention;

- something you won't let go of even if it worsens your life.

In a state of defusion, you can see a thought for what it is: nothing more or less than a bunch of words or pictures "inside your head." In a state of defusion, you recognize that a thought

- may or may not be true;

- is definitely not a command you have to obey or a rule you have to follow;

- is definitely not a threat to you;

- is not something happening in the physical world—it's merely words or pictures inside your head;

- may or may not be important—you have a choice as to how much attention you pay it;

- can be allowed to come and go of its own accord without any need for you to hold on to it or push it away.

Workability

The whole ACT model rests on a key concept: "workability." Please engrave that word—*workability*—into your cerebral cortex, because it's at the very heart of every intervention we do. To determine workability, we ask this question: "Is what you're doing working to make your life rich, full, and meaningful?" If the answer is yes, then we say it's "workable," so there's no need to change it. And if the answer is no, then we say it's "unworkable," in which case we can consider alternatives that work better.

Thus in ACT we don't focus on whether a thought is true or false, but whether it is workable. In other words, we want to know if a thought helps a client move toward a richer, fuller, and more meaningful life. To determine this, we may ask questions like these: "If you let this thought guide your behavior, will that help you create a richer, fuller, and more meaningful life? If you hold on to this thought tightly, does it help you to be the person you want to be and do the things you want to do?"

Here's a transcript that exemplifies this approach:

Client: But it's true. I really am fat. Look at me. (*She grabs hold of two large rolls of fat from around her abdomen and squeezes them to emphasize the point.*)

Therapist: One thing I can guarantee you: in this room, we're never going to have a debate about what's true and what's false. What we're interested in here is what's helpful or what's useful or what helps you to live a better life. So when your mind starts telling you "I'm fat," what happens when you get all caught up in those thoughts?

Client: I feel disgusted with myself.

Therapist: And then what?

Client: Then I get depressed.

Therapist: And if I were watching a video of you, what would I see you doing when you're feeling depressed and disgusted with yourself?

Client: I'd probably be sitting in front of the TV and eating ice cream.

Therapist: So getting all caught up in "I'm fat," doesn't seem too helpful, does it?

Client: No, but it's *true!*

Therapist: Well, let me say this again: with this approach, what we're interested in is not whether a thought is true or false, but whether it's helpful. When that thought pops into your head, does it help you to get all caught up in it? Does it motivate you to exercise, or eat well, or spend time doing the things that make life rich and rewarding?

Client: No.

Therapist: So what about if we could do something here that could make a difference; what if you could learn a skill so that next time your mind starts telling you the "I'm fat" story, you don't have to get all absorbed in it?

When we use the basic framework of "workability," we never need to judge a client's behavior as "good" or "bad," "right" or "wrong"; instead we can ask, nonjudgmentally and compassionately, "Is this working to give you the life you want?" Likewise, we never need to judge thoughts as irrational or dysfunctional, or get into debates about whether they're true or false. Instead we can simply ask, "Does holding on tightly to those thoughts help you to live the life you truly want?" or "How does it work in the long run, if you let that belief be in charge of your life?" or "If you get all caught up in those thoughts, does it help you to do the things you want?" or "If you let those thoughts push you around, does that help you to be the person you want to be?"

Note that in the transcript above, the therapist makes no attempt to change the content of the thoughts. In ACT, the content of a thought is not considered problematic; it's only *fusion* with the thought that creates the problem. In many psychology textbooks, you'll discover this quotation from the works of William Shakespeare: "There is nothing either good or bad, but thinking makes it so." The ACT stance would be fundamentally different: "Thinking does not make anything good or bad. But if you fuse with your thinking, that can create problems."

EXPERIENTIAL AVOIDANCE

Experiential avoidance means trying to avoid, get rid of, suppress, or escape from unwanted "private experiences." (As I mentioned earlier, ACT uses the term *private experience* to mean any experience you have that no one else knows about unless you tell them: for example, thoughts, feelings, memories, images, urges, and sensations.) Experiential avoidance is something that comes naturally to all humans. Why? Well, here's how we describe it to clients …

The Problem-Solving Machine: A Classic ACT Metaphor

Therapist: If we had to pick one ability of the human mind that has enabled us to be so resourceful that we've not only changed the face of the planet but also traveled outside it, it'd have to be our capacity for problem solving. The essence of problem solving is this: A problem means something unwanted. And a solution means avoid it or get rid of it. Now in the physical world, problem solving often works very well. A wolf outside your door? Get rid of it: throw rocks or spears at it, or shoot it. Snow, rain, hail? Well, you can't get rid of those things, but you can avoid them by hiding in a cave, building a shelter, or wearing protective clothes. Dry, arid ground? You can get rid of it by irrigation and fertilization, or you can avoid it by moving to a better location.

So our mind is like a problem-solving machine, and it's very good at its job. And given that problem-solving works so well in the material world, it's only natural that our mind tries to do the same with our inner world: the world of thoughts, feelings, memories, sensations, and urges. Unfortunately all too often when we try to avoid or get rid of unwanted thoughts or feelings, it doesn't work—or if it does, we end up creating a lot of extra pain for ourselves in the process.

How Experiential Avoidance Increases Suffering

We'll return to the Problem-Solving Machine Metaphor in later chapters. For now, let's consider how experiential avoidance increases suffering. Addictions provide an obvious example. Many addictions begin as an attempt to avoid or get rid of unwanted thoughts and feelings such as boredom, loneliness, anxiety, guilt, anger, sadness, and so on. In the short run, gambling, drugs, alcohol, and cigarettes will often help people to avoid or get rid of these feelings temporarily, but in the long run, a huge amount of pain and suffering results.

The more time and energy we spend trying to avoid or get rid of unwanted private experiences, the more we're likely to suffer psychologically in the long run. Anxiety disorders provide a good example. It's not the presence of anxiety that comprises the essence of an anxiety disorder. After all, anxiety is a normal human emotion that we all experience. At the core of any anxiety disorder lies excessive experiential avoidance: a life dominated by trying very hard to avoid or get rid of anxiety. For example, suppose I feel anxious in social situations, and in order to avoid those feelings of anxiety, I stop socializing. Now I have "social phobia." The short-term benefit is obvious—I get to avoid some anxious thoughts and feelings—but the long-term cost is huge: I become isolated and my life "gets smaller."

Alternatively I may try to reduce my anxiety by playing the role of "good listener." I become very empathic and caring toward others, and in social interactions, I discover lots of information about their thoughts, feelings, and desires, but I reveal little or nothing of myself. This helps in the short run to reduce my fear of being judged or rejected, but in the long run, it means my relationships lack intimacy, openness, and authenticity.

Now suppose I take Valium, or some other benzodiazepine, to reduce my anxiety. Again, the short-term benefit is obvious: less anxiety. But long-term costs of relying on benzodiazepines, anti-depressants, marijuana, or alcohol to reduce my anxiety could include (a) psychological dependence on my medication, (b) possible physical addiction, (c) other physical and emotional side effects, (d) financial costs, and (e) failure to learn more effective responses to anxiety, which therefore maintains or exacerbates the issue. Still another way I might respond to social anxiety would be to grit my teeth and socialize *despite* my anxiety—that is, to tolerate the feelings even though I'm distressed by them. From an ACT perspective, this too would be experiential avoidance. Why? Because, although I'm not avoiding the situation, I'm still struggling with my feelings and desperately hoping they'll go away. This is tolerance, not acceptance. If I truly accept my feelings, then even though they may be very unpleasant and uncomfortable, I'm not distressed by them.

To get the distinction between tolerance and acceptance, consider this: Would you want the people you love to *tolerate* you while you're present, hoping you'll soon go away and frequently checking to see if you've gone yet? Or would you prefer them to completely and totally *accept* you as you are with all your flaws and foibles, and to be willing to have you around for as long as you choose to stay?

The cost of tolerating my anxiety (that is, gritting my teeth and putting up with it) is that it takes a huge amount of effort and energy, and it makes it hard to remain fully engaged in any social interaction. As a consequence, I miss out on much of the pleasure and fulfillment that commonly accompanies social interaction. And this in turn increases my anxiety about future social events because "I won't enjoy it" or "I'll feel awful" or "It's too much effort."

Sadly the more importance we place on avoiding anxiety, the more we develop anxiety about our anxiety. It's a vicious cycle, found at the center of any anxiety disorder. (After all, what is at the core of a panic attack, if not anxiety about anxiety?) A large body of research shows that higher experiential avoidance is associated with anxiety disorders, excessive worrying, depression, poorer work performance, higher levels of substance abuse, lower quality of life, high-risk sexual behavior, borderline personality disorder, greater severity of PTSD, long-term disability, and higher degrees of overall psychopathology (Hayes, Masuda, Bissett, Luoma, & Guerrero, 2004). Indeed, it's arguably the single biggest factor in psychopathology.

So now you can see one reason why ACT doesn't focus on symptom reduction: to do so is likely to reinforce experiential avoidance, the very process that fuels most clinical issues. Another reason is that attempts to reduce symptoms can paradoxically increase them. For example, research shows that suppression of unwanted thoughts can lead to a rebound effect: an increase in both intensity and frequency of the unwanted thoughts (Wenzlaff & Wegner, 2000). Other studies show that trying to suppress a mood can actually intensify it in a self-amplifying loop (Feldner, Zvolensky, Eifert, & Spira, 2003; Wegner, Erber, & Zanakos, 1993).

One core component of most ACT protocols involves getting the client in touch with the costs and futility of experiential avoidance. This is done to undermine the *agenda of control* (that is, the agenda of trying to control our thoughts and feelings) and to create space for the alternative agenda: acceptance. However, although we want to facilitate mindful, valued living, we don't want to turn into …

"Mindfulness Fascists"

We are not "mindfulness fascists" in ACT; we don't insist that people must always be in the present moment, always defused, always accepting. Not only would that be ridiculous, it would also be self-defeating. We're all experientially avoidant to some degree. And we all fuse with our thoughts at times. And experiential avoidance and cognitive fusion in and of themselves are not inherently "bad" or "pathological"; we only target them when they get in the way of living a rich, full, and meaningful life.

In other words, it's all about workability. If we take aspirin from time to time in order to get rid of a headache, that's experiential avoidance, but it's likely to be workable—that is, it improves our quality of life in the long run. If we drink one glass of red wine at night primarily to get rid of tension and stress, that too is experiential avoidance—but unless we have certain medical conditions, it's not likely to be harmful, toxic, or life distorting. On the contrary, it will actually do our heart some good. However, if we drink two entire bottles each night, obviously that's a different story.

The same holds true for fusion. There are certain contexts—although few and far between—where fusion is actually life enhancing, such as when we allow ourselves to "get lost" in a novel or a movie. And there are other contexts where we fuse with our thoughts, and although it's not life enhancing, it's not usually problematic either—for example, when we're daydreaming while waiting in a supermarket line. But generally speaking, we're better off defusing from our thoughts at least a little. (To clarify this, recall the Hands As Thoughts Exercise you did earlier. Even a small gap between your face and your hands allows a lot more information about the world to get through to you.)

A Very Important Point about Acceptance vs. Control

In ACT, we do not advocate acceptance of all thoughts and feelings under all circumstances. That would not only be very rigid but also quite unnecessary. ACT advocates acceptance under two circumstances:

1. When control of thoughts and feelings is limited or impossible.

2. When control of thoughts and feelings *is* possible, but the methods used reduce quality of life.

If control *is* possible and assists valued living, then go for it. Please do remember this point. It is often forgotten or misunderstood by new ACT practitioners, and remembering it will save you a lot of confusion.

THE SIX CORE PATHOLOGICAL PROCESSES

Cognitive fusion and experiential avoidance together give rise to six core pathological processes, as shown in figure 2.1 below. (You can think of these as the "flip sides" of the six core therapeutic processes.) As I take you through each process, I'll use clinical depression to provide examples.

Fusion

As described above, fusion means entanglement in our thoughts so that they dominate our awareness and have a huge influence over our behavior. Depressed clients fuse with all sorts of unhelpful thoughts: *I'm bad, I don't deserve any better, I can't change, I've always been this way, Life sucks, It's all too hard, Therapy won't work, It'll never get any better, I can't get out of bed when I feel this way, I'm too tired to do anything.* They also often fuse with painful memories involving things such as rejection, disappointment, failure, or abuse.

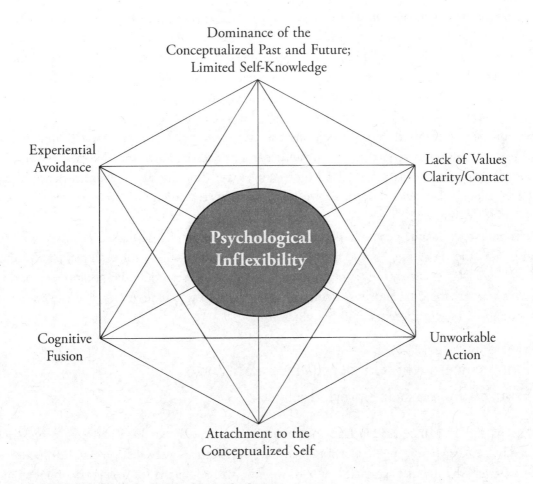

Figure 2.1 **An ACT Model of Psychopathology**

(Extreme fusion with a memory—to such an extent that it seems to be actually happening right here and now—is commonly referred to as a *flashback*.) In clinical depression, fusion often manifests as worrying, ruminating, trying to figure out "why I'm like this" or an ongoing negative commentary: "This party sucks. I'd rather be in bed. What's the point of even being here? They're all having such a good time. No one really wants me here."

Experiential Avoidance

As I've mentioned before, experiential avoidance means trying to get rid of, avoid, or escape from unwanted private experiences such as thoughts, feelings, and memories. It's the polar opposite of acceptance (which is an abbreviation of "experiential acceptance"). As an example, let's look at the role of experiential avoidance in depression. Your depressed clients commonly try very hard to avoid or get rid of painful emotions and feelings such as anxiety, sadness, fatigue, anger, guilt, loneliness, lethargy, and so on. For example, they often withdraw from socializing in order to avoid uncomfortable thoughts and feelings. This may not be apparent at first glance, so let's think it through. As a social engagement draws nearer and nearer, they're likely to fuse with all sorts of thoughts such as *I'm boring, I'm a burden, I've got nothing to say, I won't enjoy it, I'm too tired,* or *I can't be bothered,* as well as memories of previous social events that have been unsatisfactory. At the same time, their feelings of anxiety increase and they often report a sense of anticipatory "dread." However, the moment they cancel the engagement, there's instant relief: all those unpleasant thoughts and feelings instantly disappear. And even though that relief doesn't last for long, it's very reinforcing, which increases the chance of future social withdrawal.

Fusion and avoidance generally go hand in hand. For example, depressed clients often try hard to push away the very thoughts and memories they keep fusing with—for example, painful thoughts such as *I'm worthless* or *Nobody likes me,* or unpleasant memories of rejection, disappointment, and failure. They may try anything from drugs, alcohol, or cigarettes to watching TV or sleeping excessively in vain attempts to avoid these painful thoughts.

Dominance of the Conceptualized Past and Future/Limited Self-Knowledge

Fusion and avoidance readily lead to a loss of contact with our here-and-now experience. We all readily get caught up in a conceptualized past and future: we dwell on painful memories and ruminate over why things happened that way; we fantasize about the future, worry about things that haven't yet happened, and focus on all the things we have to do next. And in the process, we miss out on life in the here and now.

Contacting the present moment includes the world around us and inside us. If we lose contact with our inner psychological world—if we're out of touch with our own thoughts and feelings—then we lack self-knowledge. And without self-knowledge, it's much harder to change our behavior in adaptive ways.

Depressed clients commonly spend a lot of time fused with a conceptualized past: ruminating on painful past events, often having to do with rejection, loss, and failure. They also fuse with a conceptualized future: worrying about all the "bad stuff" that might lie ahead.

Lack of Values Clarity/Contact

As our behavior becomes increasingly driven by fusion with unhelpful thoughts, or attempts to avoid unpleasant private experiences, our values often get lost, neglected, or forgotten. If we're not clear about our values or not in psychological contact with them, then we can't use them as an effective guide for our actions. Depressed clients often lose touch with their values around connecting with and contributing to others, being productive, nurturing health and well-being, having fun, or engaging in challenging activities such as sports, work, and hobbies.

Our aim in ACT is to bring behavior increasingly under the influence of values rather than fusion or avoidance. (Note: Even values should be held lightly rather than fused with. If we fuse with values, they easily become rigid rules.) Consider the differences between going to work under these three conditions:

1. Mainly motivated by fusion with self-limiting beliefs such as "I have to do this job. It's all I'm capable of."

2. Mainly motivated by avoidance: going in to work to avoid "feeling like a loser" or to get rid of feelings of anxiety related to tension at home.

3. Mainly motivated by values: doing this work guided by values around contribution, self-development, being active, or connecting with others.

Which form of motivation is likely to bring the greatest sense of vitality, meaning, and purpose?

Unworkable Action

Unworkable action means patterns of behavior that pull us away from mindful, valued living; patterns of action that do *not* work to make our lives richer and fuller, but rather get us stuck or increase our struggles. This includes action that's impulsive, reactive, or automatic as opposed to mindful, considered, purposeful; action persistently motivated by experiential avoidance rather than values; and inaction or procrastination where effective action is required to improve quality of life. Common examples of unworkable action in depression include using drugs or alcohol excessively, withdrawing socially, being physically inactive, ceasing previously enjoyable activities, avoiding work, sleeping or watching TV excessively, attempting suicide, excessive procrastination on important tasks, and the list goes on and on.

Attachment to the Conceptualized Self

We all have a story about who we are. This story is complex and multilayered. It includes some objective facts such as our name, age, sex, cultural background, marital status, occupation, and so on. It also includes descriptions and evaluations of the roles we play, the relationships we have, our strengths and weaknesses, our likes and dislikes, and our hopes, dreams, and aspirations. If we hold this story lightly, it can give us a sense of self that helps to define who we are and what we want in life. However, if we fuse with this story—if we start to think we *are* the story—it readily creates all sorts of problems. Most ACT textbooks refer to this story as the *conceptualized self* or *self-as-content*. I prefer the term *self-as-description*, a phrase coined by psychologist Patty Bach, because that's essentially what it is: a way of describing ourselves. And when we fuse with our self-description, it seems as if we *are* that description, that all those thoughts are the very essence of who we are: self-as-description.

Note that even fusion with a very positive self-description is likely to be problematic. For example, what might be the danger of fusing with "I am strong and independent?" That will undoubtedly give me high self-esteem, but what happens when I really need help and I'm so fused with my positive self-description that I'm unwilling to ask for it or accept it? And what's the potential danger of fusing with "I am a brilliant car driver. I can drive exceedingly well even when I am drunk!"? Again, this gives me very positive self-esteem, but it can easily lead to disaster.

In depression, clients generally fuse with a very "negative" self-description: "I am (bad/worthless/hopeless/unlovable/dumb/ugly/fat/incompetent/a loser/a failure/damaged goods/disgusting/boring/unlikeable)," and so on. However, you may also get "positive" elements in there—for example, "I'm a strong person; I shouldn't be reacting like this," or "I'm a good person; why is this happening to me?" or even "I don't need any help. I can get through this on my own."

Overlap among Pathological Processes

You'll notice that there's considerable overlap among these pathological processes; as with psychological flexibility, they're all interconnected. For example, if your client ruminates on "Why am I such a failure?" you could class that as fusion or self-as-description. And if he spends the evening pacing up and down ruminating instead of doing something life enhancing, you could class it as unworkable action. And if he's lost in his thoughts while spending time with his wife and kids, then not only is he losing contact with the present moment, he's probably losing contact with his values around connecting and engaging with others. Rumination could even serve as experiential avoidance, if he's doing it primarily to avoid thinking about or dealing with other painful issues, or to distract himself from feelings in his body.

SO WHO IS ACT SUITABLE FOR?

ACT has been scientifically studied and shown to be effective with a wide range of conditions including anxiety, depression, obsessive-compulsive disorder, social phobia, generalized anxiety disorder, schizophrenia, borderline personality disorder, workplace stress, chronic pain, drug use, psychological adjustment to cancer, epilepsy, weight control, smoking cessation, and self-management of diabetes (Bach & Hayes, 2002; Bond & Bunce, 2000; Brown et al., 2008; Branstetter, Wilson, Hildebrandt & Mutch, 2004; Dahl, Wilson, & Nilsson, 2004; Dalrymple & Herbert, 2007; Gaudiano & Herbert, 2006.; Gifford et al., 2004; Gratz & Gunderson, 2006; Gregg, Callaghan, Hayes, & Glenn-Lawson, 2007; Hayes, Masuda, Bissett, Luoma, & Guerrero, 2004; Hayes, Bissett, et al., 2004; Tapper et al., 2009; Lundgren, Dahl, Yardi, & Melin, 2008; Ossman & Wilson, 2006; Twohig, Hayes, & Masuda, 2006; Zettle, 2003). When therapists ask me, "Who is ACT suitable for?" my reply is "Can you think of anyone who ACT is *not* suitable for?" Who wouldn't benefit from being more psychologically present; more in touch with their values; more able to make room for the inevitable pain of life; more able to defuse from unhelpful thoughts, beliefs, and memories; more able to take effective action in the face of emotional discomfort; more able to engage fully in what they're doing; and more able to appreciate each moment of their life, no matter how they're feeling? Psychological flexibility brings all these benefits, and more. ACT therefore seems relevant to just about everyone.

(Of course, if humans have significant deficits in their ability to use language, such as some people with autism, acquired brain injury, or other disabilities, then ACT may be of limited use. However, RFT (relational frame theory) has all sorts of useful applications for these populations.)

To help you start thinking in terms of this model, I'm going to close this chapter with an exercise in case conceptualization. I'd like you to pick one of your clients and find examples of the six core pathological processes outlined in this chapter. To help you with this task, please use the worksheet Assessing Psychological Inflexibility: Six Core Processes. (You'll find it at the end of this chapter. It's also downloadable from www.actmadesimple.com.) If you get stuck on any heading, don't fret about it, just move on to the next one. And keep in mind, there's a lot of overlap between these processes, so if you're wondering, "Is this fusion or avoidance?" then the answer is probably yes—in which case, write it down under both headings. This exercise is purely to get you started. Later on in the book, we'll focus on case conceptualization in more detail. For now, just give it a shot, and see how you do.

Better still, run through this exercise for two or three clients because (like pretty much everything) with practice, it gets easier.

And even better still: if you really want to get your head around this approach to human psychopathology, pick two or three *DSM-IV* disorders and identify the fusion, avoidance, and unworkable action going on: What kind of mental content do sufferers fuse with (in terms of worrying, ruminating, self-image, and self-defeating beliefs and attitudes)? What feelings, urges, sensations, thoughts, and memories are sufferers unwilling to have or actively trying to avoid? What unworkable actions do sufferers typically take? What core values do they lose touch with?

Last but not least: run through this exercise on yourself. If you want to learn ACT, the best person to practice on is *you*. So take some time to do this seriously: identify what you fuse with, what you avoid, what values you lose touch with, and what ineffective actions you take. The more you apply this model to your own issues and notice how it works in your own life, the more experience you can draw on in the therapy room.

ASSESSING PSYCHOLOGICAL INFLEXIBILITY: SIX CORE PROCESSES

1. *Dominance of the conceptualized past or future; limited self-knowledge*: How much time does your client spend dwelling on the past or fantasizing/worrying about the future? What elements of the past or future does she dwell on? To what extent is she disconnected from or lacking awareness of her own thoughts, feelings, and actions?

2. *Fusion*: What sort of unhelpful cognitive content is your client fusing with—rigid rules or expectations, self-limiting beliefs, criticisms and judgments, reason-giving, being right, ideas of hopelessness or worthlessness, or others?

3. *Experiential avoidance*: What private experiences (thoughts, feelings, memories, and so on) is your client avoiding? How is he doing that? How pervasive is experiential avoidance in her life?

4. *Attachment to the conceptualized self*: What is your client's "conceptualized self"? For example, does he see himself as broken/damaged/unlovable/weak/stupid, and so on, or does she perhaps see herself as strong/superior/successful? How fused is he with this self-image? Does she define herself in terms of her body, or a character trait, or a particular role, occupation, or diagnosis?

5. *Lack of values clarity/contact*: What core values is your client unclear about, neglecting or acting inconsistently with? (For example, commonly neglected values include connection, caring, contribution, authenticity, openness, self-care, self-compassion, loving, nurturing, living in the present.)

6. *Unworkable action*: What impulsive, avoidant or self-defeating actions is your client taking? Does she fail to persist when persistent action is required? Or does she inappropriately continue when such action is ineffective? What people, places, situations, and activities is he avoiding or withdrawing from?

CHAPTER 3

The House of ACT

WHAT TOOK YOU SO LONG, ACT?

Why did it take ACT so long to become popular, given that as long ago as 1986 there were randomized controlled trials showing it to be equivalent or superior to traditional cognitive behavioral therapy (CBT) for treatment of depression? Steve Hayes, the creator of ACT, answers that question like this:

"If ACT had been popular twenty years ago it could not have withstood scrutiny. The model was not well developed and its foundation was weak ... We were willing to spend years on philosophy, basic theory, measures, and applied theory before even publishing the approach in book form (in 1999) ... But because we waited and worked on the foundation, now when people peel back the layers they see how much has been done on the foundations of the work" (Harris, 2008b)

As a result of all this foundational work, ACT is now like the top floor of a three-story mansion. On the next floor down, you'll find relational frame theory (RFT), which is a behavioral theory of human language and cognition. Then on the ground floor you'll find applied behavioral analysis (ABA), a powerful model for the prediction and influence of behavior that has had an enormous impact on almost every branch of modern psychology. And the ground on which the entire mansion rests is a philosophy called functional contextualism (FC).

While the rest of this book is primarily focused on ACT, in this chapter we're going to take a quick look at functional contextualism. You don't have to know this stuff—you can skip this chapter if you wish—but I encourage you to read on because it will help your understanding of ACT. (Originally this chapter also included an introduction to ABA and RFT, but unfortunately we had to cut it for lack of space. However, you can download that introduction from www.actmadesimple .com/the _ house _ of _ ACT.)

FUNCTIONAL CONTEXTUALISM AND THE THREE-LEGGED CHAIR

I'd like you to imagine a chair that has four legs, but the moment anyone sits on it, one of the legs drops off. Would you describe this chair as "broken," "faulty," or "damaged"? Would you call it a "dysfunctional chair" or even a "maladaptive chair"? I've asked this question of many hundreds of therapists, and they always answer yes to at least one of the above descriptions. The problem is that this instinctive answer—"Yes, there is something wrong, faulty, or flawed in the chair"—forgets to take into account the all-important role of context. So I invite you now to think laterally: think of at least three or four contexts in which we could say this chair functions very effectively to serve our purposes.

* * *

Did you come up with some? Here are a few I thought of:

- Playing a practical joke.

- Creating an art exhibition of broken furniture.

- Finding props for a clown's act or a comedy show.

- Demonstrating design flaws in a furniture-making class.

- Improving balance, coordination, and muscle strength (that is, you try sitting down without making the leg fall off).

- Hoping to injure yourself at work to get a compensation claim.

In all of these contexts, this chair functions very effectively to serve our purposes. This example illustrates how *functional contextualism* gets its name: it looks at how things function in specific contexts. From the viewpoint of FC, no thought or feeling is inherently problematic, dysfunctional, or pathological. In a context that includes cognitive fusion and experiential avoidance, our thoughts, feelings, and memories often function in a manner that is toxic, harmful, or life distorting. However, in a context of defusion and acceptance (that is, mindfulness), those very same thoughts, feelings, and memories function very differently: they have much less impact and influence over us. They may still be painful, but they're no longer toxic, harmful, or life distorting—and more importantly, they don't hold us back from valued living.

Most models of psychology are based on a philosophy called *mechanism*. Mechanistic models treat the mind as if it's a machine made up of lots of separate parts. "Problematic" thoughts and feelings are seen as faulty parts of the machine or errors in the structure of the machine. The aim in such models is to repair, replace, or remove these faulty parts so the machine can function normally. Mechanistic models of psychology assume that there are such things as inherently "dysfunctional," "maladaptive," or "pathological" thoughts, feelings, and memories. In other words, there are memories, thoughts, feelings, emotions, urges, schemas, narratives, ego states, core beliefs, and so on that are fundamentally problematic, dysfunctional, or pathological, and much like a "faulty chair," they need to be either fixed, replaced, or removed.

Mechanism has been the most successful philosophy of science in most scientific fields, so it's not surprising that most models in psychology are based on some sort of mechanistic philosophy. And there is nothing "wrong" or "bad" or "inferior" or "basic" about mechanism. I'm merely emphasizing that functional contextualism is a radically different philosophical approach to the mainstream, and it naturally leads to a different way of doing therapy.

Are Clients "Damaged Goods"?

Our clients often come to therapy with mechanistic ideas. They believe that they're faulty, damaged, or flawed, and they need to be fixed up or repaired. Sometimes they even refer to themselves as "damaged goods." They often believe they're lacking important components such as "confidence" or "self-esteem." Or they believe they have faulty parts—such as feelings of anxiety, negative thoughts, or painful memories—that need to be removed. Most mechanistic models readily reinforce these notions through two processes:

1. They use words—for example, terms such as "dysfunctional," "maladaptive," "irrational," or "negative"—that imply we have faulty or damaged components in our minds.

2. They use a wide variety of tools and techniques designed to directly reduce, replace, or remove these unwanted thoughts and feelings (usually on the assumption that this is an essential step for improving quality of life).

In ACT, our attitude is very different. We don't set out to reduce or eliminate "symptoms"; instead we aim to fundamentally transform the client's relationship with her thoughts and feelings so that she no longer perceives them as "symptoms." After all, the moment we label a thought or feeling as a "symptom," that implies that it's "bad," "harmful," "abnormal," and therefore something we need to get rid of in order to be normal and healthy. This attitude readily sets us up to struggle with our own thoughts and feelings—a struggle that often has disastrous consequences.

Suppose there's a plant that you judge as "ugly," growing right in the center of your front garden. And suppose that there's no way to get rid of it without destroying your entire garden. (You may be thinking, *But there must be some way to get rid of it.* If so, just step back for a minute and make a hypothetical leap: imagine, for the purposes of this exercise, that you *can't* get rid of this plant without destroying your garden.) Now if you view this plant as a "weed," what is likely to happen to your relationship with it? Chances are you won't like it and you won't want it there. And you may well get upset or angry about it. You could easily waste lots of time thinking about how much better your garden would be without it. You might even hesitate to let people into your front garden, for fear they'll judge you on account of it. Perhaps you might even start leaving by the back of your house so you don't have to look at this "ugly weed." In other words, this "ugly weed" has become A VERY IMPORTANT THING IN YOUR LIFE—so much so, that it now has a significant impact on your behavior.

But what happens if, instead of viewing that plant as an "ugly weed," you view it as just an unfortunate fact of life: a natural part of the native environment, a common example of American indigenous flora? Now it's the same plant, in the same location, but your relationship with it has fundamentally changed. Now you no longer have to struggle with it. Now you need no longer be upset or embarrassed about it, or waste so much time thinking about it. Now you can let people into your garden without hesitation, and you can leave by the front of the house. The plant itself has not changed, but you no longer make it into A VERY IMPORTANT THING IN YOUR LIFE. It now has much less impact or influence over you.

Mindfulness enables us to make a similar attitude shift toward all those thoughts, feelings, sensations, and memories that we so readily judge as "problematic"; it enables us to choose the relationship we have with them. By changing the context from one of fusion and avoidance to one of defusion and acceptance (that is, mindfulness), we alter the function of those thoughts and feelings so they have much less impact and influence over us. In a context of mindfulness, they're no longer "symptoms" or "problems" or "things that stop us from living a rich and full life"; they're nothing more or less than thoughts, feelings, sensations, memories, and so on.

In one sense, mindfulness is the ultimate reframing tool: it moves all these painful thoughts and feelings from the old frame of "abnormal pathological symptoms that are obstacles to a rich and meaningful life" into the new frame of "normal human experiences that are natural parts of a rich and meaningful life."

What Is the Goal of Functional Contextualism?

The goal of FC is to predict and influence behavior accurately and effectively, using empirically supported principles. And what is the purpose of predicting and influencing behavior? In ACT, the purpose is specifically to help humans create rich, full, and meaningful lives—that is, to enable mindful, valued living. Thus ACT teaches people to increase awareness of their own behavior (both public and private), and to notice how it functions in the context of their life: does it improve their quality of life, or lower it? You may recall that in ACT, we refer to this concept as "workability."

Now let's take a moment to consider the word "function." It's a technical term (not one that you'd use with clients) that you'll find in most ACT textbooks. When we ask "What is the *function* of this behavior?" we mean "What effects does this behavior have? What are the consequences?" In other words, we're asking, "What purpose does this behavior serve? What is it intended to achieve?"

To clarify this, imagine five different people, in five different situations, each making cuts across their forearm with a sharp knife. Now see if you can come up with five possible functions for this behavior.

* * *

Here are some possibilities:

- Getting attention

- Self-punishment

- Release of tension

- Distraction from painful emotions

- Creating body art

- Trying to feel something if you are "totally numb"

- Attempting to get admitted to a hospital

Notice in all these scenarios the *form* of the behavior is the same—cutting one's arm—but the *function* of the behavior—the purpose it serves—is different.

Now let's suppose your partner is lost in thought, and your purpose is to gain his attention. Think of five different *forms* of behavior that might achieve this.

* * *

Here are a few ideas:

- Wave at him.

- Shout "Hello, is there anybody in there?"

- Pour a cup of water over his head.

- Bang loudly on some furniture.

- Say, "Darling, can I have your attention for a moment, please?"

In this example, you can see that many different *forms* of behavior all have the same function: they serve the purpose of getting attention. In functional contextualism, we're interested in the function of a behavior rather than the form of it. But notice, we can only know the function of a behavior if we know the context in which it occurs. If someone raises an arm up high in the air, what purpose does that serve? Is he in a lecture hall, asking a question? Is she pointing up at a plane in the sky? Or is he perhaps trying to hail a taxi? Without knowing the context, we can't know the function of the behavior and vice versa. And that brings up another important question: What do we mean by "behavior"—and "behaviorism"?

"BEHAVIORISM": A MISUNDERSTOOD WORD

When I first discovered ACT, I couldn't believe that such a spiritual, humanistic model came out of behaviorism. I thought behaviorists treated humans like robots or rats, that they had no interest in thoughts and feelings, and considered them unimportant or irrelevant. Boy, was I wrong! I soon discovered there are several different schools of behaviorism, and some of them have ideas that directly contradict essential elements of ACT and RFT. ACT comes from a branch known, somewhat unfortunately, as "radical behaviorism." But don't let the name put you off. *Radical behaviorists* do not run around in combat gear, armed with assault rifles—they get their name because of their radical viewpoint: they consider everything that an organism does is behavior. Yes, you read that correctly: *everything* that an organism does is behavior. Thus, to a radical behaviorist, processes such as thinking, feeling, and remembering are all considered to be forms of behavior—and *all* are considered very important.

Radical behaviorists talk of two broad realms of behavior. One realm is "public" behavior—that is, behavior that can directly be observed by others (provided they are present to witness it). Thus, if we watched a video of you, whatever we could see you doing or hear you saying would be public behavior. In everyday language, we commonly refer to these public behaviors as "actions." The other realm is "private" behavior—that is, behavior that can only be directly observed by the person doing it: thinking, feeling, remembering, fantasizing, worrying, tasting, smelling, and so on. Radical behaviorists are very interested in both these realms.

Behaviorism has had a profound impact on clinical psychology. Through rigorous scientific study, the behaviorists discovered a wide range of powerful methods for reliably and effectively influencing human behavior (both public and private): methods that include exposure, reinforcement, shaping, extinction, and classical and operant conditioning. Many models of therapy have been extremely influenced by these ideas, although many fail to acknowledge it or even realize it. Indeed, it's hard to imagine an effective therapist or coach that does not utilize at least some of these basic principles, given they have proven so effective for facilitating behavioral change.

Many of these ideas are hugely influential in everyday life. For example, business leadership programs advise managers to catch their coworkers "doing something right" and sincerely praise them for it. Likewise, positive parenting programs advise parents to actively notice when their children are behaving well and reward them for it. All this excellent advice is based on the powerful behavioral principle of "positive reinforcement."

The Three Waves of Behaviorism

Now let's take a quick tour of behaviorism to see how we got to where we are today. There have been three "waves" of behavioral therapies in the last century. The "first wave," which reached its peak of popularity in the 1950s and 60s, focused primarily on overt behavioral change and utilized techniques linked to operant and classical conditioning principles. Many practitioners in this first wave placed little importance on thoughts and feelings. Unfortunately this led to *all* behaviorists being painted with the same brush: that they treated humans like rats or robots.

The "second wave" of behaviorism, which took off in the 1970s, included cognitive interventions as a key strategy in behavior change. In particular, the "second wave" placed a major emphasis on challenging or disputing irrational, dysfunctional, negative, or erroneous thoughts, and replacing them with more rational, functional, positive, or realistic thoughts. Cognitive behavioral therapy (CBT) eventually came to dominate this "second wave," closely followed by rational emotive behavior therapy (REBT).

ACT is part of the so-called "third wave" of behavioral therapies—along with dialectical behavior therapy (DBT), mindfulness-based cognitive therapy (MBCT), functional analytic psychotherapy (FAP), and several others—all of which place a major emphasis on acceptance and mindfulness, in addition to traditional behavioral interventions.

AND THE REST OF THE TOUR?

If you'd like to tour the rest of the house of ACT, then I recommend you read *The ABCs of Human Behavior: Behavioral Principles for the Practicing Clinician* by Jonas Ramnerö and Niklas Törneke. This is an excellent book that takes you step-by-step, simply and clearly, through all the details of FC, ABA, and RFT, tying them all together with ACT via numerous clinical examples and annotated transcripts of therapy. There's also a free online tutorial on RFT, available at *www .contextualpsychology.org/rft_tutorial*.

But that's enough of this intellectual talk. Now it's time to start getting experiential …

CHAPTER 4

Getting Experiential

LESS TALK, MORE ACTION: ACT AS EXPERIENTIAL THERAPY

ACT is a very active therapy. We take clients through a wide array of experiential exercises, which range in duration from ten seconds to half an hour. Now, if you're already well-versed in experiential therapy, you may take this in stride. However, for many practitioners, the idea of leading such exercises is not only challenging, but it's also daunting. So in this chapter, we'll look at how to acclimatize clients to the experiential nature of ACT, and how to develop your ability to lead these exercises.

The Proof of the Pudding

There's an old saying, "The proof of the pudding is in the eating." You can talk until the cows come home, trying to describe the pudding you want me to taste, but until I actually place it in my mouth, I won't know what it tastes like. One of the most common pitfalls when we're new to ACT is trying to describe or explain ACT processes instead of actually doing them. If we're not careful, it's easy to get bogged down in wordy conversations and waste a lot of time on intellectual discussion instead of doing something that's practical and useful.

Because of this, you're better off to go through a process experientially and then talk about it later, rather than the other way around. And if you do choose to explain an exercise in advance, then preferably do so via a metaphor; I'll give you plenty of examples as we go.

A Quick Note on the Therapeutic Relationship

Throughout this book, you'll encounter a lot of techniques, metaphors, worksheets, strategies, and other interventions. None of this will be effective if you don't have a good relationship with your client. In ACT, we aim to be fully present with our clients: open, authentic, mindful, compassionate, respectful, and in touch with our own core values. In other words, we aim to live and breathe ACT ourselves, and to deliver it with heart and soul rather than coldly and mechanically using it like a fancy tool kit.

Kelly Wilson, one of the pioneers of ACT, puts this very simply. He advises us to see our clients as sunsets, not as math problems. And he reminds us that we don't do interventions *to* clients—we do interventions *with* clients. As part of this respectful stance toward our clients, we repeatedly ask their permission to begin and/or persist with experiential exercises. For example, we might say, "I'm just wondering—there's an exercise that I think could be really useful for you in dealing with this issue. Would you be willing to give it a go?"

Similarly, in the midst of some exercise where our client is in touch with strong emotions, you might ask, "I'm just checking—is it okay if we keep going with this? I don't want you to feel in any way coerced. We can stop at any point."

And if we should notice we've spent a long time discussing ACT processes as opposed to actually doing them, we might say, "I've just noticed something here. We've been doing a lot of talking in this session but not much practice. Obviously you can't learn to play a guitar by talking about it; you have to actually pick it up and strum the strings. And it's the same with this therapy. So would it be okay if we stopped talking for a while, and instead could we do a little exercise related to this issue?"

Relevance and Rationale

We want to make our metaphors and exercises directly relevant to the issues we're dealing with in the session rather than trotting out some exercise simply because we like it, it's fresh in our memory, or it worked well with our previous client. For longer exercises, it's often useful to provide a rationale. For example:

Therapist: So, in summary, it seems like you spend a lot of time caught up in all these worrying thoughts, and it's making you pretty miserable.

Client: Yes. I know it's stupid, but I can't help it. That's the way I am. We're all worriers in my family. My mom's the worst.

Therapist: What if you could learn a new skill so that when these worrying thoughts pop into your head, you could let them come and go—as if they were just cars, driving past outside your house—instead of getting all caught up in them. Would that be something you'd be interested in?

Client: I know what you're saying, but (*laughing*) I really don't think I could do that.

Therapist: Well, would it be okay to give it a go, and see how it works? It's a very simple exercise—you can do with your eyes open, or closed, whichever you prefer.

Client: I can try, I guess.

Establishing Structure

In the very first session, we generally say something like this: "One of the things that makes ACT different from many other therapies is that during our sessions, we spend a lot of time practicing skills such as learning new ways to handle difficult thoughts and feelings more effectively. And you can't learn these skills simply by talking about them—you have to actually practice them. So quite often, if it's okay with you, I'll be asking you during the session to do some simple exercises. Would you be okay with that?"

(Note: Not all clients will answer yes; some will want to know more about these exercises. We'll cover how to deal with this in the next chapter.)

Usually within the first session or two, we'll take our client through at least one mindfulness exercise that lasts five minutes or more. Until clients know what to expect, I generally introduce all exercises with a short spiel, such as this: "This exercise will take [estimate duration]. You can do it with your eyes open or closed, whichever you prefer. And there's no need to speak to me during it, but you can talk at any time if you wish, and stop me whenever you like."

Once we've done a couple of mindfulness exercises, we could say, "If it's okay with you, I'd like to start each session with a short mindfulness exercise, a bit like the one we've just done. Would that be okay?" If your client agrees—as most will—you now have a lovely way to open each session that gets both you and your client into the space of mindfulness. Of course, if you don't want to structure your sessions this way, it's by no means essential; this is merely a suggestion, not a commandment. And of course, some clients will hate this idea. So if your client's not keen, whatever you do, don't push it! Remember: if we ever find ourselves pushing, persuading, coercing, convincing, debating, or arguing with our clients, then we're not doing ACT.

Flexibility, Creativity, and Spontaneity

When leading exercises, be flexible. Make them longer or shorter, as required. Change the words to suit your own style, and adapt them for the clients you're dealing with. And feel free to interrupt any exercise at any point to check in with your client and ask how he's doing. Also use your creativity to incorporate thoughts, feelings, comments, or metaphors that your client has made in this session or previous ones.

Improving Delivery

As you work through this book, don't just read the exercises to yourself. I strongly urge you to read them out loud and pretend that you're actually working with a client. This may seem odd, but it's a simple and effective way to build your skills and confidence. When you rehearse by yourself, it prepares you for the therapy room: your words will flow more smoothly, and you'll have to exert less conscious effort. (Better still, find a colleague to practice with.)

I used to practice mindfulness scripts into a tape recorder (and as technology advanced, into an MP3 recorder). Then I played them back and analyzed them. I then worked on the bits that were shaky until I knew what I was doing. This meant that even if I was reading from a script in session, the script became just a guide to improvise around rather than something I had to slavishly follow word for word. This allows for a fluidity and spontaneity that brings scripts to life rather than making them sound stilted, awkward, and unnatural.

The same holds true for the many metaphors ACT utilizes. Some people are natural-born storytellers. They'll hear a metaphor once, and then retell it in their own way, and it will come out wonderfully. They're very lucky! Most of us aren't so talented. We need practice. I suggest that you try saying a metaphor out loud a few times. Then once you have it down pat, try telling it to someone else.

As a general rule, mindfulness exercises are best delivered at a slow, deliberate pace and in a calm, still voice. Generally it's better to go too slow than too fast. In many of the scripts in this book, I've indicated pauses of five, ten, fifteen, or twenty seconds, but these are only rough guidelines, so please don't try to slavishly follow them—find your own natural rate and rhythm. For most people, one slow deep breath all the way in and all the way out is about ten seconds. I have recorded some CDs and MP3s that you can use for guidance, if you wish (see appendix 2).

If you wish to read from a script during a session, it's a good idea to say something to your client like "There's an exercise I'd really like to take you through, but I haven't yet memorized the whole thing, so do you mind if I read it from this book?" However, don't read the text word for word as written, or it will sound stilted and unnatural; improvise around it.

Finally, remember to be yourself. I encourage you to alter the words and phrases in every exercise and metaphor within this book to suit your own style, your own way of speaking, and the clientele you work with.

THE HEXAFLEXERCISE

We're now going to look at the Hexaflexercise, which covers all elements of the hexaflex (see chapter 1) in "one hit." I use it in all my workshops, talks, and lectures; at the start of group sessions; and as a brief "refresher course" in later sessions with my individual clients. As written here, it takes from ten to fifteen minutes, depending on how fast you talk and how long you pause. Please practice it a few times before continuing on with the book because (a) it will help you to understand the model, and (b) it will give you a foundation for many of the exercises to come.

> This exercise, used in its entirety is undoubtedly too long for some clients. But you can easily do abbreviated versions or use "chunks" of it. I've numbered different sections of the exercise so we can dissect it and refer back to it in later chapters.

Now ... please read the exercise out loud. Read it in a slow, calm, steady voice, and pretend that you're saying it to a client.

SECTION 1

Therapist: I invite you now to sit up straight, let your shoulders drop and gently push your feet into the floor ... and get a sense of the ground beneath you ... and you can either fix your eyes on a spot, or close them, whichever you prefer.

    Now just take a moment to notice how you are sitting. (*Pause 5 seconds.*) And notice how you are breathing. (*Pause 5 seconds.*) Notice what you can see. (*Pause 5 seconds.*) And notice what you can hear. (*Pause 5 seconds.*) Notice what you can feel against your skin. (*Pause 5 seconds.*) And notice what you can taste or sense in your mouth. (*Pause 5 seconds.*) Notice what you can smell or sense in your nostrils. (*Pause 5 seconds.*) And notice what you are feeling. (*Pause 5 seconds.*) Notice what you are thinking. (*Pause 5 seconds.*) Notice what you are doing. (*Pause 5 seconds.*)

SECTION 2

Therapist: So there's a part of you in there that can notice everything that you see, hear, touch, taste, smell, think, and feel. (*Pause 5 seconds.*) We don't have a good word for this part of you in everyday language. I'm going to call it "the observing self," but you don't have to call it that. You can call it whatever you like. (*Pause 5 seconds.*)

    Life is like a stage show. And on that stage are all your thoughts, and all your feelings, and everything that you can see, hear, touch, taste, and smell. The observing self is that part of you that can step back and watch the stage show: focus in on any part of it, or step back and take it all in at once. (*Pause 5 seconds.*)

SECTION 3

Therapist: Now take a moment to reflect on why you came here today. There is something that matters to you, something that is important deep in your heart that motivated you to come here ... Is it about improving your life? ... Personal growth? ... Learning new skills? ... Building better relationships?

    ... Is it about improving things at work, or with your family, or your friends? ... Or perhaps it's about your health: nurturing your body or enhancing your well-being?

... Just do a search, deep inside your heart, to clarify what values led you here today. (*Pause 15 seconds.*)

SECTION 4

Therapist: And now take a moment to reflect on how you got here today. You didn't get here by magic. You are only here because of committed action. You had to organize the appointment. You had to reschedule things. You had to invest time and effort and energy to get here. And chances are that getting here today brought up some uncomfortable thoughts and feelings for you. And yet ... here you are. (*Pause 10 seconds.*) And recognize that right now, in this moment, you are taking action. You are sitting here in a chair, doing an exercise that probably seems a bit odd or unusual ... and you probably have all sorts of thoughts whizzing through your head ... and all sorts of feelings passing through your body. (*Pause 5 seconds.*) And there are all sorts of things you could be doing right that are much more fun than this, and yet here you are, taking action to improve and enrich your life. (*Pause 10 seconds.*)

SECTION 5

Therapist: Now for the next few breaths, I'd like you to focus on emptying out your lungs: push all the air out of them until there's no more left, and then allow them to gently fill, all by themselves. (*Pause 5 seconds.*) Really notice the breath—notice it flowing in and out. (*Pause 10 seconds.*) Observe it as if you're a curious scientist who has never encountered breathing before. (*Pause 10 seconds.*) Notice how once the lungs are empty, they automatically refill, all by themselves. (*Pause 5 seconds.*) You can take a deep breath in if you want to, but notice how there's really no need to: the breath just happens by itself. (*Pause 10 seconds.*) And I invite you now to undertake a challenge: for the next couple of minutes, keep your attention on your breath, observing it as it flows in and out. (*Pause 10 seconds.*)

SECTION 6

Therapist: You will find this hard, because your mind is a masterful storyteller. It will tell you all sorts of interesting stories to grab your attention and pull you away from what you're doing. (*Pause 5 seconds.*) See if you can let those thoughts come and go, as if they are merely passing cars—just cars driving past, outside your house—and keep your attention on the breath. (*Pause 10 seconds.*) Notice your breath flowing in and out. (*Pause 10 seconds.*) Notice your abdomen, rising and falling. (*Pause 10 seconds.*) Notice the rise and fall of your chest. (*Pause 10 seconds.*) Let your mind chatter away as if it's just a radio playing in the background. Don't try to turn the radio off; it's impossible—not even Zen masters can do that. Just let it play on in the background, and keep your attention on the breath. (*Pause 10 seconds.*)

From time to time, your mind will succeed in distracting you: it will hook you in with a good story, and you'll lose track of your breathing. This is normal and natural, and it will happen repeatedly. The moment you realize this has happened, take a moment to note what hooked you, and then gently refocus on your breathing. (*Pause 10 seconds.*)

Again and again and again, you will drift off into your thoughts. This is normal and natural. It happens to everyone. As soon as you realize it, gently acknowledge it and refocus on your breath. (*Pause 10 seconds.*)

SECTION 7

Therapist: As this exercise continues, the feelings and sensations in your body will change. There may be pleasant feelings showing up—such as relaxation, calm, peacefulness—and there may be unpleasant ones—such as boredom, frustration, anxiety, or backache. See if you can allow those feelings to be exactly as they are in this moment. (*Pause 10 seconds.*) Don't try to control your feelings, just let them be as they are—regardless of whether they are pleasant or unpleasant—and keep your attention on your breathing. (*Pause 10 seconds.*) Again and again, you'll drift off into your thoughts. As soon as you realize it, acknowledge it and refocus on your breath. (*Pause 10 seconds.*) This is *not* a relaxation technique. You are not trying to relax. The aim is to let your feelings be as they are, to feel whatever you feel without a struggle. So if you're noticing a difficult feeling, then silently say to yourself, *Here's a feeling of frustration* or *Here's a feeling of anxiety* or *Here's a feeling of boredom.* Acknowledge it's there, and keep your attention on the breath. (*Pause 20 seconds.*)

SECTION 8

Therapist: So life is like a stage show. And on that stage are all your thoughts and all your feelings, and everything that you can see, hear, touch, taste, and smell. In this exercise, you dimmed the lights on the stage and you focused a spotlight on your breathing. And now it's time to bring up the rest of the lights. This breathing is happening inside a body, so now bring up the lights on your body: sit up in the chair, and notice your arms and legs, head, neck, chest, and abdomen. (*Pause 5 seconds.*) And your body is inside a room, so now bring up the lights on the room around you. Look around, and notice what you can see and hear, and smell and taste and touch. (*Pause 10 seconds.*) And notice what you're feeling. (*Pause 5 seconds.*) And notice what you're thinking. (*Pause 5 seconds.*) So there's a part of you in there that can notice everything: whatever you see, hear, touch, taste, smell, think, feel, or do in any moment.

And that basically brings the exercise to an end. So let's take a good stretch, and then we can talk about it.

Pulling It All Apart

We will now analyze the Hexaflexercise, section by section. Please go back and reread each section of the exercise out loud before reading the explanation below.

SECTION 1: BE HERE NOW

Section 1 covers contact with the present moment. This section consists of the basic instruction at the core of all mindfulness exercises: "notice X." "X" can be anything that is here, right now, in this moment. It could be your breathing, the sounds in the room, the tension in your body, the thoughts in your head, the taste in your mouth, the view from the window, and so on. Common alternatives to the word "notice" include "pay attention to," "bring your awareness to," "focus on," or "observe." Note that the pauses at this point are brief—only five seconds. Later on in the exercise, they increase. You can easily adapt this section into a brief mindfulness exercise, suitable for any session as a grounding or centering technique.

SECTION 2: PURE AWARENESS

Section 2 covers self-as-context. Here we refer to it as the "observing self": the part of you that does all the noticing. I originally came up with the Stage Show Metaphor specifically to facilitate self-as-context, but as we'll see later, you can use it to enhance any other mindfulness process: acceptance, defusion, or contact with the present moment.

> **Before you take clients through this section, it's a good idea to give a brief explanation about the two parts of the mind—the thinking self and the observing self—so the term "observing self" won't take them by surprise. The following transcript exemplifies this.**

THE THINKING SELF AND THE OBSERVING SELF

Therapist: So one of the things that's important in our work here is to recognize that there are two very distinct parts of the mind. There's the part we're all very familiar with—the part that thinks, imagines, remembers, analyzes, plans, fantasizes, and so on. Let's call that the "thinking self." But there's another part of the mind that virtually never gets talked about—we don't even have a word for it in common everyday language. It's a part of your mind that doesn't think, can't think—it just notices. It notices whatever you're thinking and feeling and doing and seeing and hearing and tasting and so on. The closest words we have to it in everyday language are "awareness," "attention," or "focus." In ACT, we call it the "observing self" because it doesn't think—it merely observes. To give you an example, have you ever encountered a magnificent sunset and for a moment, your thinking self goes quiet. There are no thoughts—you're just silently observing this amazing sunset. That's your observing self in action—silently noticing. But the silence doesn't last long. Within seconds, the thinking self pipes up: "Oh, look at all those lovely colors. I wish I had my camera. This reminds me of that trip to Hawaii." And as you get more and more caught up in your thoughts, you start to disconnect from the sunset.

SECTION 3: KNOW WHAT MATTERS

Section 3 covers values: what matters enough to this client that he has bothered to come and see you? (Even if he was mandated by a court of law under threat of going to prison, he still didn't have to come: he came because he valued being free.) Ideally we individualize this section to specifically mention any core values already identified—for example, "Is it about being a better mother to your kids?"

SECTION 4: DO WHAT IT TAKES

Section 4 covers committed action: taking the action necessary to live by your values even when it's difficult and painful. Here we acknowledge and validate that the client has committed to action even though it has brought up discomfort. This is a message we'll reinforce throughout therapy: the actions we take to make our lives meaningful often give rise to pain. At times, we'll feel good as a result of them, and at other times, we won't. The question life repeatedly asks each one of us is this: "Am I willing to make room for these feelings in order to do what matters to me?"

SECTION 5: BE HERE NOW (AGAIN!)

Here we're back to the basic mindfulness instruction of "notice X." In this case, "X" is the sensations of breathing. Sections 5 and 6 taken together constitute a quick and simple mindful breathing exercise that you can use in any session.

SECTION 6: WATCH YOUR THINKING

Section 6 covers defusion: putting some distance between you and your thoughts so you can let them come and go without getting entangled in them. We're using three different metaphors here to facilitate defusion: (1) the notion of the mind as a storyteller and thoughts as stories; (2) treating your thoughts like passing cars; and (3) treating your mind as if it's a radio playing in the background. Any and all of these metaphors can be usefully added into any mindfulness exercise you do.

We also emphasize over and over that it's "normal and natural" to repeatedly drift off into your thoughts (that is, to fuse with them). This is important because many clients (like many therapists) have a strong perfectionist streak, and they'll be disappointed if they expect to maintain total focus.

Indeed, many clients (and therapists) are shocked at just how hard it is to stay focused for more than a few seconds.

SECTION 7: OPEN UP

Section 7 covers acceptance: opening up to and making room for painful private experiences. (Note: Acceptance is short for "experiential acceptance," the opposite of experiential avoidance.) Here we introduce the notion of allowing your feelings and sensations to be as they are without trying to change them or get rid of them. When you silently name and acknowledge a painful feeling, this often facilitates acceptance, so it's a useful little technique to slip into this section. And you can easily assign it as a simple technique to practice in between sessions.

You'll notice too that we emphasize that this is not a relaxation technique. This is important because many clients will find this experience calming, and they'll often mistake relaxation as the purpose of the exercise when in fact it's merely a beneficial by-product.

SECTION 8: WRAPPING IT UP

Section 8 wraps up the exercise with the Stage Show Metaphor to facilitate contact with the present moment and briefly revisit self-as-context.

Practice, Practice Practice

Now before reading on, I strongly encourage you to go back and read through every transcript in this chapter—but this time, read the words *out loud*, as if you're actually speaking to a client. This is especially important for the Hexaflexercise. I ask you to do this because only through practice will you master this model. So why wait until you're working with your clients? Start right now!

CHAPTER 5

Opening ACT

THE FIRST SESSION

Therapists come to ACT from a vast array of backgrounds and therefore often have widely differing ideas about the first session. For example, many therapists like to do an "intake session" or "pretreatment session" before the first session of "active" therapy. This could involve some or all of the following: taking a detailed history, filling in assessment forms, conducting specialized assessments such as a mental status examination, obtaining informed consent, and/or agreeing to a therapeutic contract.

Some ACT textbooks actively recommend a pretreatment session, and others implicitly assume it. However, practitioners with a background in brief therapy often prefer *not* to do a pretreatment session; instead they actively jump into therapy on the very first encounter. There are pros and cons to both approaches, and this book isn't the place to discuss them; presumably you already have your own approach, and if it's working, there's no need for you to change it. For the sake of clarity, throughout this book I treat session 1 as the very first client-therapist encounter (that is, there's no pretreatment session). If you don't work this way, just add a pretreatment session or "stretch out" the first session into two.

Ideally in session 1, we aim to

- establish rapport;

- take a history;

- obtain informed consent;

- agree on initial treatment goals; and

- agree on the number of sessions.

In addition, if time allows, we may also be able to

- do a brief experiential exercise, and

- give some simple "homework."

With high-functioning clients or those who have a very specific problem, you can often accomplish all of the above in one session. However, for low-functioning clients or those with multiple problems and complex histories, this could easily spill over into two sessions, especially if you want your client to fill in a battery of assessment forms.

Also keep in mind, if your client has a long history of trauma or repeated experiences of abuse and betrayal in intimate relationships, there may well be significant trust issues. If so, you may want to spend two or three sessions primarily taking a history and building rapport—going slowly and taking your time in order to gradually establish a trusting relationship.

Establish Rapport

All models of therapy place importance on the therapeutic relationship; in ACT, this is especially so. Most ACT textbooks ask readers to apply ACT to themselves. Why? Because ACT is far more effective when we, the practitioners, actually embody it in the therapy room. When we're fully present with our clients, open to whatever emotional content arises, defused from our own judgments, and in touch with our core values around connection, compassion, and contribution, then we'll naturally facilitate a warm, resonant, open, and authentic relationship. Indeed, when we give our full attention to another human being with openness, compassion, and curiosity—that in itself is therapeutic.

The ACT stance is that we as therapists are in the same boat as our clients: we both readily get entangled in our minds, lose touch with the present, and engage in futile battles with our own thoughts and feelings; repeatedly lose touch with our core values and act in self-defeating ways; and we both will encounter many similar struggles in our lives, including disappointment, rejection, failure, betrayal, loss, loneliness, sickness, injury, grief, resentment, anxiety, insecurity, and death. This is all part of the human experience. So given that client and therapist are fellow travelers on the same human journey, we can both learn a lot from each other.

In ACT, a compassionate, open, and respectful therapeutic relationship is of utmost importance. Without it, many of our tools, techniques, strategies, and interventions will fail, backfire, or come across as insensitive or invalidating. In particular, we need to be alert for any trace of "one-upmanship" or "superiority" in ourselves; this would be inconsistent with the ACT stance that the therapist and client are equals. The Two Mountains Metaphor (Hayes, Strosahl, & Wilson, 1999) effectively conveys this stance, and I generally share this with the client about half-way through the first session.

THE TWO MOUNTAINS METAPHOR

Therapist: You know, a lot of people come to therapy believing that the therapist is some sort of enlightened being, that he's resolved all his issues, he's got it all together—but actually, that's not the way it is. It's more like you're climbing your mountain over there, and I'm climbing my mountain over here. And from where I am on my mountain, I can see things on your mountain that you can't see—like there's an avalanche about to happen, or there's an alternative pathway you could take, or you're not using your pickax effectively.

But I'd hate for you to think that I've reached the top of my mountain, and I'm sitting back, taking it easy. Fact is, I'm still climbing, still making mistakes, and still learning from them. And basically, we're all the same. We're all climbing our mountain until the day we die. But here's the thing: you can get better and better at climbing, and better and better at learning to appreciate the journey. And that's what the work we do here is all about.

Take a History

Gathering a client history can take anything from a few minutes to an hour, depending upon the situation. For example, the excellent textbook *ACT in Practice* (Bach & Moran, 2008) recommends an entire session to take a detailed history and carefully conceptualize your client's issues. On the other hand, ACT is increasingly used in primary care settings where the therapist may have only two or three sessions of fifteen to thirty minutes each, and this obviously necessitates a brief history (Robinson, 2008).

So once again, the message is this: adapt ACT to your own way of working, your own style, and your own clientele. And as part of taking the history, you can use whatever standardized assessment tools you like. A word of caution though: many popular assessment tools measure changes in the number or severity of symptoms (that is, changes in symptom *form*) but fail to measure changes in the psychological impact or influence of symptoms (that is, changes in symptom *function*). However, in ACT, our interest is in changing symptom *function* rather than *form*. So while there's no absolute necessity for you to use ACT-specific assessment tools, such as the AAQ (Acceptance and Action Questionnaire), they can be very helpful. I won't discuss such tools in this book, but you can download a wide variety at www.contextualpsychology.org/act-specific _ measures.

Before we move on to the nuts and bolts of history taking, take a look at figure 5.1 below. This figure summarizes the essence of most clinical issues from an ACT perspective.

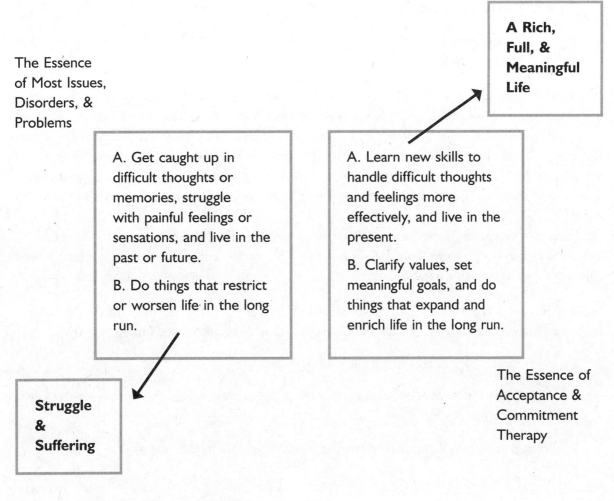

Figure 5.1 **The Essence of Clinical Issues**

This figure reminds us that the outcome we want from ACT is mindful, valued living. In other words, we want to reduce struggle and suffering (via defusion and acceptance) and create a rich, full, and meaningful life (via mindful, values-guided action). When we take a history, our clients generally find it far easier to describe their suffering and their struggles than to describe what a rich, full, and meaningful life would look like. However, we need to know both sets of information. Fortunately there are all sorts of tools and techniques to help people clarify their values, as we shall see later.

CASE CONCEPTUALIZATION: TWO KEY QUESTIONS

With regard to any client's problem, we want to find the answers to two key questions:

1. What valued direction does the client want to move in?

2. What stands in the client's way?

These two questions allow us to quickly conceptualize any issue from an ACT perspective. Let's look at them in more detail.

What valued direction does the client want to move in? Here we seek to clarify values: How does the client want to grow and develop? What personal strengths or qualities does he want to cultivate? How does she want to behave? How does he want to treat himself? What sorts of relationships does she want to build? How does he want to treat others in those relationships? What does she want to stand for in life? What does he want to stand for in the face of this crisis or challenging situation? What domains of life are most important to her? What values-congruent goals does he currently have?

Once we can answer the question "What valued direction does the client want to move in?" we can use that knowledge to set valued goals and to guide, inspire, and sustain ongoing valued action. And if we *can't* answer this question, that tells us we'll need to do some values-clarification work.

What stands in the client's way? This question is about the three main barriers to mindful, valued living: fusion, avoidance, and unworkable action. We can break it down into three smaller questions:

1. What unhelpful thoughts is the client fusing with?

2. What private experiences—thoughts, feelings, memories, urges, and so on—is the client trying to avoid or get rid of?

3. What is the client doing that restricts or worsens her life in the long run?

Put more simply:

■   What is the client fused with?

■   What private experiences is he avoiding?

■   What unworkable action is she taking?

These three questions reveal the essence of any clinical problem: fusion, experiential avoidance, and unworkable action. (A quick reminder: "unworkable" means it doesn't work to make life rich, full, and meaningful in the long run; it interferes with vital, valued living. When action is strongly influenced by fusion and avoidance, it's likely to be unworkable.)

A BASIC GUIDE TO TAKING A HISTORY

For many of us, taking a history is not a neat, orderly, linear process (and it's important to remember, we don't need to gather all our information in one session; we can always get more history later, as needed). Personally, to make this process quicker and easier, I ask my clients to fill out a couple of worksheets before the first session. (I either mail or e-mail the forms out, or ask the client to arrive twenty minutes early and complete them in the waiting room.) I give them Dissecting the Problem, and either the Bull's Eye or the Life Compass. You'll find these worksheets at the end of the chapter. Please take a quick look at them now, then come back to this point. If we want to broadly assess values in different domains of life, the quickest and easiest form is the Bull's Eye, which divides life into four domains: work/education, health/personal growth, relationships, and leisure. More complex but still very user-friendly is the Life Compass, which divides life into ten domains. You might like to experiment with both and see which works best in your practice. I personally use the Bull's Eye initially with lower-functioning clients, and the Life Compass initially with higher-functioning clients. The Dissecting the Problem worksheet breaks down the client's "struggle and suffering" into its key components: fusion, avoidance, and unworkable action. I ask my clients to complete these worksheets to the best of their ability and bring them along to the first session. I explain that even if they only write a few words, that's a good start. Alternatively, you can fill these worksheets in during the session or give them as "homework" to complete after the session.

Now let's go on to the history itself. What follows is a very basic guide to taking a history. Each of the numbered sections can be briefly covered in a few minutes or explored in depth over a much longer time frame, depending on your needs. There's no need to ask all the questions in each section: they are merely guides. (Note: The term "thoughts and feelings" is short for "thoughts, memories, images, emotions, sensations, and urges.") You can download a simplified version of this history guide from www.actmadesimple.com. Read through the guide now, and then we'll explore it in more detail.

HISTORY: A BASIC GUIDE

1. The Presenting Complaint

    a. What is your client's conceptualization of (1) the main problem and (2) how it evolved?

    b. According to your client, how does the presenting complaint interfere with her life? What does it stop him from doing or being?

    c. *Questions to identify problematic thoughts and feelings:* What are the most difficult feelings or emotions showing up for you that are tied into this issue? When your mind wants to get you all worked up over this, what are the scariest, nastiest, or most hurtful things it says to you? Do you ever find yourself dwelling on this issue or worrying about it? If I could listen in to your mind at those times, what would I hear? Does your mind ever beat you up over this? If so, what are the nastiest judgments it makes about you?

    d. *Questions to identify unworkable actions*: What happens when you get caught up in all these painful thoughts and feelings? What do you do differently at those times—how does your behavior change? If I were watching you on a video camera during those times when you get caught up in these thoughts and feelings, what would I see you doing or hear you saying?

    e. *Questions to identify experiential avoidance and unworkable actions:* What have you tried doing to get rid of these painful thoughts and feelings? Is there anything you do that makes you feel stuck or makes the situation worse? Is there anything you do that impacts negatively on your health, or hurts your relationships, or just makes you feel worse? Is there anything you do that wastes your time, energy, or money? Is there anything you do that gives you some relief in the short run but makes the problem worse in the long run?

2. Initial Values Assessment
    You can ask your client some or all of the following questions. In addition (or as an alternative), you can ask the client to fill in a simple assessment tool such as the Bull's Eye or the Life Compass. (You'll find these worksheets at end of this chapter.)

    a. If I could wave a magic wand so that all these problematic thoughts and feelings no longer had any impact on you, what would you start doing, or do more of? What would you stop doing, or do less of? How would you behave differently toward your friends, partner, children, parents, relatives, work colleagues, and so on? How would you act differently at home, at work, and at play?

    b. Do you ever feel a sense of purpose, meaning, vitality, or fulfillment—even for just a moment? Doing what? What, when, where, how, and with whom?

c. If, in the process of dealing with this unwanted, painful issue, you could develop some personal strengths or qualities or abilities that would help you in some way to become a "better person," or to "grow as a human being," or "make a difference in the lives of others," what might those strengths, qualities, or abilities be?

d. What are you doing in your life right now that is inconsistent with the person, deep in your heart, that you truly want to be? What would you like to do differently?

e. If the work we do here could have a positive impact on the most important relationships in your life, which relationships would improve? And how? How would you like to be in those relationships if you could be the ideal you?

f. *For clients in crisis or extremely painful life situations:* What do you want to stand for in the face of this? If at some point in the future you were to look back at the way you handled this situation now, then what would you like to say about the way you handled it? What would you like to say about how you grew or developed as a result of it?

g. *For suicidal clients:* What has stopped you from killing yourself?

h. *For mandated/coerced/reluctant clients:* For a moment, let's forget about the person(s) who sent you here and focus on what's in this for you. If there were something useful you could get out of our sessions so that they weren't just a hassle, a stress, a nuisance, a waste of your time; if there were some way this time could help you improve your life and make it better in some way, what area of your life would you most want to improve? In what ways would you like to improve it? What matters to you in this area of your life?

3. The Current Life Context, Family History, Social History, Other Assessment Tools
   Current life context includes health, medications, work, finances, relationships, family, culture, and so on. Also look for factors that reinforce the problem—for example, secondary gains. Family history and social history include significant relationships from the past and present, and how the clients perceive they have been impacted by this history. Other assessment tools depend on your practice and clientele. You may prefer to keep this brief initially and gather more data as necessary in later sessions.

4. Psychological Inflexibility

   a. *Dominance of the conceptualized past or future; limited self-knowledge:* How much time does your client spend dwelling on the past or fantasizing/worrying about the future? How easily does he lose contact with the present (that is, how distractible is he)? How difficult does she find it to "know" what she's thinking and feeling?

   b. *Fusion:* What sort of unhelpful cognitive content is your client fusing with—rigid rules, self-limiting beliefs, harsh judgments, reason-giving, being right, ideas of hopelessness or worthlessness, or others?

c. *Experiential avoidance:* What private experiences (thoughts, feelings, memories, and so on) is your client avoiding—and how? How pervasive is experiential avoidance in your client's life?

d. *Attachment to the conceptualized self:* What is your client's "conceptualized self"? For example, does he see himself as broken/damaged/unlovable/weak/stupid, and so on, or does she perhaps see herself as strong/superior/successful? How fused is your client to this self-image?

e. *Lack of values clarity/contact:* What core values is this client unclear about, neglecting or acting inconsistently with (for example, connection, caring, contribution, self-care, self-compassion, loving, nurturing, or others)?

f. *Unworkable action:* What self-defeating actions is your client taking? Does he lack necessary skills for change? Does she fail to persist when persistent action is required, or does she inappropriately continue when such action is ineffective? What people, places, situations, and activities is he avoiding or withdrawing from?

5. Motivational Factors

Assess positive factors—for example, goals, dreams, desires, visions, values. Also assess negative factors: internal barriers to change (that is, fusion and avoidance) and external barriers to change (for example, financial or social situation).

6. Psychological Flexibility and Client Strengths

Assess areas of life in which the client already exhibits psychological flexibility through defusion, acceptance, self-as-context, contacting the present moment, connection with values, and committed action. Also identify personal strengths and useful life skills that your client already has which can be utilized in therapy.

A FEW NOTES ON TAKING A HISTORY

Notes on section 1: The Presenting Complaint. In this section, you may also include a question such as this: what do you hope to get from therapy? The answer will usually tell you a lot about the client's emotional control agenda. She's likely to tell you how she wants to feel (happy, more confident, more self-esteem, and so on) or what feelings he wants to get rid of (anxiety, depression, bad memories, and so on).

The questions in 1b are very useful: How does this issue interfere with your life? What does it stop you from doing or being? Clients' answers usually fall into three categories; the issue is problematic because:

1. *"I can't stand feeling this way."* This answer points to the experiential avoidance agenda. You may follow up by asking which thoughts/feelings/memories and so on are hardest to feel, or most unwanted, or have the greatest impact.

2. *"I just want to be normal."* This answer points to fusion with the conceptualized self. The client is likely fused with "I am abnormal/weird/weak [or others]." You may follow up by asking, "So what does your mind say this problem means about you?"

3. *"It stops me from being or doing X, Y, Z."* This answer often points to values and goals. You may follow up by asking for more information about X, Y, Z.

Notes on section 2: Initial Values Assessment. I've included lots of questions in this section to give you a variety of options for eliciting values. You wouldn't ask all of these questions of one client; you can pick and choose which are most relevant or likely to be useful for a given client. (If you get answers like "I don't know" to every single question you ask, and your client is unwilling or unable to fill in the Bull's Eye or Life Compass worksheets, that's useful information; it tells you you're almost certainly dealing with a client at the upper end of the experiential avoidance spectrum, and you'll probably need to develop defusion and acceptance skills before you can get to values in depth.) The Bull's Eye is a simpler assessment tool than the Life Compass and is a better initial choice if you suspect your client is highly experientially avoidant.

Notes on section 3: The Current Life Context, Family History, Social History, Other Assessment Tools. Current life context includes health, medications, work, finances, relationships, family, culture, and so on. Also look for factors that reinforce the problem—for example, getting attention, manipulating others, obtaining disability benefits, avoiding fears of rejection/intimacy/failure, adhering to cultural beliefs, and so on. Identify these factors as soon as possible as they will likely provide barriers to moving forward. Keep your eyes and ears open for "secondary gains." For example, if Dad only helps out with their three young kids when Mom is in bed feeling "too depressed to do anything," then this secondary gain could act as a barrier to Mom's recovery.

Family history and social history also includes significant relationships from the past and present, and how the client perceives he has been impacted by this history. Here we're looking at the broad context of the client's life as it is today, as well as key events from the past that have shaped the client's current behavior and contributed to the problematic thoughts, feelings, memories, and so on that are showing up in her life today. In particular, note social and financial factors playing a role in the client's current problems.

Personally I tend to zip through this quite rapidly with most clients, knowing I can gather more information whenever I need to. However, as with everything in ACT, modify this to your own preferences and needs. Thus, if you want to conceptualize in depth how current behavior has been shaped by past experience, then you'll obviously take much longer to explore the client's past history.

Notes on section 4: Psychological Inflexibility. This section is pretty much self-explanatory: we are on the lookout for core pathological processes that we'll later target with mindfulness and valued action.

Notes on section 5: Motivational Factors. Hopefully you will already have gathered a lot of this information via sections 1, 2, and 3. Of course, with some clients you'll initially have little or no helpful responses to questions about values and goals. But that's okay: it just tells you this client is likely to need work around defusion and acceptance before he can readily do values work. The very fact that such clients have come to therapy points in the direction of values. For example, in an extreme case such as a client mandated by the court to either attend therapy or go to prison, the very fact that she has come to see you points to values around freedom. (You can also use the FEAR acronym to identify barriers to change: see chapter 12.)

Notes on section 6: Psychological Flexibility and Client Strengths. Assess areas of life in which the client already exhibits psychological flexibility through defusion, acceptance, a sense of self-as-context, contacting the present moment, connection with values, and taking committed action. This is a vitally important part of the history. If we imagine psychological flexibility as a scale of 0 to 100, presumably there would be no such thing as a client who rated zero. So let's find what elements of psychological flexibility he is already using, in what contexts, with what results. You may want to ask direct questions, such as these:

- Do you ever find you're able to detach from your thoughts or not take them so seriously? Do you ever find your mind starts criticizing you, but you don't buy into it?

- Do you ever find you can tolerate your feelings even though they're very unpleasant?

- Do you ever get a sense of being able to step back and observe painful thoughts and feelings rather than struggling with them?

- Do you have any spiritual, religious, or meditative practices? (You might specifically inquire about yoga, tai chi, martial arts, meditation, prayer, and so on.)

- When do you feel connected with life, yourself, or the world? When do you get a sense of meaning, purpose, vitality? Doing what sorts of activities? Where? When? With whom? When do you get a sense that you're making the most of your life, or contributing to something important, or connecting with something that "pulls you out of yourself"?

- When do you push on and do what you need to do regardless of how you're feeling?

- When are you fully present—that is, conscious, aware, and engaged in what you're doing instead of being "off in your head"? Doing what sorts of activities? With whom? Where? And when?

Obtain Informed Consent

Ideally informed consent includes some discussion of

- the ACT model: what ACT is and what it involves;

- the importance of experiential exercises and practicing skills; and

- possible adverse experiences.

To move from taking a history to informed consent, you could say something like, "There's a lot more I could ask you about all this, but you've given me enough for us to make a start. What I'd like to do at this point is tell you a bit about the sort of therapy I do, what it involves, and how long it takes, and basically make sure it's the right approach for you. Is that okay?"

THE ACT MODEL: WHAT ACT IS AND WHAT IT INVOLVES

Next you can provide a brief summary of the ACT approach, as detailed below. (I suggest you take this "spiel," rewrite it or modify it into your own words, and then practice it until it rolls off the tip of your tongue so that you can quickly summarize ACT to colleagues, allied health professionals, clients, friends, relatives, and people you meet at dinner parties.)

Therapist: Do you know anything at all about the model I work with?

Client: No.

Therapist: Well, it's a scientifically based therapy that has a rather unusual name. It's called acceptance and commitment therapy—or ACT, for short. And it gets its name from one of its core messages: accept what's out of your personal control and commit to taking action that improves your life. And the aim of ACT is basically very simple: to help you create a rich, full, and meaningful life while effectively handling the pain and stress that goes with it. And ACT achieves this in two main ways. First, it helps you develop psychological skills to *deal with your painful thoughts and feelings more effectively, in such a way that they have much less impact and influence over you.* We call these "mindfulness skills." Second, ACT helps you to clarify what is truly important and meaningful to you—what we call your "values"—and then use that knowledge to guide, inspire, and motivate you when making changes in your life.

Notice the italicized phrase: *deal with your painful thoughts and feelings effectively, in such a way that they have much less impact and influence over you.* This wording is very important. ACT is not about trying to reduce, avoid, eliminate, or control these thoughts and feelings—it's about reducing their impact and influence over behavior (in order to facilitate valued living).

Practical Tip You don't have to use the word "mindfulness." Most clients are fine with it, but some people associate mindfulness with hypnosis, religion, or the New Age movement. So you could talk instead about "psychological skills" or "new ways to handle thoughts and feelings"; and you could use alternative terms such as "noticing," "observing," "opening up," "centering," "being present," "focusing," "paying attention," "awareness," and so on.

THE IMPORTANCE OF EXPERIENTIAL EXERCISES AND PRACTICING SKILLS

After the spiel above, you could say something like this:

Therapist: As I just mentioned, ACT is a scientifically based model. It's been proven to be effective with a wide range of issues from depression, anxiety, and work stress to drug addiction and schizophrenia. And it's a very active model of therapy. We don't just talk in these sessions; we actually practice psychological skills so you can learn how to handle all those difficult thoughts and feelings more effectively. And like any skill, the more you practice, the better you'll get. So what we do during these sessions will be useful, but what really makes the difference is practicing these new skills in between sessions. After all, if you wanted to learn the guitar, you wouldn't expect to have a few lessons and then become a great guitarist—you'd expect to do some practice.

If clients want more detail. At this point, some clients will ask for more detail about what's involved. If so, you could say something like the following (tailoring your response to specifically address the client's issues): "Well, what we do varies enormously from session to session. In some sessions, we'll focus on how you can let go of painful thoughts or memories or worries, or free yourself up from self-limiting beliefs. Sometimes we'll look at new ways to handle strong feelings like fear or anger or sadness or guilt. At times, we'll focus on getting in touch with what's important to you, setting goals, or constructing an effective plan of action. It varies enormously, depending upon what the issue is, and how you're going along, and what you've found helpful."

A small number of clients will still ask you for more information at this point about what sort of skills they'll be learning or what exercises they'll be doing. If so, you could answer, "I think it's great that you're eager to know more, but trying to describe exactly what we do in ACT is like trying to describe skiing or scuba diving or horse riding: you can talk about those things until the cows come home, but you'll never know what they're really like until you actually start doing them. In the same way, I can't do justice to ACT in words. But what I'd like to do a bit later is take you through a short exercise to give you a taste of what's involved. And if we don't have time today, then we'll leave it for next session. Would that be okay?"

(Alternatively, you could take the client through the ACT in a Nutshell Metaphor from chapter 1. However, before you do this, there are several things you need to consider. First, is the metaphor appropriate for this client at this point in therapy? I'm wary of using it for very low-functioning clients or those that I suspect are extremely experientially avoidant because they may misinterpret it, criticize it, or insist it won't work for them. In contrast, high-functioning clients typically warm to it. Second, do you have time in the session? You should allow several minutes to run through the metaphor and also ensure you have at least another five minutes to address any questions or concerns. And last but not least, I wouldn't advocate the use of this metaphor as part of informed consent until you have quite a bit of practice at ACT and a sound grasp of the model so you can address any concerns or queries that arise in an effective, ACT-consistent manner.)

If the client is doubtful. Suppose your client says, "I don't think this will work for me." Thoughts like this are perfectly natural, and they're only problematic if the client fuses with them. So here you have a perfect opportunity to establish a context of acceptance and defusion. For example, you might say, "That's a perfectly natural thought. Many people feel doubtful at first. And the fact is there is no known treatment that is guaranteed to work for everyone. So I can't promise that this *will* work for you. I could tell you it's worked for lots of other people, and I could pull out all the published studies and the research papers, and so on, but that still wouldn't guarantee it will work for you. However, here's something I can guarantee: if we stop the session whenever you have the thought *This won't work*, then I can absolutely guarantee that we WON'T get anywhere. So even though you're having the thought that this won't work, are you willing to give it a go anyway?"

Notice that we're not challenging the client's thought. Rather we're validating it as natural and normal. And we're establishing a context where (a) it's okay for the client to have that thought (acceptance), and (b) the thought is just a thought and doesn't control the client's actions (defusion).

POSSIBLE ADVERSE EXPERIENCES

Next we move on to discussing possible adverse consequences of therapy. I like to use a roller-coaster metaphor: "There are a couple more things I want to discuss with you. One thing is, in order to learn new skills for handling painful thoughts and feelings, we're going to have to bring up some of those thoughts and feelings in session so that you have something to practice with. This means that at times therapy might seem like a bit of a roller-coaster ride. But here's my guarantee: I will be there in the roller-coaster car alongside you." If you know that your client is highly experientially avoidant or has a tendency to drop out of therapy, then it's useful to say something like this: "You may find that at times you feel a strong urge to drop out of therapy. This is completely normal and natural, and if it happens, then it's almost always when you're facing up to some very important issue—usually something that can have a huge impact on your life. So if you ever do start feeling that way, I hope you'll be willing to share it with me so we can work with those feelings during our sessions."

Agree on Treatment Goals

Agreeing on goals and formulating a treatment plan may not come naturally to you, but it is important; otherwise how do you know where to go in your sessions? Of course, while obtaining informed consent, you've already agreed on some basic treatment goals: that during sessions the client will learn mindfulness skills, clarify values, and use values to guide behavioral change, and between sessions, she'll practice and apply these new skills. For some clients, this may be about as specific as you can get during a first session.

If you've had your client fill in the Bull's Eye or Life Compass worksheets, you can ask him, "If you had to pick just one of these life domains to start working on, which one would it be? What sort of changes do you want to make in that area of your life? How do you want to improve it?" If you're lucky, this will give you some useful values-guided goals to agree on as treatment goals. However, many clients will initially give you "emotional goals," "dead person's goals," or "insight goals." Let's take a quick look at each of these.

EMOTIONAL GOALS

"I just want to be happy," "I don't want to be depressed," "I want to stop feeling anxious," "I want more self-confidence," "I need more self-esteem," "I want to move on," "I want to feel calm," or "I want to stop worrying." In ACT, we call these "emotional goals" because in each case, the goal is to control how one feels: to get rid of "bad" thoughts and feelings and replace them with "good" ones.

If we agree to these goals, we'll reinforce experiential avoidance, a core pathological process that is the very opposite of mindfulness. However, if we bluntly announce this to the client, it will probably be counterproductive. So it's better to say something like, "Okay. So can I put it this way? There are painful thoughts and feelings that you've been struggling with, and one goal of therapy is to learn better ways of handling them."

Having said all that, there are a few special circumstances in which it's probably better to be crystal clear from the outset that our agenda is *not* to eliminate unwanted thoughts and feelings. For example, suppose you have a client with PTSD who says, "I just want to get rid of these memories." A useful response to this might include the Horror Movie Metaphor.

THE HORROR MOVIE METAPHOR

Therapist: You know, there are quite a few scientifically proven models for treating PTSD—we call them "empirically supported" treatments—but not one of them works by *eliminating* bad memories. What they all do is help you to respond to your memories differently so they have less impact and influence over you. If I can give you an analogy: right now when these memories show up, it's like watching a terrifying horror movie late at night, all alone by yourself, in a rickety old house, with all the lights off. Now suppose you have exactly the same movie playing, but this time the TV's in the corner of the room, it's broad daylight, sunlight's streaming in through the windows, your house is full of friends and family, and you're all interacting together—talking, laughing, eating, having fun. The movie hasn't changed one bit—it's still playing on the TV in the corner of the room—but now it's having much less effect on you. Mindfulness skills will enable you to do this sort of thing. I don't know any way to permanently delete these memories, but we can change your relationship with them so you can get on with your life and do the things you really want to do.

DEAD PERSON'S GOALS

Often your client's goals will be to stop feeling or behaving a certain way—for example, "I want to stop using drugs," "I want to stop yelling at my kids," "I don't want to have any more panic attacks," or "I don't want to feel depressed." In ACT, these are called a "dead person's goals" (Lindsley, 1968). A dead person's goal is anything that a corpse can do better than a live human being. For example, a corpse will never use drugs, never yell at the kids, never have a panic attack, and never feel depressed.

In ACT, we want to set "living person's goals"—things that a live human being can do better than a corpse. To move from a dead person's goal to a living person's goal, you can ask simple questions like these:

- "So let's suppose that happens. Then what would you do differently? What would you start or do more of? And how would you behave differently with friends or family?"

- "If you weren't using drugs, what *would* you be doing instead?"

- "If you weren't yelling at your kids, how *would* you be interacting with them?"

- "If you weren't having panic attacks or feeling depressed, what would you be doing differently with your life?"

Two useful questions to turn emotional goals and dead person's goals into values-congruent goals are the magic wand question and the seven-day documentary question. Let's take a quick look at each of these now.

The magic wand question. This is a good question for cutting through the emotional control agenda. Note the phrase "are no longer a problem for you"; this is very different to saying "have all disappeared."

Therapist: Suppose I had a magic wand here. I wave this wand, and all the thoughts and feelings you've been struggling with are no longer a problem for you. What would you then do differently? What sort of things would you start doing or perhaps do more of? How would you behave differently toward others? What would you do differently at work, at home, on weekends?

The Seven-Day Documentary Question. This is a good question for helping the client become more specific about the changes she wants to make in her life.

Therapist: Suppose we followed you around with a camera crew for a week, filmed everything you did, and edited it into a documentary. And then suppose we did the same at some point in the future, after our work together has finished. What would we see or hear on the new video that would show that therapy had been helpful? What would we see you doing or hear you saying? What would we notice differently about the way you interact with other people or the way you spend your time?

INSIGHT GOALS

"I want to understand why I'm like this," "I need to figure out why I keep doing this," or "I want to discover who I really am." Treatment goals like these easily lead to "analysis paralysis"—to session after session of intellectual/theoretical/conceptual discussions and endless reflections on the past instead of to the development of new skills for mindful, valued living.

As it happens during ACT, clients *will* develop a lot of understanding and insight into their own behavior, thoughts, feelings, personality, and identity. They will generally have powerful realizations around who they are, how their mind works, what they really want in life, how the past has influenced them, and why they do the things they do. But in ACT, they develop this insight via experiential work, not through lengthy analytical discussions. Furthermore, this insight is not an end in itself: it's simply something that happens on the journey toward the desired outcome of mindful, valued living.

Thus to move to a more useful treatment goal, I say, "As part of the work we do together, you'll certainly get a lot more insight into who you are, how your mind works, why you do the things you do, and what you really want in life. All of that is already a given; it happens as part of the process in ACT. When I ask what you want out of therapy, what I mean is, once you have that insight and understanding, what do you want to do differently? If you had that knowledge, what would you do that you're not doing now? How would you behave differently? What would others notice that was different about you?"

TREATMENT GOALS: A FEW EXAMPLES

Here are some examples of treatment goals, as summarized by the therapist.

Treatment Goals for Depression. In response to the magic wand question, this client replied that what she'd do differently is get back to work, start exercising again, and spend more time with her friends and family.

Therapist: So can we say it like this: It seems that what you mean by depression is partly that you're getting caught up in a lot of unpleasant thoughts—negative self-judgments, a sense of hopelessness, and thoughts and memories about painful events from the past. And another part of it is that you're struggling with some really painful feelings including guilt, sadness, anxiety, and physical tiredness. And a third part of it is, you're doing things that make your life worse, such as spending a lot of time in bed, socially isolating yourself, staying indoors, giving up exercise, avoiding going to work, and so on. So we may well change the goals as we go, but for now can we agree that what we're aiming for is (a) to learn some new skills to handle all those difficult thoughts and feelings, and (b) to get you back into doing things that used to matter to you, such as socializing, working, exercising, and generally doing things that fulfill you? Is that about right?

Notice how the therapist breaks the issue down into three elements: (1) getting caught up in thoughts, (2) struggling with feelings, and (3) unworkable actions. This is intentional. Right from the word "go," we can subtly lay the groundwork for two key insights:

1. Our thoughts and feelings are not the main problem; it's getting caught up in them (fusion) and struggling with them (avoidance) that creates our problems.

2. Our thoughts and feelings do not *control* our actions.

This second key insight often takes therapists by surprise, so let's take a moment to explore it. Our thoughts and feelings certainly *influence* our actions, but they don't *control* our actions. Our behavior in any moment is under the influence of multiple streams of stimuli, coming both from the world inside our skin and from the world outside us. Think back to the Stage Show Metaphor: our actions are influenced by everything on the stage—whatever we can see, hear, smell, touch, taste, sense, feel, and think.

So when do thoughts and feelings have the most influence over our actions? You guessed it: in a context of fusion and avoidance. However, in a context of defusion and acceptance (that is, mindfulness), those same thoughts and feelings have much less influence over our behavior, which frees us up to act on our values. What this means is the greater our psychological flexibility, the greater our capacity to choose the actions we take regardless of the thoughts and feelings we're having. With this in mind, we want to repeatedly draw a distinction between (a) the client's thoughts and feelings, and (b) the actions the client takes when those thoughts and feelings show up. Ultimately we want to shatter the illusion that the former *controls* the latter. (And this approach is only likely to succeed when we do it experientially, not didactically.)

Treatment goals for alcohol addiction. This client wanted to quit drinking because (a) his wife was threatening to leave him, and (b) at a recent medical checkup his liver was in bad shape. In response to the magic wand question, he wanted to be a "better husband" and "fix up" his liver.

Therapist: So to summarize: when you've tried to quit drinking in the past, it never lasted long because you'd get strong cravings or you'd have feelings of anxiety and depression, and then you'd start drinking to make them go away. So our goals here in therapy are (a) to learn some new skills so you can handle these cravings and feelings more effectively, (b) to build a better relationship your wife, and (c) to start looking after your liver and make it as healthy as possible. Is that about right?

Notice how the therapist has moved from a dead person's goal—stop drinking—to several living person's goals.

> **Practical Tip**   Some clients have so many issues, they don't know where to start, or they feel overwhelmed. Here the Bull's Eye or Life Compass worksheets are very useful: you can say, "Just pick one of these domains, and we'll start there. What would you like to do differently in this area of your life?"

Generic treatment goals. Sometimes, despite all your best efforts, your client will be unable or unwilling to give you any specific values-oriented treatment goals. She may just keep answering, "I don't know," "Nothing matters," or "I just want to stop feeling like this," or "I just want to feel happy." In such cases, don't try to force the point; just accept that for now your treatment goals will be vague and generic. Below are two alternatives you could use in these cases.

Therapist: So how about we agree to this? The work we do here will be about two things. First, learning new ways to handle your thoughts and feelings more effectively so they can't hold you back from living the life you want. Second, even though right now you have no idea what you want and you feel like nothing matters, let's make this a place where you get to discover what *does* matter to you and what sort of life you *do* want to have. And once we've discovered that, let's set about making it happen.

***

Therapist: So for now, let's just say that the work we do here will be about giving you a life that grabs you, a life that you feel is worth living. At this point, you don't know what that life looks like, but that's okay. We'll find out as we go along. So one aim of our work here will be to discover what's important to you and what sort of life you want to live. And another aim will be to learn better ways to deal with the pain that life is currently giving you. And both of those aims are ultimately to serve one purpose: creating a rich and meaningful life.

> **Practical Tip**   Notice in all of these examples how the therapist uses terms like "handle" or "deal with" pain as opposed to "manage," "control," "reduce," or "eliminate." Mindfulness is not a way to control, manage, reduce, or eliminate thoughts and feelings; it's a way of "handling them gently" or "dealing with them compassionately" or "holding them lightly." Other terms you could use include "stepping out of the battle," or "dropping the struggle," or "changing your relationship" with your thoughts and feelings.

Agree on the Number of Sessions

How many sessions of ACT does a client need? Well, how long is a piece of string? I've seen amazing things happen from a single session of ACT, and I've also had clients that I worked with on a regular basis for three or four years! As a general rule, the greater your clients' problems in number, duration, severity, and impact on their quality of life, the longer the duration of therapy. However this is not *necessarily* so; ACT can be delivered in many different formats, including these:

- **Long-term therapy:** for example, one protocol for ACT with borderline personality disorder goes for forty group sessions, each two-hours long (Brann, Gopold, Guymer, Morton, & Snowdon, 2007).

- **Brief therapy:** for example, a popular protocol for ACT with anxiety disorders is based on twelve one-hour sessions (Eifert & Forsyth, 2005) and one published study for ACT with chronic stress and pain is based on an eight-hour protocol (Dahl et al., 2004).

- **Very brief therapy:** for example, one published study on ACT for chronic schizophrenia consisted of only three or four one-hour sessions. That very brief intervention lead to an almost 50 percent reduction in hospital readmission rates (Bach & Hayes, 2002).

(Obviously with these very brief ACT interventions, it's not as if the client fully and completely embraces mindful, valued living and never has any issues ever again. It's more the case that we can deliver the core elements of ACT—be present, open up, do what matters—quite quickly and with significant benefits. The client then becomes his own ACT therapist, and life throws up all sorts of problems and challenges, which provide opportunities to further develop his skills.)

Quite a few ACT textbooks suggest you agree to twelve sessions initially, but there is nothing magical about this number, so you can adjust it to suit your clientele. For example, in Australia, the country where I live and practice, there's not the same degree of openness to therapy as there is in the United States; therefore I typically contract for only six sessions initially.

At this juncture, we tell the client that therapy isn't a smooth journey but involves ups and downs. For example, you might say, "One thing I should mention is that therapy doesn't always progress smoothly. Sometimes you make a huge leap forward; and sometimes you take a big step backward. So because it can be a bit up and down, I wonder if you would commit to six sessions initially—and at the end of that time, we'll assess how it's going and see if you need more. And you'll be the one who makes the call on that, not me. You'll judge whether we're making progress or not. Now obviously, some people don't need a full six sessions, and others end up needing more than that. At this point, it's hard for me to predict how many you'll need, so would you be willing to initially commit to six?"

Do a Brief Experiential Exercise

If time permits, I like to do a brief experiential exercise during the first session. Any mindfulness exercise will suffice—ideally one that goes for about five minutes. For example, you might run through a chunk of the Hexaflexercise (see chapter 4), or exercises such as Dropping an Anchor or Ten Mindful Breaths (see chapter 9). Then once you've done this exercise at the first session, you could ask permission to start each session with a similar one.

Give Homework

Ask your clients to do a little bit of homework between this session and the next. This reinforces the notion that ACT involves active work both in session and between sessions. For example, if you took your client through a simple mindfulness exercise, then for homework you could ask her to practice it once a day. Alternatively you might ask her to keep a diary or fill in a worksheet, such as those at the end of this chapter.

Practical Tip   Many people don't like the sound of "homework." It carries all sorts of negative connotations. I prefer the term "practice" or "experiment." For example, you might say, "Would you be willing to practice something between now and next session?" or "Would you be willing to experiment with doing this and see what happens?"

WORKSHEETS

This book contains a lot of client worksheets. They're often helpful because they act as a reminder of the session, increase the chance that your client will follow through, and provide good material for the next session. (But they aren't essential, and you can certainly do ACT effectively without using worksheets, if you prefer not to.)

At the end of the first session, if you didn't get much information about values, and you didn't get the client to fill out a Life Compass or Bull's Eye worksheet, then you could now ask them to do so for homework. For example, you might say, "We've talked quite a lot about your problems today—the thoughts and feelings you struggle with, and the things you do that make your life worse—but we haven't talked much about what sort of life you want to live, what really matters to you in the big picture. So I'm wondering, between now and next session, would you be willing to fill in this worksheet, which asks you to think about these things?" Other worksheets you might give out are the Vitality vs. Suffering Diary or the Problems and Values Worksheet. You can explain that these worksheets help gather more information to guide therapy. (Worksheets are located at the end of the chapter, or they can be downloaded at no cost from www.actmadesimple.com.)

ALTERNATIVES TO WORKSHEETS

Some clients—and some therapists—don't like using worksheets and forms. This is not too surprising. Try filling in a few yourself, especially those that require daily completion, and you'll soon see how challenging it is. If clients strongly oppose filling in forms, or if you as a therapist intensely dislike using them, then you don't have to use them. They are simply aids to ACT, not essentials.

So instead of giving her a worksheet, you could ask your client simply to notice over the next week (a) what she does that drains or restricts her life, and (b) what she does that enriches and expands her life.

Alternatively you could ask your client to think a bit more about his values or practice a simple mindfulness technique such as mindful breathing. You might even ask him to notice some of the most distressing thoughts that he has, and to notice what happens when he gets caught up in them.

HOMEWORK FOR YOU

If you're anything like me, you have a tendency to read textbooks and hope everything "sinks in" so you can readily trot it out in the therapy room. If only!! There's no two ways about it: you won't learn ACT simply by reading a book. So from now on at the end of each chapter, you'll find a homework section. If you do these exercises, they'll help you to learn ACT in a way that far surpasses mere reading. And because you're the best person to practice on, many of these exercises ask you to work on your own issues.

So here are a few things I recommend:

1. Read out loud and paraphrase all of the therapist's "spiels" in the transcripts above—especially on informed consent—to get yourself used to ACT-speak.

2. Do a couple of quick case conceptualizations. Pick two clients and write brief answers to these four questions: What valued direction does the client want to move in? What is she fused with? What is he avoiding? What unworkable action is she taking?

3. Practice summarizing treatment goals. Pick two clients and imagine how you would summarize the treatment goals, using the suggestions in this chapter.

As you do these exercises, and all the other ones in this book, please give yourself permission to do them poorly. You're learning a new model of therapy, so allow yourself to be a beginner, a novice, a learner. Beginners make mistakes (and so do experts). It's an essential part of the learning process. And if your mind starts beating you up, then make a note of what it says, so you can work with those thoughts in chapter 7.

SUBSEQUENT SESSIONS

One of the hardest decisions for new ACT practitioners is this: after session 1, where on the hexaflex do I start? There is no "correct" answer to this question. There's really no such thing as the "right" or "wrong" starting point, as all six core processes are interconnected and overlapping. (If you're brand-new to ACT, this interconnectedness may not become clear until the end of this book.) Indeed, as you become more familiar with ACT, you'll typically find yourself covering most or all points on the hexaflex in most or all sessions. As you do this, some processes will be explicit—that is, you directly focus on them in the session—while the others remain implicit—that is, present but "in the background."

In terms of subsequent sessions, traditional ACT protocols follow a particular sequence:

1.   Defusion and acceptance

2.   Contacting the present moment

3.   Self-as-context

4.   Values and committed action

A less common sequence but one that I recommend for coaching, couples work, high-functioning clients, mandated clients, or clients lacking in motivation is this:

1.   Values and committed action

2.   Defusion and acceptance

3.   Contacting the present moment

4.   Self-as-context

There is also an optional component of ACT called *creative hopelessness*, which means getting in touch with the costs and futility of experiential avoidance. Creative hopelessness is only *essential* if and when clients are so deeply attached to the agenda of emotional control that they aren't open to mindfulness and acceptance. You can bring creative hopelessness in at any point in therapy where it becomes necessary—however, traditional ACT protocols start with it in order to lay the foundation for acceptance.

As I'm a traditional kind of guy (did you notice my conceptualized self there?), in the next seven chapters, I'm going to take you through the traditional sequence, starting with creative hopelessness. However, please keep in mind there are no clean-cut divisions between different components of the model: when we talk about the "sequence of components," it's a convenient way of describing the major emphasis in each of those sessions. For example, it's hard to imagine a session focused purely on acceptance without an element of values or a session purely on values without some defusion.

Also remember that once you know what you're doing, you can dance around the hexaflex in any sequence that's likely to be clinically effective. For example, if you have a client who dissociates easily, you might start active therapy with contacting the present moment: teaching him simple mindfulness exercises for grounding and centering himself.

What Do We Do in Each Session?

Recall that the aim of ACT is to cultivate psychological flexibility: the ability to be fully conscious and open to your experience while acting on your values—or, said more simply, the ability to "be present, open up, and do what matters." The outcome we're looking for is mindful, valued living, which means doing what is meaningful while embracing each moment of life.

As figure 5.2 (below) illustrates, we aim to help clients move from mindless, fused, avoidant, ineffective action—which leads to suffering—to mindful, valued, willing, effective action—which leads to vitality. And when we use the term *vitality* in ACT, we're not referring to a feeling or an emotion; we mean a sense of being fully alive and embracing each moment even if it's painful.

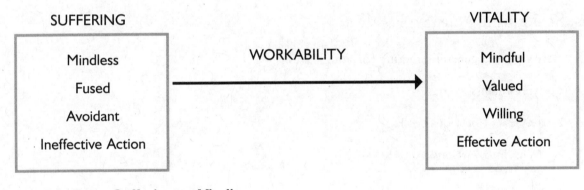

Figure 5.2 **From Suffering to Vitality**

In each session, we aim to increase psychological flexibility: that is, to help the client move from the left (suffering) to the right (vitality). Behavior that takes the client from left to right is "workable"—and behavior that takes her in the opposite direction is "unworkable." Whether the session is fifteen minutes long or an hour long, we aim to make a shift in any or all of the dimensions in this diagram:

■ Where unworkable behavior is mindless (that is, done impulsively or on autopilot), we can work on mindfulness: helping the client become fully conscious of and engaged in what he is doing.

■ Where unworkable behavior is heavily influenced by fusion with unhelpful beliefs, we can work on both defusion from those beliefs and values clarification as an alternative source of motivation.

- Where unworkable behavior is heavily influenced by avoidance of unwanted private experiences, we can work on willingness to have those private experiences.

- Where unworkable behavior is due to ineffectiveness—that is, due to deficits in skills or failure to use appropriate skills—we can work on building and applying necessary skills.

What Interventions Do We Use?

Any intervention that helps the client to move from the left to the right in the figure above is useful. No matter how tiny the move is, if the client moves in the direction of "workability," the intervention can be said to be "effective." Of course this isn't always a smooth linear process. Often your clients will get stuck or "backslide," and will start moving in the opposite direction. Your aim is then to compassionately and nonjudgmentally help the client connect with the costs of doing so and to help her get back "on track" as fast as possible.

Structuring Your Sessions

Here's a good general structure for your sessions:

1. Mindfulness exercise

2. Review of previous session

3. Main interventions

4. Homework

Let's take a quick look at each of these now.

Mindfulness exercise. It's often helpful to start each session with a brief mindfulness exercise such as mindful breathing. (This is not essential, just often helpful!)

Review of previous session. Review the previous session, including key content covered, exercises practiced, and any thoughts or reactions the client has had since. If your client followed through on his homework, what happened, and what difference did it make? And if not, what got in the way?

In later sessions, once values work has been done, specifically ask about valued living. For example, "So how have you done living by your values this week?" or "What valued actions have you been taking?"

Main interventions. If you're following a protocol, you'll have a good idea in advance of what you wish to cover in session. It's important though to be flexible—to respond to what's happening in session. Be willing to let go of everything you had preplanned, if needs be. (You can always come back to it in a later session.) If you're not following a protocol, you will either pick up from wherever you left off in the previous session or address a new issue that has just arisen.

Homework. It's important to repeatedly emphasize to clients that what they do in between sessions is what will really make all the difference in their lives. Mindfulness skills require practice. Valued action requires effort. You need to collaboratively agree before the end of each session what the client is going to practice, do, or experiment with in between sessions. (But be careful—don't get too pushy or use values coercively.)

SUMMARY

To sum it all up, the main tasks for a first session are to build rapport, obtain informed consent, and make a basic assessment. When assessing the current problems, look for fusion, avoidance, and unworkable action. And when assessing desired outcomes of therapy, look for values and values-congruent goals. And that's basically it; that's the main information you'll need to help your client move from suffering to vitality.

Of course, it's not as easy as it sounds in a four-sentence summary. To do ACT effectively requires practice—and plenty of it. And the fact is, there's a lot of information in this chapter; most readers will not take it all in the first time around. So I strongly suggest that as soon as you've finished the book, come back and read through this chapter again. And I guarantee it'll all seem much simpler then.

The worksheets for clients mentioned in this chapter are presented below in alphabetical order:

- The Bull's Eye

- Dissecting the Problem

- The Life Compass

- The Problems and Values Worksheet

- Vitality vs. Suffering Diary

THE BULL'S EYE

YOUR VALUES: *What do you want to do with your time on this planet? What sort of person do you want to be? What personal strengths or qualities do you want to develop? Please write a few words under each heading below.*

1. **Work/Education:** includes workplace, career, education, skills development.

2. **Relationships:** includes your partner, children, parents, relatives, friends, co-workers.

3. **Personal Growth/Health:** may include religion, spirituality, creativity, life skills, meditation, yoga, nature; exercise, nutrition, and/or addressing health-risk factors.

4. **Leisure:** how you play, relax, or enjoy yourself; activities for rest, recreation, fun, and creativity.

THE BULL'S EYE: make an X in each area of the dart board, to represent where you stand today.

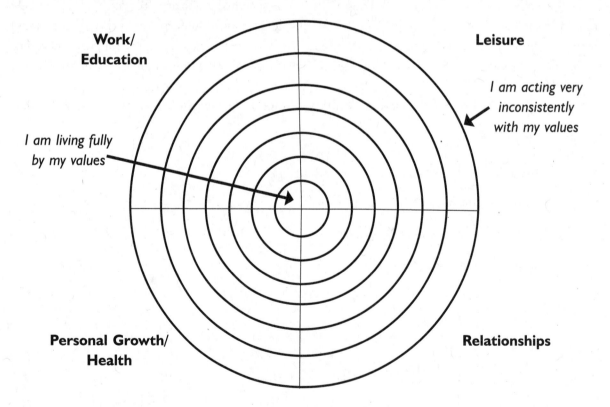

Adapted from *Living Beyond Your Pain* by J. Dahl and T. Lundren by permission of New Harbinger Publications (Oakland, CA), www.newharbinger.com.

DISSECTING THE PROBLEM

This form is to help gather information about the nature of the main challenge, issue, or problem facing you. First, please summarize, in one or two sentences, what the main issue or problem is:

Second, please describe, in one or two sentences, how it affects your life, and what it stops you from doing or being:

Regardless of what your problem is—whether it is a physical illness, a difficult relationship, a work situation, a financial crisis, a performance issue, the loss of a loved one, a severe injury, or a clinical disorder such as depression—when we dissect the problem, we usually find four major elements that contribute significantly to the issue. These are represented in the boxes below. Please write as much as you can in each box about the thoughts, feelings, and actions that contribute to or worsen the challenge, problem, or issue facing you:

Entanglement with Thoughts What memories, worries, fears, self-criticisms, or other unhelpful thoughts do you dwell on or get "caught up" in that are related to this issue? What thoughts do you allow to hold you back or push you around or bring you down?	**Life-draining Actions:** What are you currently doing that makes your life worse in the long run: keeps you stuck; wastes your time or money; drains your energy; restricts your life; impacts negatively on your health, work, or relationships; maintains or worsens the problems you are dealing with?
Struggle with Feelings What emotions, feelings, urges, impulses, or sensations (associated with this issue) do you fight with, avoid, suppress, try to get rid of, or otherwise struggle with?	**Avoiding Challenging Situations:** What situations, activities, people, or places are you avoiding or staying away from? What have you quit, withdrawn from, dropped out of? What do you keep "putting off" until later?

THE LIFE COMPASS

In the main part of each large box, write a few key words about what is important or meaningful to you in this domain of life: What sort of person do you want to be? What do you want to do? What sort of strengths or qualities do you want to develop? What do you want to stand for?

(If a box seems irrelevant to you, that's okay: just leave it blank. If you get stuck on a box, skip it and come back to it later. And it's okay if the same words appear in several or all boxes.)

Then in the upper small square of each large box, mark on a scale of 0 to 10 how important these values are to you at this point in your life (0 = no importance, 10 = extremely important). It's okay if several squares all have the same score. Finally, in the lower small square of each large box, mark on a scale of 0 to 10 how effectively you are living by these values right now (0 = not at all, 10 = living by them fully). Again, it's okay if several squares all have the same score.

Now have a good look at what you've written. What does this tell you about (a) what is important in your life? (b) what you are currently neglecting?

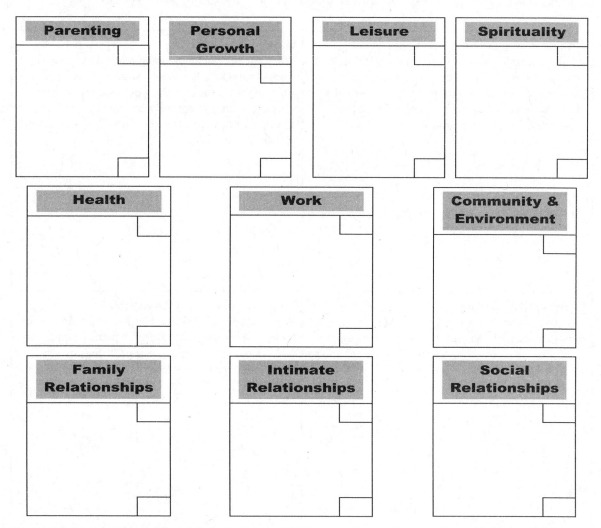

Adapted from *Living Beyond Your Pain* by J. Dahl and T. Lundren by permission of New Harbinger Publications (Oakland, CA), www.newharbinger.com.

THE PROBLEMS AND VALUES WORKSHEET

Acceptance and commitment therapy aims to reduce struggle and suffering and make life rich, full, and meaningful. To help this process, four types of information—represented in the four columns below—are particularly important. Between now and the next session, see what you can write in or add to each column.

STRUGGLE & SUFFERING		RICH & MEANINGFUL LIFE	
Problematic Thoughts and Feelings: What memories, worries, fears, self-criticisms, or other thoughts do you get "caught up" in? What emotions, feelings, urges, or sensations do you struggle with?	**Problematic Actions:** What are you doing that makes your life worse in the long run—that keeps you stuck, wastes your time or money, drains your energy, impacts negatively on your health or your relationships, or leads to you "missing out" on life?	**Values:** What matters to you in the "big picture"? What do you want to stand for? What personal qualities and strengths do you want to develop? How do you want to enrich or improve your relationships? How would you like to "grow" or develop through addressing your issue(s) or problem(s)?	**Goals and Actions:** What are you currently doing that improves your life in the long run? What do you want to start or do more of? What life-enriching goals do you want to achieve? What life-enhancing actions do you want to take? What life-improving skills would you like to develop?

This worksheet has been reformatted to fit the layout of this book. Rather than photocopying it, we recommend you use the original version, downloadable from www.actmadesimple.com

VITALITY VS. SUFFERING DIARY

Between now and next session, keep a record of what you do when painful thoughts and feelings arise, and notice if these actions lead to increased vitality or increased suffering.

Painful Thoughts/Feelings/ Urges/Sensations/Memories that showed up today	Things I did—when those thoughts and feelings showed up—that led to **VITALITY** (that is, expanded or enriched my life, or improved my health, well-being, or relationships)	Things I did—when those thoughts and feelings showed up—that lead to **SUFFERING** (that is, restricted or worsened my life, or hurt my health, well-being, or relationships)

CHAPTER 6

Creative What??!!

CREATIVE HOPELESSNESS IN A NUTSHELL

In Plain Language: *Creative hopelessness* means fully opening to the reality that trying too hard to control how we feel gets in the way of living a rich, full life.

Aim: To increase awareness of the emotional control agenda; to experience that it's basically unworkable, and discover why this is so.

Synonym: Confronting the agenda.

Method: Look at what the client has done to try to control how he feels, examine whether it's made his life better or worse, and get him in touch with the unworkability of his actions. This creates openness to an alternative way of handling thoughts and feelings.

When to Use: When the client is strongly attached to an agenda of emotional control. In many ACT protocols, it's a precursor to the rest of the work.

CONFRONTING THE AGENDA

Creative hopelessness (which is not a term we use with clients) or "CH" is also known as "confronting the agenda," which is short for "confronting the agenda of emotional control." The emotional control agenda is based on this idea: the more you can control how you feel, the better your life will be. In any session we may, at times, need to confront the control agenda of our client.

What Do We Mean by "Control"?

When clients come in to therapy, they usually want to feel better. This isn't surprising. Everyone likes to feel good. No one likes to feel bad. So quite naturally we try hard to avoid or get rid of "bad" or "negative" thoughts and feelings. This is the agenda of emotional control.

Our culture strongly reinforces this agenda with the popular notion that happiness is the same as feeling good. If you buy into that notion, then you're going to invest a lot of time and energy in emotional control strategies—that is, trying to reduce the "bad" feelings and increase the "good" ones. (In ACT, we stay away from the word "happiness" as it is such a loaded term. But if we *were* to define it, we'd say, "Happiness means living a rich, full, and meaningful life in which you willingly feel the full range of human emotions." This is very different than Happiness = Feeling Good. Indeed, we often say to clients, "It's not about feeling good; it's about feeling what you feel without a struggle" or "It's not about feeling good; it's about feeling alive.")

A *control strategy* therefore means anything we do primarily to try to get rid of "bad" thoughts and feelings: it is action motivated primarily by experiential avoidance. Control strategies can include everything from exercise, prayer, and meditation to alcohol, heroin, and suicide attempts. In creative hopelessness work, we ask the client to look openly and nonjudgmentally at all the control strategies she's using. But we don't judge these strategies as good or bad, right or wrong, positive or negative; our aim is purely and simply to see how these strategies are working in terms of creating a better life.

Does ACT Target All Control Strategies?

In a word: no! Recall that the whole ACT model rests on the concept of workability: is this behavior working to improve quality of life? So if control strategies *are* working to enrich and enhance life, it makes sense to keep doing them! However, the reality is most, if not all, human beings over-rely on control strategies; and when we use them excessively or inappropriately, our quality of life suffers.

Take eating chocolate, for example. When we eat a piece of good-quality chocolate, we feel good (assuming we like chocolate, that is). Use this simple control strategy in moderation, and it enriches our life: it's workable. But do it excessively, and it may well start to have costs to our health, such as weight gain.

Exercise is another example. When we exercise, we often feel better (at least, afterward, if not at the time). And exercise also improves our quality of life. Therefore, as a control strategy, it's generally workable. But if it becomes *excessive*—like the anorexic client who spends three hours in the gym each day to keep her body in a state of wasted thinness—then even something as positive as exercise can have costs.

Furthermore, ACT postulates that even life-enhancing activities (such as exercise, prayer, meditation, healthy eating) will be more satisfying and rewarding when they're motivated by values (such as looking after health and well-being and building rich relationships) rather than motivated by experiential avoidance.

For example, have you ever eaten food primarily to push away "bad" feelings such as boredom, stress, or anxiety? Was it a deeply satisfying experience? Contrast that with occasions when your eating was motivated by values around savoring your food, or sharing with friends, or trying out a new recipe. Which was more rewarding?

Similarly, if you do charity work motivated by values around sharing, giving, and contributing to the community, you'll likely find that far more rewarding than if you're mainly motivated by trying to avoid feelings of guilt or worthlessness.

Therefore we aim to help clients take action guided by their values rather than by experiential avoidance: we want to get them consciously moving toward what is meaningful rather than simply running from what is unwanted.

To really hammer this point home: Suppose you exercise primarily motivated by values such as looking after health and fitness, or you pray motivated by values around connecting with God. We wouldn't class those as *control* strategies because your primary aim isn't to control how you feel. We would only call them control strategies if your main purpose in doing them is to get rid of unwanted thoughts and feelings.

Creative hopelessness is an intervention based on workability. We ask the client to take a good, long, honest, and mindful look at what he's doing to avoid or get rid of unwanted thoughts and feelings, and to see what that is costing him. We want him to connect with the reality that what he's doing often works in the short run to make him feel better, but it does *not* work in the long run to make his life rich, full, and meaningful.

Is CH Necessary for Everyone?

Again, the answer is no. Our aim is to loosen the client's attachment to the agenda of emotional control (that is, trying to get rid of "bad" thoughts and feelings). We hope thereby to open her to an alternative agenda of acceptance or willingness. However, if she's highly motivated to change and not deeply attached to an agenda of emotional control, or if she's already familiar with mindfulness or ACT and open to the approach, then there's no need for CH, and we can therefore skip it. However, if we do skip it, we may still use some of the exercises and metaphors that traditionally follow immediately after CH, especially those about the illusion of control.

How Long Does It Take?

CH interventions vary enormously in length. In Zettle's sample protocol for depression (Zettle, 2007), CH lasts for 20 minutes. In Walser's protocol for PTSD, it lasts for one to two sessions (Walser & Westrup, 2007). We can also do CH very quickly, in the space of a few minutes (Strosahl, 2005).

Ideally we'll "titrate" the intervention to suit our client's issues. A high-functioning client with plenty of self-awareness and openness to new ideas is a very different story than the client with a lifelong history of substance abuse who clings desperately to the control agenda. The latter will likely need a far more extensive CH intervention than the former.

THREE SIMPLE QUESTIONS

Creative hopelessness interventions are constructed around three simple questions:

1. What have you tried?

2. How has it worked?

3. What has it cost?

First we ask, "What have you tried doing to get rid of these difficult thoughts and feelings?" We ask the client to come up with every single control strategy he has ever used.

Next we ask, "How has it worked in the long run?" We ask the client to assess whether in the long run it has actually worked: Has it reduced her pain? Has it enriched his life?

Finally we ask, "What has it cost you when you have over-relied on these methods?" We ask the client to notice the costs—when these methods are used excessively or inappropriately—in terms of health, well-being, relationships, work, leisure, energy, money, and wasted time.

Join the DOTS

The Join the DOTS worksheet given below simplifies CH. It is self-explanatory. You can fill this in with the client in session, prompting her and giving feedback. Or you can draw it up on a whiteboard (especially useful with groups). Or you can simply talk through it with the client without using the worksheet.

JOIN THE DOTS

What are the main thoughts and feelings that are problematic for you? Write these down under "Body" and "Mind." Next, write down everything you have tried to get rid of, avoid, suppress, escape, or distract yourself from these thoughts or feelings.

BODY
Feelings, sensations, urges

MIND
Thoughts, memories, beliefs, worries

D - Distraction: How have you tried to distract yourself from these thoughts and feelings (for example, watching TV, shopping, and so on)?

O - Opting out: We often opt out (quit, avoid, procrastinate, or withdraw from) people, places, activities, and situations when we don't like the thoughts and feelings they bring up for us. What are some of the things you opt out of?

T - Thinking: How have you tried to think your way out of it (for example, blaming others, worrying, rehashing the past, fantasizing, positive thinking, problem solving, planning, self-criticism, analyzing, trying to make sense of it, debating with yourself, denial, beating yourself up, pretending it's not important, and so on)? Have you dwelled on thoughts such as "What if?", "If only …," "Why me?", "Not fair!", or similar things?

S - Substances, Self-harm, Other Strategies: What substances have you tried putting into your body (including food and prescription medication)? Have you ever tried self-harming activities—for example, suicide attempts, reckless risk-tasking? Are there any other strategies you have ever tried—for example, excessive sleeping?

Did these strategies get rid of your painful thoughts and feelings in the long run so that they never came back?

When you have used these strategies excessively, rigidly, or inappropriately, what have they cost you in terms of health, vitality, energy, relationships, work, leisure, money, missed opportunities, wasted time, or emotional pain?

Alternatively, you might just use the DOTS acronym as a memory aid for yourself. Because most clients can't readily reel off a list of control strategies, you'll generally need to prompt them. DOTS helps you remember the most common strategies used:

D – Distraction

O – Opting out

T – Thinking strategies

S – Substances, self-harm, other strategies

There's considerable overlap between these elements: eating junk food and drinking wine could come under distraction or substances. Under "other strategies," you can put anything from sleeping all day long to punching the wall to yoga or therapy. With this acronym in the back of your mind, you can keep asking the client, "Have you ever tried doing this?" Make sure to ask about previous therapies tried.

As an alternative to Join the DOTS, you might prefer the worksheet Attempted Solutions and Their Long-Term Effects (adapted from Hayes et al., 1999; see below). You can download free copies of both of these forms from www.actmadesimple.com.

ATTEMPTED SOLUTIONS AND THEIR LONG-TERM EFFECTS

ATTEMPTED SOLUTIONS AND THEIR LONG-TERM EFFECTS			
What have you done to avoid or get rid of problematic thoughts, feelings, memories, emotions, or sensations? List everything you can think of whether it was intentional or not.	a. Did your thoughts and feelings go away? b. Did they return in the long run? c. Did they worsen?	Has this brought you closer to a rich, full, and meaningful life?	What has this cost you in terms of wasted time, energy, or money; or negative effects on health, well-being, work, leisure, or relationships?

Question 1: What have you tried?

Here the therapist helps the client identify control strategies, using the DOTS acronym.

Therapist: So far, we've identified quite a few thoughts and feelings that are problematic for you. Now, by the time most folks get to therapy, they've already tried doing a lot of different things to feel better or not feel so bad. And one of the things I want to ensure is that we don't do more of what doesn't work. So I'd like to spend a bit of time recapping all the things you've tried to avoid or get rid of these painful thoughts and feelings. Is that okay?

Client: To be honest, I can't really think of anything.

Therapist: Well, let me help you out here. One of the most common things people do is try to distract themselves to take their mind off it. What sort of things do you do to distract yourself from how you're feeling?

Client: I watch TV. Listen to music. Read. Smoke dope.

Therapist: Computers?

Client: Yeah—computer games, surfing the Net, a lot of time on YouTube, just watching crap.

Therapist: What else?

Client: (*pauses, shakes his head*)

Therapist: Well, another thing people often do is they start opting out of things that bring up painful feelings. Are there any people, places, situations, activities that you've withdrawn from or are staying away from?

The therapist continues in this manner, working through the DOTS acronym. Once complete, she moves to the next question.

Question 2: How Has It Worked?

We now aim to validate that the client has invested a lot of time and effort in the control agenda—and clearly it has not worked.

Therapist: So you've put a lot of time and effort into trying to get rid of these thoughts and feelings. No one can call you lazy. And most of those strategies are things that all of us commonly do. We all avoid uncomfortable situations, put stuff into our bodies, or use all sorts of different ways to distract ourselves. And in the short run, these things often make us feel better for a little while. But let me ask you this: in the long run, did these things get rid of your painful thoughts and feelings so that they never came back again?

Client: (*hesitates*) No. That's why I'm here.

Therapist: Right. You've come here to try and get rid of them once and for all.

Client: Yeah. I hate feeling this way.

Therapist: Okay, so can I add that to the list—thinking about how much you hate these feelings?

Client: Well, wouldn't you?

Therapist: I have to say, I don't know anyone who likes painful feelings. The question we're interested in here is this: what's the best way of dealing with them? Have your efforts to get rid of these feelings taken you in the direction of a rich, full, and meaningful life, or have they taken you in the direction of struggle and suffering?

Question 3: What Has It Cost?

We now move on to asking what all the costs have been, and we'll often have to prompt our client to think about different areas of life: health, well-being, relationships, work, money, wasted time, missed opportunities, and so on. You can do this through conversation alone—but if you're up for something more adventurous, you can do this using the interactive physical metaphor of Pushing Against the Clipboard. Note: the clipboard metaphor is very effective, but don't ever use it with people who have neck/shoulder/arm issues, and always be careful you don't push too hard!

PUSHING AGAINST THE CLIPBOARD: AN INTERACTIVE METAPHOR

Therapist: Can I stand up and demonstrate something to you? (*Client nods. Therapist picks up a clipboard, stands up, and walks over to the client.*) You don't have shoulder or neck problems? Good, because I want you to imagine that this clipboard is all those painful thoughts and feelings you've been trying to get rid of for so long, and I want you to place both your hands flat on this clipboard and push against it, trying to get rid of it. Don't push so hard that you knock me over, but do push firmly. (*Client pushes; therapist pushes back.*) That's it—keep pushing. You hate this stuff. You want it to go away. (*As the client tries hard to push the clipboard away, the therapist pushes back. The harder the client pushes, the more the therapist leans into it.*) Notice how much effort and energy it requires—trying to make them go away. (*The therapist eases off on the pushing, but retains enough gentle counterpressure to keep the clipboard suspended in midair, resting between the client's hands and the therapist's hands.*) So here you are, trying very hard to push away all these painful thoughts and feelings. You've tried distracting yourself with TV, music, computers, books, avoiding friends and family, staying home all by yourself, avoiding work, beating yourself up, analyzing why you're like this, telling yourself life sucks, smoking dope, drinking beer, punching the wall, jogging, reading self-help books—the list goes on and on. You've been doing this for years: pushing and pushing and pushing. And are those painful thoughts and feelings going anywhere? Sure, you're keeping them at arm's length, but what's the cost to you? How does it feel in your shoulders? (*Therapist pushes a bit harder.*) We've only been doing this for a minute or two, but you've been doing this for over twenty years. This is tiring, isn't it?

Client: Yes. I'm tired.

Therapist: (*easing off the pressure*) Okay, well I'm easing off the pressure here, but just for a while longer, would you be willing to keep gently pressing? (*Client presses very gently against the board.*) Now I want you to notice—while you're doing this—if I asked you to do your job effectively, or socialize with your friends, or cook dinner, could you do it?

Client: No way.

Therapist: And what's it like trying to have a conversation with me while you're doing this?

Client: Annoying.

Therapist: Annoying. Frustrating. Exhausting. Right? And do you feel a bit closed in or cut off from the world around you?

Client: Yes.

Therapist: So trying to push all these feelings away is eating up a lot of effort and energy. Now let me take the clipboard back for a moment. (*Therapist takes the clipboard back and sits down.*) So this is what you've been doing for soooo long now—trying to get rid of these thoughts and feelings. And yet, they're still showing up, still pushing you around, still having an impact on your life.

Client: Yes. I know that. So how do I get rid of them?

Therapist: Well, we're going come to that shortly. But first let's take a look at what it's cost you, trying so hard to get rid of this stuff. What has it cost you in terms of health, relationships, money, wasted time? (*The therapist now prompts the client through all the different costs of his control strategies.*)

Therapist: So trying to get rid of all this stuff (*holds the clipboard at the edges and pushes it out in front of her as far away as she can possibly stretch*) is not only tiring, not only costly, but it doesn't even work. These thoughts and feelings are still showing up! And each time you ask me how to get rid of it, you're asking me to help you do more of this. Do you really want to do more of what doesn't work?

Client: No. But then—what are you saying? I just have to put up with it?

Therapist: Not at all. Putting up with it is doing more of the same. It's like you're still trying to push it away, but you're so tired, you stop pushing so hard. Putting up with it is like doing this. (*Therapist again pushes the clipboard out in front of her, but this time her arms are half bent instead of fully outstretched.*) It's still tiring, still costing you, still getting in the way of your life.

Client: So what do I do then?

Therapist: Good question. I'll come back to that. But let's just acknowledge you have already tried very hard to sort this out. You certainly haven't been lazy. And you haven't been stupid either; most of the things you've tried are commonsense strategies that almost everyone uses. And some of them, such as distraction techniques, are frequently recommended by doctors and psychologists. And yet it doesn't seem to be working. You're trying very hard, but it's not having the effect that you want.

> **Practical Tip**   For this work to be effective, we need to come from a space of compassion, equality, and respect. We aim to validate the client's experience—that she's trying very hard, but what she's doing isn't working. If we come from a space of one-upmanship or arrogance, if we come across as critical or judgmental, if we adopt the role of the expert with "all the answers," then our client will feel irritated, demeaned, or belittled.

PLEASE, TELL ME WHAT TO DO!

At some point toward the end of CH, your client is likely to say something like, "Are you saying I should just put up with it?" As in the transcript above, we'd reply, "Putting up with it/tolerating it/giving up/resignation is just doing more of the same. Your agenda is still to get rid of it—you're just putting less effort into it. It's still tiring, still draining away your health and vitality." Your client is likely to then ask you for a solution: "So what do I do?"

At that point, you have to make a judgment call. Has the client really acknowledged the unworkability of the control agenda? If so, you could go straight into active work on the hexaflex, typically moving on to defusion and acceptance. (In chapter 8, we'll look at how you can revisit the clipboard metaphor and use it to illustrate the move from avoidance to acceptance.) More commonly at this point, you'd move on to identifying that control is the problem, not the solution, and then go on to two psychoeducational components: normalizing control and the illusion of control.

Here's an example of how that might go:

Client: So what do I do then?

Therapist:	Good question. You already know we're going to be learning some new skills here for handling thoughts and feelings. But this approach is so different from everything else you've tried, from everything our society tells us, from almost everything you read in pop psychology, it would probably backfire if we just leaped straight into it. So if you're willing to bear with me a little longer, what I'd like to do is lay a bit of groundwork for what comes next. Perhaps you could think about it this way ... (*The therapist now uses metaphor of choice to convey that control is the problem.*)

Control Is the Problem, Not the Solution

In this phase, we use a metaphor to increase our client's awareness that emotional control strategies are largely responsible for her problems; that as long as she's fixated on trying to control how she feels, she's trapped in a vicious cycle of increasing suffering. Two popular metaphors are the Tug of War with a Monster and Struggling in Quicksand (Hayes et al., 1999).

STRUGGLING IN QUICKSAND METAPHOR

Therapist:	Remember those old movies where the bad guy falls into a pool of quicksand, and the more he struggles, the faster it sucks him under? In quicksand, the worst thing you can possibly do is struggle. The way to survive is to lie back, spread out your arms and legs, and float on the surface. This is very tricky, because every instinct in your body tells you to struggle, but if you do what comes naturally and instinctively, you'll drown. And notice, lying back and floating is psychologically tricky—it doesn't come naturally—but it's a lot less physical effort than struggling."

TUG OF WAR WITH A MONSTER METAPHOR

Therapist:	Imagine you're in a tug-of-war with some huge anxiety monster. (*Alter the name the monster to suit the issue, for example, the depression monster.*) You've got one end of the rope, and the monster has the other end. And in between you, there's a huge bottomless pit. And you're pulling backward as hard as you can, but the monster keeps on pulling you ever closer to the pit. What's the best thing to do in that situation?
Client:	Pull harder.
Therapist:	Well, that's what comes naturally, but the harder you pull, the harder the monster pulls. You're stuck. What do you need to do?
Client:	Drop the rope?
Therapist:	That's it. When you drop the rope, the monster's still there, but now you're no longer tied up in a struggle with it. Now you can do something more useful.

> **Practical Tip**   It's effective—and fun—to act this metaphor out with the client, using a belt or a rope. (The therapist should play the monster and hold one end of the belt tightly, while the client tugs on the other end.)

OTHER METAPHORS

There are numerous other metaphors you could use. Basically you can use anything that conveys this message: the more you do what comes naturally and instinctively in this problematic situation, the worse the situation gets. Well-known examples include slamming on the brakes when your car skids, swimming against a rip tide, trying to dig your way out of a hole, and scratching a nasty rash.

IS THIS THE END OF THE SESSION?

In more traditional protocols, you end the session at this point, and for homework you ask the client to notice (a) all the different ways he tries to avoid or get rid of unwanted feelings, (b) how that works, and (c) what it costs. Of course, as with anything in ACT, you don't have to do it the traditional way, so if you have time in the session, you may prefer to move straight on to the next two components—the normality of control and the illusion of control. (And even if you skip CH altogether, these components are often useful to bring into later sessions.)

The Normality of Control

In this component, we address why control comes naturally.

Therapist: I'd hate for you to get the wrong impression here—that I'm criticizing you in any way for what you've been doing. If that's how I've come across, I sincerely apologize because the truth is we're all in the same boat. Most of the things on your list are things that I do at times; almost everyone does. We all get caught up in the same agenda. We live in a feel-good society: everyone likes to feel good, no one likes to feel bad. So we try hard to get rid of unpleasant feelings. And we all keep on doing it—doing whatever we can to avoid or get rid of unpleasant thoughts and feelings—even though it doesn't work in the long run and we often end up suffering as a result. And there are at least four reasons why we do that. One, because we've all fallen into "the happiness trap"; we've bought into the myth that humans are naturally happy, and we should feel good most of the time. Two, because the things we do to control our feelings often *do* work quite well in the short run. Three, because we believe these methods work for other people. And four—and this is the one reason above and beyond all the others: it's the way our mind has evolved to solve problems. (*At this point, the therapist launches into the Problem-Solving Machine Metaphor from chapter 1.*)

The Illusion of Control

In this component, we shatter the myth or illusion that humans can control how they feel. You could lead into it like this: "So we're all walking around, trying to control how we feel, and it just doesn't work. It's not that we've got *no* control at all, but we've got a lot less than we'd like to have. And what I'd like to do, if you're okay with it, is just take you through a few little exercises so you can check this out for yourself and see how much control you actually have." You could then take the client through any or all of the following exercises, in any combination or order. (Except for the first two, they all come from Hayes et al., 1999.)

DELETE A MEMORY

Therapist: Just take a moment to remember how you got here today. Done that? Okay, now delete that memory. Just get rid of it. (*pause*) How'd you do?

NUMB YOUR LEG

Therapist: Now make your left leg go completely numb. So numb, that I could cut it off with a hacksaw and you wouldn't feel a thing. (*pause*) How'd you do?

DON'T THINK ABOUT …

Therapist: For the next exercise, you must not think about what I say. Not even for one microsecond. Don't think about … ice cream. Don't think about your favorite flavor. Don't think about how it melts in your mouth on a warm hot summer's day. (*pause*) How're you doing?

THE POLYGRAPH METAPHOR

Therapist: Imagine I'm a mad scientist and I've kidnapped you for an experiment. And I've wired you up to a supersensitive polygraph, or lie detector. This machine will detect the tiniest bit of anxiety in your body. You can't kid it. Even the tiniest hint of anxiety and all the alarm bells will ring. And in this experiment I'm about to do on you, you must not feel any anxiety at all. And if you do, then I'll pull this lever, which will electrocute you. (*Pause.*) What would happen?

Client: I'd be fried.

Therapist: Right. Even though your life depends on it, you can't control the anxiety.

FALLING IN LOVE

Therapist:	Now suppose I were to offer you one billion dollars—one billion—if you can do what I ask. I'm going to bring someone into this room—someone you've never met before—and if you can instantly fall head over heels in love with that person, then I'll give you the money. Could you do it?
Client:	If it were Brad Pitt, I could.
Therapist:	It's a little old man in a wheelchair, and he hasn't had a bath for three months.
Client:	No.
Therapist:	Not even for one billion dollars?
Client:	I could try.
Therapist:	Sure. You could put on an act. Hug him and kiss him and say, "I love you, I love you!" Because you've got a lot of control over your actions, but could you control your feelings?
Client:	No.

Brief Creative Hopelessness

As mentioned earlier, we don't have to do CH with all clients. With motivated high-functioning clients who are not overly attached to control, we may well skip it or do a brief version. In the brief version, we ask, "So all these painful feelings are showing up. What have you tried doing to get rid of them?" Next we elicit a few of the main control strategies. Then we say, "Okay, so seems like you've tried quite a few things to get rid of these thoughts and feelings, and that's not working too well, so how about we try something different?"

And if we take this approach initially, but down the line it turns out our client is more attached to the control agenda than we thought—no problem: we can simply return to CH and do a more extensive intervention.

HOMEWORK AND THE NEXT SESSION

At this point, your client will hopefully be curious about the alternative you're offering. She may even ask again, "So what do I do?" If you have time remaining in this session, you can then move on to the next phase. If not, explain that you'll move on to it in the next session. Traditionally, after creative hopelessness and naming control as the problem, you would move on to defusion and acceptance.

As mentioned before, for homework you could ask the client to notice all the different ways he tries to avoid or get rid of unwanted feelings, and how that works, and what it costs. Either of the worksheets above—Join the Dots or Attempted Solutions and Their Long-Term Effects—can facilitate this.

Alternatively, depending on the metaphor you've used, you may ask your client to notice when she's "tugging on the rope" or "struggling in the quicksand" and when, if ever, she stops tugging or struggling.

Better still, if she's willing, have her keep a daily journal: When does the struggle happen? What triggers it? What are the consequences?

And if you started this session with a simple mindfulness exercise, you can also ask your client to practice it on a daily basis.

HOMEWORK FOR YOU

- Pick some thoughts and feelings you've been struggling with and complete both the worksheets on your own issues.

- Read through all the exercises and metaphors out aloud, as if taking a client through them.

- Reflect on your current client caseload. Do you have any clients who are clinging to the control agenda? Mentally rehearse running through a CH intervention with them.

SUMMARY

Creative hopelessness is an optional component of ACT that we use when a client seems overly attached to the emotional control agenda. We basically want the client to take a good honest look at how the control agenda is working: is it taking her in the direction of a rich, full, and meaningful life, or is it taking her in the direction of struggle and suffering? We can do this as an extensive intervention taking up a whole session, or as a brief intervention taking only a few minutes. It boils down to asking three simple questions: What have you tried? How has it worked? What has it cost?

And please keep in mind: in all creative hopelessness work, brief or long, we do not try to convince the client of unworkability. Ultimately it is up to him to judge for himself, based on his own experience, whether or not control is enriching his life.

CHAPTER 7

Watch Your Thinking

DEFUSION IN A NUTSHELL

In Plain Language: *Fusion* means getting caught up in our thoughts and allowing them to dominate our behavior. *Defusion* means separating or distancing from our thoughts, letting them come and go instead of being caught up in them. In other words, defusion means

- looking *at* thoughts rather than *from* thoughts;

- noticing thoughts rather than being caught up in thoughts; and

- letting thoughts come and go rather than holding on to them.

Synonym: Deliteralization (this term is rarely used nowadays).

Aim: To see the true nature of thoughts: they are nothing more or less than words and pictures; and to respond to thoughts in terms of workability rather than literality (that is, in terms of how helpful they are rather than how true they are).

Method: Notice the process of thinking; learn experientially that our thoughts do not control our actions.

When to Use: When thoughts function as barriers to valued living.

GETTING TO DEFUSION

We facilitate defusion throughout every single session in ACT. In some sessions, defusion is the central focus, and we formally take our clients through a variety of metaphors and experiential exercises to help them develop defusion skills. Most of this chapter focuses on such interventions. However, we also facilitate defusion informally in every session, even when the session is predominantly focused on other core processes such as values clarification. We do this in three main ways:

1. We ask clients to notice their thoughts:

    ■   "So what's your mind telling you now?"

    ■   "And what does your thinking self have to say about that?"

    ■   "Can you notice what you're thinking right now?"

    ■   "Notice what your mind is doing."

2. We ask clients to look at the workability of their thoughts:

    ■   "So is that a helpful thought? If you hold on tightly to it, does it help you deal with the situation effectively?"

    ■   "If you let that thought tell you what to do, will it take you in the direction of a rich, full, and meaningful life, or in the direction of being stuck and suffering?"

    ■   "If we stop the session just because your mind says *This won't work* or *I can't do it*, will that help you change your life—or will it just keep you stuck?"

3. We ask clients to notice when they are fused with or defused from their thoughts:

    ■   "So right now, how caught up are you in that thought?"

    ■   "Did you notice how your mind just hooked you then?"

If we want to make defusion the main focus of a session, we can lead into it in many ways. For example, if we've started therapy by identifying values and setting specific goals, then we could ask questions such as these: "So what's getting in the way of you taking action?" "What's stopping you from acting on these values/achieving these goals/being the person you want to be/building the relationships you want?" "What's your mind telling you that holds you back/keeps you stuck/makes life difficult for you?"

Alternatively, if we find in the first session that every attempt to clarify values meets with a block, then defusion is a good choice for the first step in active therapy. (Once our client has developed good defusion and acceptance skills, we can then return to work on values and goals.)

Yet another option, if we suspect or know that our client is deeply attached to the control agenda, is to do creative hopelessness before actively focusing on defusion. In this case, after a creative hopelessness intervention, we could say something like this: "So you're probably wondering if trying to get rid of these thoughts doesn't work, what's the alternative?"

Identifying Fusion

When we take a history, we watch for fusion in six key areas: rules, reasons, judgments, past, future, and self. Let's take a quick look at each of these areas now.

Rules. What sort of rigid rules does the client have about life, work, relationships, and so on? In particular, look for rules about how someone needs to feel before she can take action. Watch for key words like should, must, have to, ought, right, wrong, can't, don't, and key phrases such as shouldn't have to; if I feel X, then I can't do Y; if I do A, then you should do B. These words and phrases often alert you to rigid ideas about how life should operate or what's necessary before change can happen. These rules usually create a lot of suffering if the client fuses with them. Here are some common examples: "I shouldn't be feeling this way," "I can't go the party when I feel anxious," "If I can't do it perfectly, there's no point in trying," "This shouldn't be so difficult," "My kids should do what I tell them," and "Normal people don't feel this way."

Reasons. What reasons does the client give you for why change is impossible, undesirable, or impractical? Humans are excellent at coming up with reasons why they can't or shouldn't change: "I'm too busy/tired/anxious/depressed," "I might fail," "I shouldn't have to," "It's too hard," "It's genetic," "We're all alcoholics in my family," "It's a chemical imbalance," "I'll get hurt," "I've always been like this," "I can't cope with loneliness," "It'll all go wrong," "I'll do it when I have more time/energy/money," and so on. If we or our clients fuse with these thoughts, they often hold us back from making changes.

Judgments. Humans judge. And many of the judgments we make are useful and important: Is this person trustworthy or untrustworthy? Is this car good value for money? Is this fruit ripe or not? Unfortunately, though, many of our judgments are unhelpful. Of course, if we hold our judgments lightly, they present no problem. But if we fuse with those judgments—"I'm bad," "You're mean," "Anxiety is awful," "I'm too fat," "Being rejected is unbearable," "He's so selfish," "Life sucks," "Men are liars"—we readily end up struggling and suffering. What sort of judgmental or evaluative thinking is your client fusing with?

Past. How is your client fusing with the past? Ruminating on old hurts, failures, mistakes, missed opportunities? Reliving the "good old days" before life turned bad? Having flashbacks? (A flashback is extreme fusion with a memory.)

Future. How is your client fusing with the future? Worrying? Fantasizing about a better life? Constantly caught up in thinking about all the things he has to do later?

Self. What sort of self-description is your client fusing with? Here are some common ones: "I am weak/useless/unlovable," "I don't need help," "I am nothing without my job," "I can't cope," "I don't tolerate fools gladly," "I don't need help," "I'm right and they are wrong," and so on. Is she fusing with her diagnosis or her body image—"I am bipolar," "I am fat"? Is he perhaps fusing with his job title or his role in the family?

Obviously we could describe many different categories of thinking—black-and-white thinking, catastrophizing, overgeneralization, and so on—but the above six help to keep it simple. (We'll look in detail at fusion with past and future in chapter 9, fusion with self-description in chapter 10, and fusion with reason-giving in chapter 13.)

"Setting the Mood"

To "set the mood" for defusion, I initially recap some of the painful thoughts or memories the client has been getting caught up in or struggling with, and I compassionately acknowledge how difficult this has been for her, and how much pain and suffering she has experienced. Then I say something like this: "As you know, one of our aims in this work is to develop psychological skills that will help you to handle your mind more effectively when it starts doing things that hold you back from living a full life. And that's what I'd like to focus on today. Would that be okay with you?"

At this point, it's useful to do some psychoeducation about the nature of the mind. Typically I start with a brief discussion of the two parts of the mind: the thinking self and the observing self, as described in chapter 4. Upon conclusion, I say something like, "So in the work we do here, whenever I use the word "mind," I'm talking about "the thinking self"—the part of you that chatters away inside your head, never shuts up, and always has something to say. Can you notice it chattering away, right now?" The client usually says yes, and I then ask, "So what's your mind saying to you?" Whatever the answer, I reply, "See what I mean? It's always got something to say. Sometimes it's helpful to imagine that there are four of us in the room here: there's you and me, and your mind and my mind. My mind's going to chatter away to me, and your mind's going to chatter away to you. What's really important here is what happens between you and me rather than what our minds have to say."

Typically we next do a bit of psychoeducation about how our minds have evolved to think negatively, as in the transcript below. This sets the scene for active defusion interventions.

> Many ACT therapists don't introduce the observing self until later in therapy, following work on defusion and acceptance, but some therapists prefer to introduce it up front. I prefer the latter approach, but if you prefer the former, then simply skip introducing the observing self for now and bring it in later in therapy.

HOW OUR MINDS HAVE EVOLVED TO THINK NEGATIVELY

Therapist: So you've told me some of the painful or unhelpful thoughts that hold you back or make your life harder. And I'm willing to bet we've only just scratched the surface—because if your mind is anything like my mind, then it's got no shortage of negative thoughts. And there's actually a very good reason for that, and I'd like to take a few minutes to explain it. Would that be okay with you? (*Wait for client's response.*) You see, the human mind has evolved to think negatively. Our primitive ancestors lived in a world of constant danger—big animals with big teeth lurked around every corner. So back then, your mind had to constantly be on the lookout for danger, anticipating anything that could hurt you or harm you in any way: "Watch out. There could be a bear in that cave. There could be a wolf in those bushes. Is that person in the distance a friend or an enemy?" If you were a caveman and your mind didn't do this job well, you'd soon be dead. And that's what we've inherited from our ancestors: our modern mind is basically a "don't get killed" machine. It's constantly trying to warn you of anything that could possibly go wrong: "You'll get fat," "You'll screw up the exam," "He might reject you." This is normal. Everyone's mind does this. Our mind has evolved to think negatively. It's just trying to do its number one job, which is to protect us and keep us alive.

There's no absolute necessity to use the above spiel (or any other metaphor/exercise in this book), but it does makes a good transition into learning defusion skills. The next step is to recap some of the client's problematic thoughts, clarify what it costs him when he gets entangled in or pushed around by these thoughts, and then invite him to learn a new way of handling them. The transcript that follows illustrates only one way of many that you can do this; when you read other ACT textbooks, you'll discover many other methods.

Introducing Defusion: Part 1

The client in this transcript is a twenty-four-year-old single, female chiropractor. We are about fifteen minutes into session 2, following (1) a brief mindful breathing exercise (see chapter 9), (2) a quick review of the previous session, and (3) a quick discussion of the two parts of the mind and how the mind evolved to think negatively.

Therapist: So one thing we identified last week, a big part of the problem, is that you have a lot of thoughts about being worthless or useless.

Client: Yeah, I do. I feel like I'm a waste of space. I don't even know why you're wasting your time with me.

Therapist: And I notice that as you're saying that, you're slumping down—almost as if you're sinking into the chair. I'm getting a sense that these thoughts really drag you down.

(*Client nods.*) That must hurt. (*The client nods again, and her eyes tear up.*) What're you feeling right now?

Client: (*shaking her head*) It's silly.

Therapist: What's silly?

Client: I am. This is. (*wiping her eyes*) I don't think you can help me.

Therapist: Well, that's a perfectly natural thought to have. Lots of people have thoughts like that, especially at the start of therapy. And the truth is I can't actually guarantee that it will help. But I can guarantee that I'll do my very best to help you create a better life. So, how about we give it a go, even though you're having the thought that it's hopeless, and let's see what happens?

Client: Okay.

Therapist: Okay, well, we agreed last session that one of your goals here is to learn new ways to handle difficult thoughts and feelings. Is that still important to you?

Client: Yeah.

> **At this point, the therapist could move on to pretty much any defusion intervention he prefers.**

Therapist: Okay. (*He pulls out a white index card.*) Well, what I'd like to do, if it's okay with you, is jot down some of your thoughts on this card so we've got something to work with. Would that be okay with you?

Client: Sure.

Therapist: Thanks. So, when your mind is really beating you up, really getting stuck into you about what's wrong with you, and what's wrong with your life—if I could listen in at those times, sort of plug into your mind and listen in to what it's saying, what it's telling you, what would I hear?

Client: Oh. Um. Just really negative stuff, like, um, you're stupid, you're lazy, nobody likes you.

Therapist: Okay. So let me get this down. (*He starts writing the thoughts down on the index card.*) Your mind says, "I'm stupid ... I'm lazy ... Nobody likes me." What else?

Client: I don't know.

Therapist: Well, you mentioned "silly" and "waste of space" today, and "worthless" and "useless" last week. Are those names your mind often calls you?

Client:	Yeah.
Therapist:	(*writing them down*) Okay. So your mind tells you "I'm silly ... I'm worthless ... I'm useless ... I'm a waste of space." What else?
Client:	(*chuckles*) Isn't that enough?
Therapist:	Yes, it is—but I was just wondering if your mind tells you any really dark or scary stories about the future? You know, when it really wants to make you feel hopeless, what are the scariest things it says to you?
Client:	Um. Just that I'm f****ed. There is no future. Life is f****ed and then you die.
Therapist:	Okay, so your mind likes to swear a bit. Let's get that down. "I'm f****ed ... There is no future ... Life is f****ed and then you die!"

Now Let's Unpack That: Part 1

Before continuing this chapter, read through the above transcript again and identify the various ways the therapist subtly establishes a context of defusion, including normalizing and allowing thoughts, treating the mind as an "entity," listening to the mind, writing thoughts down, and describing thoughts as "stories." Let's take a quick look at each of these.

NORMALIZING AND ALLOWING THOUGHTS

Notice how the therapist responds to "I don't think you can help me" by saying "Well, that's a perfectly natural thought." We facilitate defusion when we describe a thought as normal, natural, typical, or common, and make no attempt to judge it, challenge it, or get rid of it.

TREATING THE MIND AS AN "ENTITY"

Defusion involves separating from your thoughts, so we often find it useful in ACT to talk, playfully and metaphorically, about the mind as if it's a separate entity. For example, we may ask questions like, "What does your mind tell you about that?" or "Who's talking here—you or your mind?" (Hayes et al., 1999). In the transcript above, the therapist also talks about the mind "getting stuck into you," "beating you up," "calling you names," and also notes that it "likes to swear."

LISTENING TO THE MIND

Many defusion techniques involve noticing or playing with the auditory properties of thoughts. Here the therapist talks about "listening in to the mind," "hearing what it is saying," and "what it sounds like."

WRITING THOUGHTS DOWN

One of the simplest ways of separating from thoughts is to write them down. This helps you to take a step back and see the thoughts for what they are: strings of words. The therapist can do the writing and then pass it on to the client, or the client can write the thoughts down.

THOUGHTS AS STORIES

In ACT, we often talk about thoughts as "stories." This ties in nicely to metaphors about the mind as a storyteller (more on this below) and getting absorbed or lost in the story. The therapist specifically asks about any "dark or scary stories" about the future.

> **Practical Tip** Once in a blue moon, a client will object to the term "stories." If so, immediately apologize and explain, "No offense intended. All I meant by the term "story" is that it's a bunch of words that conveys information. If the term bothers you, I'm more than happy to call these words 'thoughts,' 'beliefs,' or 'cognitions.'"

Now before reading part 2, I encourage you to go back to chapter 1 and reread the ACT in a Nutshell Metaphor. In the transcript below, the therapist adapts sections 1 and 3 of that metaphor.

Introducing Defusion: Part 2

The transcript below continues immediately from where part 1 left off.

Therapist: (*handing the card to the client*) So this is the sort of stuff your mind says to you when it's beating you up?

Client: (*looking down at the card*) Yeah.

Therapist: I'm going to ask you to do a couple of things with this card. They may seem a bit odd, but I think you'll get a lot out of them. Is that okay?

Client: What sort of things?

Therapist: Well, first I'd like you to hold it tightly, with both hands, and hold it right up in front of your face like this so you can't see me, so all you can see are those thoughts on the card. (*Client holds the card in front of her face.*) That's right—and hold it up so close that it's almost touching your nose. (*The client does so.*) Now what's it like trying to have a conversation with me while you're all caught up in those thoughts?

> *The therapist is now doing section 1 of the ACT in a Nutshell Metaphor.*

Client: Bloody hard.

Therapist: Do you feel connected with me?

Client: I can hear you okay.

Therapist: Sure, but can you read the expressions on my face? Do you feel truly engaged with me? If I was juggling balls right now, or doing a mime act, would you be able to see what I was doing?

Client: I guess not.

Therapist: And what's your view of the room like while you're all wrapped up in those thoughts?"

Client: (*grinning*) What room?

Therapist: So notice what's going on here. Here's your mind telling you all these nasty stories, and the more absorbed you become, the more you're missing out on. You're cut off from the world around you; you're cut off from me; you're cut off from everything except these thoughts.

Client: Yeah. That's what it's like.

Therapist: Notice, too, that while you're clutching this stuff, it's hard to do anything that enriches your life. Check it out: hold the card as tightly as you possibly can with both hands so I can't pull it from you. (*The client holds the card tightly with both hands.*) Now if I asked you to take an exam or go for an interview, or go for a swim or hug someone you love, or ride a bike, engage with your friends and family, or have a deep and meaningful conversation with a close friend while you're holding on tightly to this, could you do it?"

Client: I could give it a shot.

Therapist: Okay, you could try. And would doing it this way—all caught up in those thoughts—make it easier or harder for you?

Client: Yeah, it'd be bloody difficult.

Therapist: Right. So when your mind hooks you with these thoughts, not only do you get cut off from the world around you and disconnected from other people, but it's also much, much harder to do the things that make your life work.

Client:	(nodding) I get the point.
Therapist:	Okay, now let's try something else. Can I take the card back? (Client hands it over.) Now, is it okay if I just place this card on your lap? (Client nods. The therapist leans forward and places the card on the client's lap.) And can you just let it sit there for a moment?

The therapist is now doing section 3 of the ACT in a Nutshell Metaphor.

Therapist:	Now how's that, compared to having it right in front of your face? Do you feel more connected with me? More engaged in the world around you?
Client:	Yes.
Therapist:	Now notice those thoughts haven't gone anyway. They're still there. And if you want to, you can still get all absorbed in them. Check it out for yourself. Look down at the card and give it all your attention. (Client looks down at the card in her lap.) Notice how as you get absorbed in those thoughts, you get cut off from me—and you lose touch with the world around you. (Client nods.) Now look back at me. (Client looks up at the therapist.) And notice the room around you. (Client looks around the room.) Now which do you prefer—to get sucked into your thoughts down there or to be out here in the world interacting with me?
Client:	(smiling) I prefer this.
Therapist:	Me too.
Client:	But I keep wanting to look at it.
Therapist:	Of course you do. Our minds train us to believe that everything they say to us is *very* important and we *must* pay attention. The thing is there's nothing written on that card that's new, is there? I mean you've had those thoughts, what hundreds, thousands of times?
Client:	Try millions.
Therapist:	So notice, you have a choice here. You can either look down and get all absorbed in this stuff, in all these thoughts that you've had zillions of times, or you can just let it sit there and you can engage with the world. The choice is yours. Which do you choose?
Client:	Um ... (She seems unsure. She glances down at the card.)

Therapist:	(*warmly, humorously*) Oh, I've lost you. (*Client looks up again at the therapist.*) Ahh, you're back again. See how easily those thoughts hook you?
Client:	Yeah. I know. That happens all the time.
Therapist:	Yeah—to you, me, and everyone else on the planet. That's what we're up against. That's what minds do. They hook you. But notice how different it is when you unhook yourself. Notice that if now I asked you to take an exam, or go for an interview, or go for a swim, or hug someone you love—now you could do it so much more easily. And now you can also take in the room and appreciate all this fantastic furniture and wonderful decor from IKEA. And if I start juggling balls or doing a mime show—now you'll be able to see it.
Client:	Well, that sounds good, but I—I don't know if I could do that.
Therapist:	Well, there's really only one way to find out, and that's to give it a go. We have a fancy name for this process. We call it "defusion." And what I'd like to do, if you're willing, is take you through a couple of simple defusion techniques, and let's just see what happens. Would you be willing to do that? Just give it a go?
Client:	Okay.

Now Let's Unpack That: Part 2

When we write thoughts down on a card and then turn the card into a physical metaphor, that is a defusion technique in itself: the client is probably already starting to defuse a little from some of the thoughts on that card.

There is some psychoeducation here too: the metaphor illustrates the difference between fusion and defusion, and shows how fusion hinders effective action. It also draws out the connection between defusion and contacting the present moment: defusion enables the client to contact and engage with the therapist and the room, whereas fusion interferes with this.

At the end of the transcript, the therapist asks, "Would you be willing to do that?" and the client answers, "Okay." The therapist can now take the client through any defusion technique(s) he prefers. As a general rule, it's best to start with some quick and easy techniques rather than the longer, more meditative ones.

But suppose the client is not so willing. Suppose she says she doesn't want to let the thoughts just sit there—she wants to get rid of them! Or suppose she says okay, but her tone of voice and body language suggest that she's really not keen on the idea. What could do we do then?

You got it. In both cases, we would confront the agenda: run through everything she's tried to get rid of these thoughts, assess how well it worked, and look at what it cost. Then we'd come back and ask something like, "So given that you've been trying for years to get rid of these thoughts, and clearly it hasn't worked, are you open to exploring a different approach?"

Please keep in mind, you don't have to use the thoughts-on-cards technique above. I've used it purely as an example because I find it so effective. However, we could run through the process conversationally. First, we'd ask our client to identify the thoughts she fuses with. Then we'd clarify what happens when she gets caught up in those thoughts. Finally we'd ask about how her life would be different if those thoughts lost all their impact; if she could let them come and go without getting caught up in them.

DEFUSION IN EVERYDAY LANGUAGE

In the transcript above, the therapist uses the term "defusion." However, should you for any reason prefer not to use the technical term, there are many ways to talk about fusion and defusion in everyday language. To convey the concept of fusion, you might talk about being hooked or reeled in by thoughts, getting entangled or caught up in thoughts, or getting lost or swept away by them. Or you might talk about holding on tightly to your thoughts, refusing to let them go, dwelling on them, stewing on them, buying into them, or being absorbed by them. Or you could speak of struggling with thoughts, getting bogged down in them, or allowing them to push you around. And the list goes on. These metaphorical ways of speaking all convey the same theme: that our thoughts have a major impact on us, and we invest a lot of time, energy, and effort in responding to them.

To convey the concept of defusion, you could talk about noticing thoughts, observing thoughts, taking a step back and watching your thoughts; or letting thoughts come and go, holding them lightly, or loosening your grip on them; or unhooking yourself, disentangling yourself, dropping the story, and so on. These all convey the idea of separating from your thoughts and allowing them to do their own thing instead of investing your time and energy and effort in responding to them.

THE DEFUSION SMORGASBORD

Once you have permission from the client to do an experiential exercise, there's a smorgasbord of options available to you. However, as you read on, there are two things to keep in mind:

1. Defusion is not a technique. There are well over a hundred defusion techniques transcribed in ACT textbooks and articles, and scores of others that have never been written up. But remember: defusion is a process, not a technique. All those differing techniques are there to help learn the process.

2. Be wary of invalidation. When we do work around defusion, we need to stay in touch with our compassion and respect for the client, and to ensure that we don't get into a position of one-upmanship. When a client shares painful thoughts with us, there's a potential danger in referring to them as "stories" or doing some of the more zany defusion techniques (such as saying thoughts in silly voices or singing them—more on this below). If we do this work carelessly, it can come across as invalidating, uncaring, trivializing, or demeaning.

So it's important that we compassionately join with the client: we connect with his suffering, and we validate how much pain he's experienced. From a stance of compassion, equality, and respect, we form an alliance with the client. We work together as a team to find a new way of responding to these thoughts and to develop a new attitude that enables mindful, valued living. When we do our work with this attitude, the risk of invalidating a client is low. But without this attitude, the risk is high—especially with the zanier techniques. Compassionate, respectful playfulness is the quality we aim for in all these exchanges.

A Taste of Defusion

I'm now going to take you through several defusion techniques as if you were a client so you can get a taste of them. So pull out a scrap of paper, and write down two or three negative, self-judgmental thoughts your mind throws up from time to time to give you a good thrashing. You'll need these to work with during the exercises. (If you need any help coming up with some, consider these questions: What does your mind say about your body when you see yourself naked in the mirror? What does your mind tell you about your abilities as a therapist when you've just had a really challenging session where nothing went right? What does your mind tell you when it really wants to beat you up and tell you you're not good enough?)

Have you done that? Okay, now pick the thought that bothers you the most and use it to work through the following exercises. (At the start of each exercise, I'll ask you to fuse with your thought for ten seconds. You generally won't need to ask your clients to do that as they'll already be fused!)

I'M HAVING THE THOUGHT THAT ...

- Put your negative self-judgment into a short sentence—in the form "I am X." For example, *I'm a loser* or *I'm not smart enough*.

- Now fuse with this thought for ten seconds. In other words, get all caught up in it and believe it as much as you possibly can.

- Now silently replay the thought with this phrase in front of it: "I'm having the thought that ..." For example, *I'm having the thought that I'm a loser.*

- Now replay it one more time, but this time add this phrase "I notice I'm having the thought that ..." For example, *I notice I'm having the thought that I'm a loser.*

What happened? Did you notice a sense of separation or distance from the thought? If not, run through the exercise again with a different thought. This is a nice simple exercise (adapted from Hayes et al., 1999) that gives an experience of defusion to almost everyone.

In a therapy session, you could follow up as below:

Therapist:	So what happened to the thought?
Client:	It sort of lost some of its sting.
Therapist:	Did you get some sense of separation or distance from it?
Client:	Yeah. It sort of backed off a bit.
Therapist:	Could you just show me with your hands and your arms where the thought seemed to move to?
Client:	Out here. (*The client stretches his arms out in front of his chest.*)
Therapist:	So that's part of what we mean by defusion: you start to separate from your thoughts and give them some space to move around in.

You could follow up in other ways too. For example, you could ask the client, "I wonder if you'd be willing to try talking this way in our sessions. Suppose you have some sort of distressing, painful, or unhelpful thought like *This is all too hard.* When you have a thought like that, could you say to me, "I'm having the thought that this is all too hard?"

Once this convention is established, you can come back to it again and again and play with it as a brief intervention. Here are two examples:

Client:	I can't handle this.
Therapist:	So you're having the thought that you can't handle this.

* * *

Therapist:	Could you say that again, but this time, preface it with "I'm having the thought that ..."
Client:	I'm having the thought that I'm a stupid idiot.
Therapist:	Did you notice any difference?
Client:	Yes, it didn't bother me so much the second time.

Of course, you can use this technique with feelings and urges too: "I'm having a feeling of anxiety" or "I'm having the urge to run away."

SINGING AND SILLY VOICES

For these two exercises (taken from Hayes et al., 1999), use the same negative self-judgment as you used above, or try a new one if the old one has lost its impact:

- Put your negative self-judgment into a short sentence—in the form "I am X"—and fuse with it for ten seconds.

■ Now, inside your head, silently sing the thought to the tune "Happy Birthday."

■ Now, inside your head, hear it in the voice of a cartoon character, movie character, or sports commentator.

What happened that time? Did you notice a sense of separation or distance from the thought? If not, run through the exercise again with a different thought.

Variations on the theme include singing the thoughts out loud, saying them out loud in a silly voice, or saying them in exaggerated slow motion (for example, "I'mmmmmm stuuuuuuupiiiddddddddd"). Keep in mind that in the right context, zany techniques like these can be very powerful, but in the wrong context, they can be invalidating or demeaning. For example, you probably wouldn't ask a client with terminal cancer to sing her thoughts about dying to the tune "Happy Birthday."

Practical Tip   Often with these zany defusion techniques your client will chuckle or laugh. We're not specifically aiming for that outcome, but when it happens, it's usually a sign of significant defusion, and it's often useful to highlight it: "You're smiling. What's going on? This is a really nasty negative thought, isn't it? How come you're laughing?" However, if your client starts judging the thought harshly—"It seems so silly" or "It's stupid, isn't it?"—then we want to defuse those judgments too.

For example, we may say, "Well, the point is to notice it's just a bunch of words. We don't need to judge it. Let's just see it for what it is: a bunch of words that popped into your head."

TITCHENER'S REPETITION: LEMONS, LEMONS, LEMONS

This exercise (Titchener, 1916) involves three steps:

1. Pick a simple noun, such as "lemon." Say it out loud once or twice, and notice what shows up psychologically—what thoughts, images, smells, tastes, or memories come to mind.

2. Now repeat the word over and over out loud as fast as possible for thirty seconds— until it becomes just a meaningless sound. Please try this now with the word "lemon," before reading on. You must do it out loud for it to be effective.

3. Now run through the exercise again with an evocative judgmental word—a word that you tend to use when you judge yourself harshly, for example, "bad," "fat," "idiot," "selfish," "loser," "incompetent,"—or a two-word phrase such as "bad mother."

Please try this now and notice what happens. Most people find the word or phrase becomes meaningless within about thirty seconds. Then we see it for what it truly is: an odd sound, a vibration, a movement of mouth and tongue. But when that very same word pops into our head and we fuse with it, it has a lot of impact on us.

COMPUTER SCREEN

This exercise (Harris, 2006) is particularly useful for people who are good at visualizing. You can also convert it into a written exercise, using sheets of paper and different colored pens:

- Fuse with your negative self-judgment for ten seconds.

- Now imagine a computer screen and imagine your thought written up there as plain black text.

- Now in your mind's eye, play around with the color. See it written in green, then blue, then yellow.

- Now in your imagination, play around with the font. See it written in italics, then in stylish graphics, then in one of those big playful fonts you see in children's books.

- Now put it back as plain black text, and this time play around with the format. Run the words together. Then space them out far apart. Then run them vertically down the screen.

- Now put it back as plain black text, and this time, in your mind's eye, animate the words like those cartoons on *Sesame Street*. Have the words jump up and down, or wriggle like a caterpillar, or spin in a circle.

- Now put it back as plain black text, and this time imagine a karaoke ball bouncing from word to word. (And if you like, at the same time, hear it sung to "Happy Birthday.")

"Meditative" Techniques

You'll notice in this book I talk about mindfulness *skills*, not mindfulness *meditation*. That's because, from an ACT perspective, formal meditation is only one way among hundreds of learning the basic mindfulness skills of defusion, acceptance, and contact with the present moment. If clients want to take up meditation or other formal mindfulness practices such as yoga or tai chi, that's great—when it comes to learning new skills, the more practice the better—but it's definitely not something we expect or ask for.

Having said that, some defusion techniques, such as the two that follow—Leaves on a Stream (Hayes et al., 1999) and Watch Your Thinking—do have a meditative feel to them. In these exercises, we observe our thoughts with openness and curiosity; we watch them come and go without reacting to them—without judging them, holding on to them, or pushing them away.

LEAVES ON A STREAM

1. Find a comfortable position, and either close your eyes or fix your eyes on a spot, whichever you prefer.

2. Imagine you're sitting by the side of a gently flowing stream, and there are leaves flowing past on the surface of the stream. Imagine it however you like—it's your imagination. (*Pause 10 seconds.*)

3. Now, for the next few minutes, take every thought that pops into your head, place it on a leaf, and let it float on by. Do this regardless of whether the thoughts are positive or negative, pleasurable or painful. Even if they're the most wonderful thoughts, place them on the leaf and let them float on by. (*Pause 10 seconds.*)

4. If your thoughts stop, just watch the stream. Sooner or later your thoughts will start up again. (*Pause 20 seconds.*)

5. Allow the stream to flow at its own rate. Don't speed it up. You're not trying to wash the leaves away—you're allowing them to come and go in their own good time. (*Pause 20 seconds.*)

6. If your mind says, *This is stupid* or *I can't do it*, place those thoughts on a leaf. (*Pause 20 seconds.*)

7. If a leaf gets stuck, let it hang around. Don't force it to float away. (*Pause 20 seconds.*)

8. If a difficult feeling arises, such as boredom or impatience, simply acknowledge it. Say to yourself, "Here's a feeling of boredom" or "Here's a feeling of impatience." Then place those words on a leaf, and let the leaf float on by.

9. From time to time, your thoughts will hook you, and you'll lose track of the exercise. This is normal and natural, and it will keep happening. As soon as you realize it's happened, gently acknowledge it and then start the exercise again.

After instruction 9, continue the exercise for several minutes or so, periodically punctuating the silence with this reminder: "Again and again, your thoughts will hook you. This is normal. As soon as you realize it, start the exercise again from the beginning."

Afterward debrief the exercise with the client: What sort of thoughts hooked her? What was it like to let thoughts come and go without holding on? Was it hard to let go of any thoughts in particular? (Clients often want to hold on to positive thoughts, but that defeats the purpose of the exercise; the aim is to learn how to let thoughts come and go.) What feelings showed up? Was acknowledging the feeling (as in instruction 8) useful? (This is an acceptance technique.)

Did she speed up the stream, trying to wash the thoughts away? If so, she's probably turning it into a control technique, trying to get rid of thoughts. This is not the aim. The aim is to observe the natural "flow of thoughts," allowing them to come and go in their own good time. That's why I've put instruction 5 in there.

You can end the exercise with a simple instruction such as this: "And now, bring the exercise to an end ... and sit up in your chair .... and open your eyes. Look around the room ... and notice what you can see and hear ... and take a stretch. Welcome back!"

Practical Tip   Some people find visualization very hard. I'm one of them. So it's a good idea at the start of any exercise requiring imagination to say, "Different people imagine in different ways. Some see very vivid pictures as on a TV screen. Other people imagine with words, sounds, feelings, or ideas. However you imagine is absolutely fine."

For the Leaves on a Stream exercise, I always offer the alternative of imagining a "moving blackness" or a "moving black strip"—just a sense of something black and expansive that just keeps on rolling gently by. You place your thoughts on the moving blackness rather than on the leaves.

WATCH YOUR THINKING

1. I invite you now to sit up straight, and let your shoulders drop. Gently push your feet into the floor and get a sense of the ground beneath you. You can either fix your eyes on a spot or close them.

2. Now just take a moment to notice how you're sitting. (*Pause 5 seconds.*) And notice how you're breathing. (*Pause 5 seconds.*) And for the next few breaths, really observe the breath—study it—notice it flowing in and out. (*Pause 10 seconds.*) Observe it as if you're a curious scientist who has never encountered breathing before. (*Pause 10 seconds.*)

3. Now shift your attention from your breathing to your thoughts, and see if you can notice your thoughts: Where are your thoughts? Where do they seem to be located in space? (*Pause 10 seconds.*) If your thoughts are like a voice, where is that voice located? Is it in the center of your head or to one side? (*Pause 10 seconds.*)

4. Notice the form of your thoughts: Are they more like pictures, words, or sounds? (*Pause 10 seconds.*)

5. Are your thoughts moving or still? If moving, at what speed and in what direction? If still, where are they hovering?

6. What is above and below your thoughts? Are there any gaps in between them?

7. For the next few minutes, observe your thoughts coming and going as if you're a curious scientist who has never encountered anything like this before.

8. From time to time, you'll get caught up in your thoughts, and you'll lose track of the exercise. This is normal and natural, and it will keep happening. As soon as you realize it's happened, gently acknowledge it, then start the exercise again.

You could continue this for several minutes, with periodic reminders of the last instruction—or if you only want to do a quick exercise, you could bring it to an end at this point, as suggested in the last exercise. Debrief the exercise afterward, as with Leaves on a Stream.

Accentuating Defusion: "Letting Go" Metaphors

Defusion is implicit in any mindfulness exercise or practice: the more we enter into the world of direct experience, the more we leave behind the world of language. However, as you'll see in the next three chapters, some mindfulness exercises are more heavily geared toward acceptance, contacting the present moment, or the observing self. We can accentuate defusion in any mindfulness exercise by adding a metaphor or two about "letting go." A few examples follow.

Allow your thoughts to come and go like

- passing cars, driving past outside your house;

- clouds drifting across the sky;

- people walking by on the other side of the street;

- suitcases on a conveyor belt;

- bubbles rising to the surface of a pond;

- waves washing gently onto the beach;

- birds flying across the sky;

- trains pulling in and out of the station; or

- leaves blowing gently in the wind.

Common Client Misconceptions

Clients often have misconceptions about defusion (as do many new therapists). They may think the point of defusion is to get rid of painful thoughts, images, or memories, or to reduce the painful feelings associated with them. But it is not. Please remember:

- The aim of defusion is **NOT** to feel better or to get rid of unwanted thoughts.

■ The aim of defusion IS to reduce the influence of unhelpful cognitive processes upon behavior and to facilitate being psychologically present and engaged in experience.

■ In other words, the aim of defusion is to enable mindful, valued living.

Clients often find that when they defuse from a painful thought, it disappears, or they feel better, or both. When this happens, the therapist needs to clarify that (1) this is merely a bonus, not the primary purpose, and (2) it won't always happen, so don't expect it. If the therapist doesn't do this, clients will start using defusion to try to control their thoughts and feelings. And then, of course, it no longer functions as a mindfulness technique but as a control technique. And then it's only a matter of time before the client becomes frustrated or disappointed. Here are two examples of how the therapist may handle this:

Client: That was great. The thought just went away.

Therapist: Well, sometimes that happens, and sometimes it doesn't. Sometimes a thought just keeps on hanging around. Our aim is not to try and make it go away; our aim is to stop getting caught up in it, make some room for it, allow it to be there without struggling—so that if and when it does hang around for a while, it doesn't stop you from doing what matters and engaging fully in your life.

***

Client: That's good. I feel less anxious now.

Therapist: Yes, well that quite often happens with defusion, but certainly not all the time. Defusion is not some magical way to control your feelings. The aim of is to disentangle yourself from your thoughts so that you can be in the present moment and do the things you consider important. So if you feel better, by all means enjoy it. But please, consider it a bonus, not the main intention. If you start using these techniques to control how you feel, I guarantee you'll soon be disappointed.

If your client seems disappointed or surprised when you say this, it means she has misunderstood the purpose of defusion, in which case you'll need to recap it—and you may need to visit (or revisit) creative hopelessness. One way to do a quick recap is to "replay" the ACT in a Nutshell Metaphor from chapter 1 or the Hands As Thoughts Metaphor from chapter 2.

IT'S NOT WORKING!

Sometimes you won't realize that your client has missed the point of defusion. That's okay; he'll soon come back and tell you. He'll say something like, "It's not working!" In which case, we ask, "What do you mean it's not working?" He says, "Well, I tried all those defusion techniques, but I still felt really anxious." And hey, presto! There we have the control agenda. We can now recap the purpose of defusion and clarify that it is not a tool to control our feelings. The fact is our emotions may or may not change when we defuse from painful thoughts. (If this seems odd to you, keep in mind that it's a myth that our thoughts create our emotions. Our emotions are under multiple sources of influence at any time, and our thoughts are only one influence among many, so defusing from them may have little or no impact on our emotional state.)

BUT IT'S TRUE!

From time to time, a client will resist or criticize a defusion technique on the grounds that the thought is true. It's generally easiest to respond to this in terms of workability: "The thing is, in ACT, we're not so much interested in whether your thoughts are true or false, but whether they're helpful. If you hold this thought tightly, will it help you to live the life you want? Will it help you achieve your goals, improve your relationships, or act like the person you want to be?"

Below is an example from a therapy session:

Client: But it's true. I am a bad mother.

Therapist: Well, one thing I never intend to do here is debate with you about what's true and what's false. What we're interested in is, is this thought helpful? When you get all caught up in it, does it help you to be the sort of mother you'd like to be?

Client: Sometimes it kicks my butt into action.

Therapist: Sometimes, yes. But most of the time it just drags you down, doesn't it?

Client: Yes.

Therapist: And once it's dragged you down into the depths, that's when you're most likely to neglect the kids, right? So most of the time, getting caught up in this thought doesn't help you to be the mother you want to be.

Client: No.

Therapist: Suppose you're in the middle of the sea, your boat's capsized, and you're holding on tightly to a heavy suitcase. You don't want to let go because it's full of precious belongings. But it's dragging you down, pulling you under the water. What would you do?

Client: Let go of it.

Therapist: Right. And once you let go, you could put your energy into doing something useful—like swimming toward the shore. So how about doing the same for the "bad mother" story? Regardless of whether it's true or false, let go of it so you can put your energy into being the sort of mother you really want to be.

> *At this point, the therapist might well choose to change tack and explore values a little: to find out what sort of mother the client would like to be.*
>
> *The Suitcase in the Sea Metaphor, as given in the transcript above, is useful for both defusion and acceptance.*

When Defusion Backfires

Occasionally you'll take a client through a defusion technique, and it'll have the opposite effect to what you intended: your client will become even more fused than before. Luckily this won't happen often, but if and when it does, it's really not a problem. Simply turn it into an opportunity to help your client discriminate between fusion and defusion—for example:

Therapist: Oh, I'm sorry. That didn't turn out the way I expected. Usually that exercise helps people step back and get some distance from their thoughts, but in this case it seems to have had the opposite effect. So given that this has happened, let's learn from it. Notice how you're even more caught up in that thought than before. Notice the impact it's having on you. This is what we mean by "fusion."

Then, after debriefing, you can suggest a different defusion exercise.

Techniques Galore

There are currently well over a hundred defusion techniques documented in ACT textbooks and self-help books, and many more that have never been written up. And there's plenty of opportunity for you or your clients to modify old techniques or create new ones. You can do anything that puts the thought into a new context, where you can see it for what it is: nothing more or less than words or pictures; nothing you need to fight with, cling to, or run from.

For example, you might visualize the thought as a caption on a greeting card, written in frosting on a birthday cake, or popping up inside the speech bubble of a comic book character. Or you might imagine the thought coming from a radio, or hear it in the voice of a well-known politician or sports commentator. Or you might imagine yourself dancing with the thought, walking hand-in-hand with it down the street, or bouncing it up and down like a ball. You might draw or paint the thought, write it out in different colors, or sculpt it in clay. You might visualize it on the T-shirt of a jogger, imagine it as a text message on your cell phone, or see it as a pop-up on your computer. You might sing it in different musical styles (for example, opera, jazz, rock 'n' roll), say it in an outrageous foreign accent, or have a hand puppet say it out loud. The options are endless. So before reading on, see if you can think up a few techniques of your own. And have some fun with it. (How often do you hear that in a textbook?!)

Metaphors Galore

You can also use all sorts of metaphors to help with defusion. One of the most useful is comparing the mind to "a master storyteller" because this ties in very nicely with talking of thoughts as "stories."

THE MASTER STORYTELLER METAPHOR

Therapist: Our mind is like the world's greatest storyteller. It never shuts up. It's always got a story to tell and guess what it wants more than anything else?

Client: (*shrugs, then shakes his head*)

Therapist: It wants what any good storyteller wants. It wants us to listen. It wants our full attention. And it'll say whatever it can to get our attention. Even if it's painful or nasty or scary. And some of the stories it tells us are true. We call those "facts." But most of the stories it tells us, we can't really call "facts." They're more like opinions, beliefs, ideas, attitudes, assumptions, judgments, predictions, and so forth. They're stories about how we see the world, and what we want to do, and what we think is right and wrong or fair and unfair, and so on. And one of the things we want to do here is learn how to recognize when a story is helpful, and when it isn't. So if you're willing to do an exercise here, I'd like you to just close your eyes—don't say anything for about thirty seconds—and just listen to the story your mind is telling you right now.

OTHER METAPHORS

You can also usefully compare the mind to

- a word machine: it manufactures a never-ending stream of words;

- radio "doom and gloom": it likes to broadcast a lot of gloom about the past, a lot of doom about the future, and a lot of dissatisfaction with the present;

- a spoiled brat: it makes all sorts of demands and throws a tantrum if it doesn't get its way;

- a reason-giving machine: it churns out a never-ending list of reasons why you can't or shouldn't change;

- a fascist dictator: it constantly orders you about and tells you what you can and can't do; or

- a judgment factory: it spends all day long making judgments.

And so on and so forth. Once you've used these metaphors with a client—and assuming the client has embraced them—you can come back to them again and again in subsequent sessions as brief defusion interventions. For example, in response to a client who comes out with a whole stream of negative self-judgments you might say, "There goes the judgment factory again; it's really pumping them out today." Or in response to a client who keeps saying, "I should do X, I have to do Y!" you might say, "Wow! Seems like that little fascist dictator inside your head is really laying down the law today."

You probably already know quite a few metaphors for the mind: for example, the "chatterbox" and the "inner critic" are both in common usage. Before reading on, why not take a few moments to see if you can come up with a metaphor or two of your own.

Don't Forget About the Client

When I was new to ACT, there were times when I got so caught up in playing around with all these wonderful new defusion techniques that I forgot about the human being in front of me. So we need to remember: we do techniques *with* clients, not *on* clients. And ACT is not about delivering techniques: it's about building a vital, valued life.

So a mindful, attuned connection with the client is essential in all this work. We need to be watchful of our clients, respectful of where they are at, and open to their responses. And if we get so caught up in delivering techniques that we neglect the relationship, then as soon as we notice it, we should apologize: "Whoa! I'm so sorry. I just realized what I've been doing here. I got so caught up in my own enthusiasm, I lost touch with you. Can we just pause and rewind a little, back to before I started bombarding you with all this stuff?"

These sorts of interactions not only build a trusting and open relationship; they also allow us to model self-awareness and self-acceptance. And they demonstrate that we're in the same boat as our clients: that we too can get caught up in our heads and lose touch with the present moment—*and* we can bring ourselves back to the present and act effectively!

PSYCHOEDUCATION

Many ACT protocols include significant amounts of psychoeducation. Wherever possible, this is done via experiential exercises or metaphors rather than didactically. Metaphors are particularly useful for teaching because (a) they convey a lot of information in a short space of time; (b) clients tend to accept them because they are truisms; and (c) clients tend to remember them.

Two psychoeducational components commonly linked to defusion were covered in the last chapter: "the illusion of control" and "the normality of control." Two other components often used are "the normality of negative thinking" and "the illusion that thoughts control actions."

The Normality of Negative Thinking

Normalizing negative thinking often facilitates acceptance and defusion. Clients become more willing to have their thoughts and less intent on getting rid of them. As a bonus, clients often feel a sense of relief to know that they're "normal." We're sending them a powerful message: "Your mind's not dysfunctional; it's just doing what all minds do. Our minds evolved to judge, compare, and predict the worst. Your mind's just doing its job." The transcript that follows, on the inevitability of comparison, can also usefully be tagged on to a creative hopelessness intervention. It is written below as we might deliver it to clients, except in real life we would pause from time to time and check in with the client: "Does this sound a bit like your mind?"

THE INEVITABILITY OF COMPARISON

Therapist: We've already talked a bit about how our mind has evolved to think negatively, but there's more to it. You see, in prehistoric times, one absolute essential for survival was belonging to the group. If the group kicked you out, it wouldn't be long before the wolves ate you. So how does the mind prevent that happening? It compares you to every member of the tribe: "Am I fitting in? Am I doing the right thing? Am I doing it well enough? Am I doing anything that could get me thrown out?" As a result, our modern-day mind always compares us to others. But now, there's not just a small group or tribe. Now we can compare ourselves to everyone on the planet—the rich, famous, and beautiful, movie stars, top athletes, even fictitious superheroes. And we don't have to look far before we find someone who is "better" than us in some way—richer, taller, older, younger, more hair, better skin, more status, smarter clothes, bigger car, and so on. As a result of all this comparing, we're all walking around with some version of the "I'm not good enough" story. For most of us, it starts in childhood; for a few people, it doesn't start until the teenage years. And it's the best-kept secret on the planet. Everyone's got multiple versions of this story—"I'm too old/fat/stupid/boring/fake/ unlikeable/lazy/incompetent, blah, blah, blah" or "I'm not smart enough/rich enough/ slim enough, and so on." We've all got this story, but almost no one talks about it.

The Illusion That Our Thoughts Control Our Actions

One of the key insights that we want our clients to understand experientially is that our thoughts do not control our actions. Thoughts have a lot of influence on our actions when we fuse with them;

they have much less influence when we defuse. Once clients understand this, it enables us to do brief interventions such as these:

Client: I don't think I can do it.

Therapist: Can you have that thought and do it anyway?

***

Client: I just know this is going to turn out badly.

Therapist: Well, that's what your mind's going to tell you. Can you let your mind tell you that, and still go ahead with it?

The transcripts that follow highlight a more realistic view of the relationship among thoughts, feelings, and actions. They're written as we might deliver them to our clients.

IF OUR THOUGHTS AND FEELINGS CONTROLLED OUR ACTIONS

Therapist: If our thoughts and feelings really controlled our actions, where would we be? Think of all those angry, resentful, vengeful thoughts and feelings you've had. Remember all those nasty things you thought about saying or doing to the people you were angry with. Imagine if those thoughts and feelings had controlled your actions—if you had actually gone and done all those things. Where would we all be if our thoughts and feelings controlled our actions? (*Wait for the client to answer. She will usually say "in prison," "in the hospital," or "dead." If she doesn't, you can supply these answers for her.*)

HAVE YOU EVER HAD THOUGHTS AND FEELINGS YOU DIDN'T ACT ON?

Therapist: Have you ever had thoughts and feelings you didn't act on? For example, did you ever have the thought "I can't do this," but you went ahead and did it anyway? (*After this and each subsequent question, try to elicit answers from the client.*) Did you ever have thoughts about yelling at someone or leaving your partner or quitting your job or calling in sick, but you didn't act on them? Did you ever feel angry but act calmly? Did you ever feel frightened but act confidently? Did you ever feel sad but act as if you were happy? Did you ever feel like running away from an awkward or stressful situation, but you stayed? What does this show you? Do your thoughts and feelings truly control your actions, or do you have some choice in how you act?

I CAN'T LIFT MY ARM

Therapist: I'd like you to silently repeat to yourself, *I can't lift my arm.* Say it over and over in your head and as you're saying it, lift your arm up. (*Wait until the client lifts his arm up. Usually there will be a pause of a second or two.*) So you can lift your arm up even though your mind says you can't. Did you notice how you hesitated though? We're so used to believing whatever our minds tell us, for a moment there you actually believed it. Now repeat to yourself, "I have to stand up," and, as you say it, remain seated.

SUMMARY OF DEFUSION TECHNIQUES

The diagram below (see figure 7.1) encapsulates many common defusion techniques (but not even close to all of them). The box at the very bottom is entitled "The Classics" because these all come from the very first ACT textbook ever written, *Acceptance and Commitment Therapy: An Experiential Approach to Behavior Change* (Hayes et al., 1999), and they represent some of the oldest ACT techniques in use. Most of the boxes are self-explanatory, but I'd like to quickly touch on a few of them.

PRAGMATISM
If you go along with that thought, buy into it, and let it control you, where does that leave you? What do you get for buying into it? Where do you go from here? Can you give it a go anyway, even though your mind says it won't work?

INTERESTED
That's an interesting thought.

MEDITATIVE
Let your thoughts come and go like: passing clouds; cars driving past your house; etc.

YOUR MIND IS LIKE ....
- a "don't get killed" machine
- a word machine
- radio "doom and gloom"
- a masterful salesman
- the world's greatest story teller
- a fascist dictator
- a judgment factory

BULLYING REFRAME
What's it like to be pushed around by that thought/belief/idea? Do you want to have it run your life, tell you what to do all the time?

PROBLEM SOLVING
This is just your mind problem solving. You're in pain, so your mind tries to figure out a way to stop the pain. Your mind evolved to solve problems. This is its job. It's not defective; it's doing what it evolved to do. But some of those solutions are not very effective. Your job is to assess whether your mind's solutions are effective: do they give you a rich and full life in the long run?

WORKABILITY
If you let that thought dictate what you do, how does it work in the long run? Does buying into it help you create a rich, full, and meaningful life?

THOUGHTS

THE CLASSICS
I'm having the thought that ...
Say it in a silly voice.
Sing it.
Say it very slowly.
Repeat it quickly over and over.
Write thoughts on cards.
Passengers on the Bus Metaphor.
Thank your mind for that thought.
Who's talking here: you or your mind?
Leaves on a Stream Exercise.
How old is that story?

SECONDARY GAINS
When this thought shows up, if you take it at face value/go along with it/let it tell you what to do, what feelings, thoughts, or situations might it help you avoid or escape from (in the short run)?

FORM AND LOCATION
What does that thought look like? How big is it? What does it sound like? Your voice or someone else's? Close your eyes and tell me, where is it located in space? Is it moving or still? If moving, in what direction and at what speed?

COMPUTER SCREEN
Imagine this thought on a computer screen. Change the font, color, and format. Animate the words. Add in a bouncing ball.

INSIGHT
When you buy into this thought, or give it all your attention, how does your behavior change? What do you start or stop doing when it shows up?

NAMING THE STORY
If all these thoughts and feelings were put into a book or movie, titled "the something something story," what would you call it? Each time this story shows up, name it: "Aha, there's the XYZ story again!"

NOTICING
Notice what your mind is telling you right now.
Notice what you're thinking.

THE OBSERVING SELF
Take a step back and look at this thought from your observing self.

Figure 7.1 **Summary of Defusion Techniques**

Problem Solving

A client will often feel very guilty if she has thoughts about killing herself, or wishing she were dead, or leaving her partner, or running away from her kids. These are common thoughts that many people have when under stress, and we can normalize, validate, and reframe them by pointing out, "This is just your mind problem solving. This is what it evolved to do." Defusion happens when the client can recognize the thought as merely an automatic product of that amazing "problem-solving machine" we call the mind. (You can link this to the Problem-Solving Machine Metaphor in chapter 2.)

Workability/Pragmatism

The questions in these boxes look at the *function* of thoughts as opposed to the *content*. They all ask the same question: how does it work for you, in terms of living a rich and full life, if you fuse with a thought—that is, if you allow it to have a major influence over your actions? This neatly sidesteps the issue of whether thoughts are true or false. Below are a few more useful questions for clients to ask themselves.

Helpful Questions for Unhelpful Thoughts

- Is this thought in any way useful or helpful?

- Is this an old story? Have I heard this one before?

- What would I get for buying into this story?

- Could this be helpful, or is my mind just babbling on?

- Does this thought help me take effective action?

- If I let this thought guide my actions, which direction will it take me? Towards vital, valued living, or struggle and suffering?

- Does this thought help me to be who I want to be?

Insight/Secondary Gains

The questions in these boxes also look at the function of thoughts. The client develops insight into how her behavior changes when she fuses with thoughts and becomes aware of the costs and benefits of allowing this to happen. This approach to thoughts also sidesteps the true/false issue.

The Observing Self

Although we've already touched on self-as-context, commonly known as the "observing self," several times in previous chapters, we won't cover it in depth until chapter 10. I just want to mention here that once we've introduced the observing self and run through some of the brief exercises in chapter 10, we have a way of instantly facilitating defusion: "Can you look at this thought from the perspective of the observing self?" "Take a step back and see if you can look at your thoughts from the viewpoint of your observing self," "Notice, this is your mind in full flight—it desperately wants you to get all caught up in what it's telling you. See if you can go into the psychological space of your observing self and, from that space, notice what your thoughts are doing." Or simplest of all: "Let's look at that thought from the observing self."

Keeping Defusion Simple

As we've seen, there are all sorts of defusion techniques and you can certainly have a lot of fun inventing your own, and/or getting your clients to do so. However, I find there are plenty of times where, for one reason or another, I just like to keep it all very simple. So here are a few of the simplest defusion interventions I know:

"Notice what your mind is telling you right now." This simple phrase—or the shorter version, "Notice that thought"—is usually instantly defusing. It instantly gets your client to notice his thoughts rather than being caught up in them. Sure, it may not give him a huge degree of defusion, but it rapidly creates a little distance from his thoughts. This can then be increased by adding in any number of brief defusion techniques. For example, you can ask questions like these: "Is this a helpful thought?" "How old is this story?" "What would happen if you allowed yourself to get all caught up in this? Would it be a good use of your time and energy?" Alternatively you might go for responses in which the client notices the form (see below).

Notice the form. You can ask your client to notice the form of the thought: "Is it made up of words, sounds, or pictures? Do you see it or hear it or just sense it?" You may choose to focus on the sound: "What does that thought sound like in your head? Is it your own voice or somebody else's? Is it loud or soft? What emotion can you hear in that voice?" Or you may focus on location and movement: "Just close your eyes for a moment and notice where that thought seems to be: Is it in front of you, above you, behind you, inside your head, inside your body? Is it moving or still? If moving, in what direction and at what speed is it moving?"

Hands As Thoughts Metaphor. You'll find this little exercise in chapter 2. It's a simple metaphor for fusion and defusion, and, once established, you can use it to help clients gage how fused they are, as in this transcript:

Client: I don't deserve any better.

Therapist: So your mind's telling you don't deserve any better. Right now, how caught up in that thought are you? Are you like this (*holds her hands over her eyes*) or like this (*rests her hands in her lap*), or somewhere in between?

"That's an interesting thought." This is what I say when I don't know what to say. When a client says something that throws me, triggers a strong reaction, or sets my mind in a frenzy trying to figure out how to respond, I find this little phrase stops me from rushing in and getting caught up in the content. It's a simple phrase that reminds both me and the client that no matter what she has just said, what we're dealing with is a thought. And it invites us both to stop and look at the thought rather than leaping straight into the content of the thought. I often follow this statement with a long pause, which allows me to center myself so I can respond effectively and mindfully.

Thank Your Mind. Encourage your client to thank his mind for its input (Hayes et al., 1999). You might say, "Whatever your mind says to you, no matter how nasty or scary, see if you can simply reply, 'Thanks, mind!'" Do this with a sense of humor and an appreciation of your mind's amazing capacity for grabbing your attention with any means at its disposal."

Short phrases. When your client expresses a particularly negative, critical, or unhelpful thought, you could say "Nice one!" with a sort of nonchalant, humorous openness. Or you can use other words such as "lovely," "neat," "beautiful," or "very creative." Once the client "gets" the concept, purpose, and experience of defusion—and provided there is a good therapeutic rapport so there's no chance of the client feeling invalidated or belittled—then you can say these words in response to a wide variety of harsh criticisms, judgments, catastrophic thoughts, or other "nasty stories." Accompanied by a compassionate grimace, saying "Ouch!" can also work well.

Introducing Defusion: Part 3

The third and final part of this transcript picks up about twenty minutes after the end of part 2. During that time, the therapist took the client through several brief defusion techniques, asking her to work with some of the thoughts written on the card. Once she could discriminate fusion and defusion experientially, he then didactically explained it as in the Simple Summary of Fusion vs. Defusion from chapter 2. During all that time, the client had the card sitting on her lap, an ongoing metaphor for defusion and acceptance. Occasionally she would look down at the card, and the therapist would ask, "Has it hooked you?" When the client looked up again, the therapist would make a light-hearted comment like, "Ah. You're back again."

Now, in part 3, the therapist ties the whole session together with another defusion technique called Naming the Story (Harris, 2007) that neatly doubles up as homework.

Therapist: So let's come back to all these thoughts on the card there. I'm going to ask you something and it may seem a bit odd.

Client: I'm getting used to it.

Therapist:	Suppose we took all these thoughts, and all the painful feelings and memories that go with them, and we put them all into a documentary of your life, or an autobiography. And suppose you were to give that film or book a short title—the something something story, for example, the "I'm no good" story or the "life sucks" story—then what would you call it? And please make sure the title acknowledges and honors just how much you have suffered; don't pick a title that trivializes or makes light of it.
Client:	Um. How about the "useless Jane" story.
Therapist:	Okay. And you're quite sure that title acknowledges your suffering and doesn't trivialize it?
Client:	Yeah.
Therapist:	Okay. Can I have the card back for a moment? (*The client passes it over.*) I'm going to write that title on the back here. (*The therapist flips the card over and writes,* AHA! HERE IT IS AGAIN! THE "USELESS JANE" STORY!) Okay, now here's what I'd like you to do, if you're willing. First, I'm going to ask you to read through all of these negative thoughts on this side. Then flip the card over and read what's written on the back, and just notice what happens.
Client:	Do you mean read it out loud?
Therapist:	No. Just do it in your head. And I honestly don't know what will happen. Are you willing to just do it as an experiment?
Client:	Sure. (*The therapist passes the card to the client. She silently reads through all the negative thoughts, a frown on her face. Then she flips the card over and reads the statement on the back. Then she grins.*)
Therapist:	You're smiling. How come?
Client:	It's sort of amusing, I think. It's like you said. I can see it as a story. That's what it is. It's the "useless Jane" story.
Therapist:	And are you caught up in this story?
Client:	No. It's—this card sort of contains it.
Therapist:	So let me ask you, is it okay to have that story? Have you got room for it?
Client:	When it's like this.
Therapist:	When you're defused from it?
Client:	Yeah.
Therapist:	Well, that's what we're aiming for. You can't get rid of the story—not without major brain surgery anyway—but you can learn to hold it lightly.

Client: Well, I can do it in here. But I don't know about outside.

Therapist: I'm glad you said that. Because defusion is a skill, and it needs practice. Like I said to you last session, if you want to become a good guitarist, you need to practice in between your guitar lessons. So if you want to get better at doing this, would you be willing to practice a couple of things between this session and the next?

Client: Like what?

Therapist: Well, the first thing is to practice naming the story. For the next week, anytime a thought or a feeling or a memory that is linked to this story shows up, the moment you notice it, I'd like you to say to yourself, "Aha! There's the 'useless Jane' story" or something like that. But that's all you do. Just name it. Sometimes it'll hook you before you're aware of it. That's normal. We expect it. As soon as you realize it's happened, say to yourself, "Oh. Just got hooked by the 'useless Jane' story." Does that sound doable?

Client: Yeah. I'll give it a go.

Therapist: There's another thing too. And this may seem a bit odd, so please feel free to say no if you don't want to do it.

Client: Okay.

Therapist: Okay. Well, what I'd like you to do is carry this card around in your purse for the next week and pull it out at least four or five times a day. Read through all these negative thoughts, and then flip the card over and read what's written on the back.

Client: I hope no one gets into my purse.

Therapist: (chuckles) Would you be willing to do that? It's fine if you don't want to. There are plenty of other things I can suggest.

Client: No. That's fine.

Therapist: Great.

Now Let's Unpack That: Part 3

Okay, before we wrap up, here are a few things to consider:

1. It doesn't always go that smoothly. This client readily embraced defusion. A few may find it difficult or miss the point. Others may return to the control agenda. If the latter, your best bet is to jump back to creative hopelessness.

2. The therapist could have used any number of defusion techniques in this session. There's nothing essential about writing thoughts on a card or naming the story. However, as you've probably guessed, the therapist is me—and this double-combo is my personal favorite. I particularly like using an index card because (a) it provides a great physical metaphor to work with in session; (b) when your client takes it away, it reminds him of the session and jogs his memory about homework; (c) carrying the card around in a purse or wallet is an ongoing metaphor for defusion and acceptance; and (d) you can write several defusion techniques on the back of the card, if you like, to jog the client's memory.

3. Suppose the client is reluctant to take the card away. Suppose she says, "No, I don't want it." That would indicate both fusion and experiential avoidance. In this case, you wouldn't try to coerce her. Instead put the card in her file and keep it for more work in the next session.

FUSION VS. BELIEVABILITY

Fusion isn't the same as believability. You can fuse with a thought you don't believe, and you can defuse from a thought that you do believe. A couple of years ago I gave a workshop and one of the attendees—let's call her Naomi—came up to me at the morning coffee break and told me that she had a malignant brain tumor. The tumor was untreatable, and Naomi had only a few months to live. She was attending the workshop for personal reasons: to help cope with her fear, and come to terms with her impending death. Naomi said it was hard to stay focused in the workshop. She kept thinking about dying: losing her loved ones, the tumor spreading through her brain, the inevitable deterioration to paralysis and coma, then death.

Now clearly if you have a terminal illness there's a time and a place when it's useful to think about dying: if you're writing a will, planning a funeral, making medical care arrangements, or sharing your fears with a loved one. But if you're attending a workshop for personal growth, it's not useful to be so fused with your thoughts about dying that you're missing out on the workshop. So after listening compassionately, I talked to Naomi about naming the story, and she chose this title: the "scary death" story.

I asked her to practice naming the "scary death" story throughout the workshop. By midway through the second day, she had significantly defused from those thoughts about death and dying. They had not altered in believability one tiny bit, but she was now able to let them come and go without getting caught up in them.

When we defuse from thoughts, they often do reduce in believability—but from an ACT perspective, it's not that important. After all, believing a thought simply means taking it to be true. In ACT, we're interested not in whether a thought is true or false, but whether it can help us with valued living.

HOMEWORK AND THE NEXT SESSION

Homework is essential. Defusion, like any skill, requires practice. Not all clients will do it, of course, but we should at least ask them. Homework could involve a quick technique to practice intermittently throughout the day—like Naming the Story. Alternatively, if you took the client through Leaves on a Stream or a mindful breathing exercise, you could ask him to practice that each day. You might like to record these exercises while you're doing them in session, then burn them onto a CD and give them to your clients to assist their practice at home. Most clients find this very helpful. (These days I have prerecorded CDs that I give to all my clients on the first session. The CDs are imaginatively titled *Mindfulness Skills Volume 1* and *Mindfulness Skills Volume 2*, and, if interested, you can purchase them from www.actmadesimple.com.)

Another type of homework involves asking clients to fill in a worksheet such as Getting Hooked, which you'll find at the end of this chapter.

For a more informal homework, you might say something as below:

Therapist: Between now and next session, I wonder if you'd be willing to practice a few things. First, I'd like you to learn more about how your mind hooks you and reels you in. In what situations does it happen? What sort of things does it say to you? And as soon as you realize you've been hooked, just acknowledge it: "Aha! Hooked again." Second, I'd like you to play around with one of those defusion techniques we covered. (*Select one or ask the client to pick one.*) Then whenever you're feeling wound up, stressed, anxious, or whatever, identify the "hot" thought—the one that burns you the most—and try defusing from it. Third, I'd like you to notice any times that your mind tries to hook you, but you don't take the bait—you just let the mind do its thing, but you don't get caught up in it.

Practical Tip   You can make homework a win-win experience. First, when you introduce the homework, you could say, "Do this as an experiment to see what happens," or "Do this to learn more about how your mind works," or "Do this to discover more about yourself and how you operate." Second, say something like, "Let's make this a win-win proposition. I hope you follow through because, as I said earlier, practice is important. However, if you don't do it, I'd like you to notice what stopped you. What thoughts did you get caught up in, what feelings did you get into a struggle with, or what kind of things did you do that got in the way?"

During the next session, if the client hasn't followed through, you would address these barriers as in chapter 13.

The first thing to do on the next session—preferably after a brief check-in and mindfulness exercise—is review the homework and see what happened. We may need to do more work around defusion, or if the client has fallen into the control agenda, we may need to move to creative hopelessness. If he's making progress (that is, he's finding it easier to defuse from unhelpful thoughts), we traditionally move on to acceptance and contacting the present moment—but we could move to any other part of the hexaflex.

Of course, it's not as if defusion is covered entirely in one or two sessions and then never mentioned again. As mentioned at the start of this chapter, in every single session, we help our clients defuse from unhelpful cognitions with simple interventions like these: "Notice what your mind is telling you. Is this an old story or a new one?" or "So if you let that thought dictate what you do, will it lead you to vitality or suffering?"

HOMEWORK FOR YOU

Is this the end of defusion? No way. We'll be revisiting it throughout the book. But before reading on, let's talk about your homework for this chapter. Here are a few suggestions:

1. Try out all the defusion techniques on yourself. You're the best person to practice on!

2. Read all the exercises, metaphors, and psychoeducational components out loud, as if taking a client through them.

3. Review the cases of two or three clients, and identify key thoughts that they're fusing with. Especially look for fusion with past, future, self, rules, reasons, and judgments. Then consider which defusion techniques you might try with them.

And if you don't do any of this, identify what's stopping you, in terms of fusion, experiential avoidance, and ineffective action. What thoughts are you fusing with? (For example, "I can't be bothered" or "I'll do it later" or "I don't need to do this stuff; reading is enough.") What feelings are you avoiding—reluctance, impatience, apathy, anxiety? What ineffective actions are you taking— procrastinating, distracting yourself, skim reading?

SUMMARY

The ability to think is very, very useful, but the greater the degree of fusion with our thoughts, the more inflexible our behavior becomes. We facilitate defusion in every session of ACT by repeatedly asking clients to notice what they're thinking, discriminate fusion from defusion, and look at their thoughts in terms of workability. And we never need to debate whether a thought is true or false— all we need to ask is something like this: "If you hold on tightly to this thought, will it help you to live the life you want?"

GETTING HOOKED

In ACT, we talk colloquially of being "hooked by your mind" or "hooked by thoughts." By this, we mean you get all caught up in your thoughts and they exert a strong influence over your actions. In what situations does your mind manage to hook you? What sort of things does it say in order to hook you? How do you manage to unhook yourself?

Date/Time Triggering events or situation	What did your mind say or do to hook you?	How did your behavior change when you got hooked? What did those actions cost you?	Did you manage to unhook yourself? If so, how?

CHAPTER 8

Open Up

ACCEPTANCE IN A NUTSHELL

In Plain Language: *Acceptance* means allowing our thoughts and feelings to be as they are, regardless of whether they are pleasant or painful; opening up and making room for them; dropping the struggle with them; and letting them come and go as they naturally do.

Aim: To allow ourselves to have painful private experiences if and when doing so enables us to act on our values.

Synonyms: Willingness, expansion.

Method: Make full, open, undefended psychological contact with unwanted private experiences.

When to Use: When experiential avoidance becomes a barrier to values-congruent action.

A FEW WORDS ON ACCEPTANCE

Clients often don't understand what acceptance is; they commonly think it means resignation, tolerance, "gritting your teeth and putting up with it," or even liking it. Therefore, early on in therapy, it's best to avoid the word. Traditionally "willingness" is used as an alternative—that is, the willingness to have your thoughts and feelings as they are, in this moment. Another term you can use is "expansion"; this fits nicely with the metaphorical talk of opening up, creating space, and making room. Here are a few others to play around with:

- Allow it to be there.

- Open up and make room for it.

- Expand around it.

- Give it permission to be where it already is.

- Let go of struggling with it.

- Stop fighting with it.

- Make peace with it.

- Give it some space.

- Soften up around it.

- Let it be.

- Breathe into it.

- Stop wasting your energy on pushing it away.

A Quick Reminder

Sorry to keep harping about this, but it's very important, and many new practitioners get the wrong idea: for the third (and final) time, we're not mindfulness fascists in ACT. We don't advocate acceptance of every single thought and feeling. We advocate acceptance if and when it enables us to act on our values.

Also, acceptance is short for "experiential acceptance." It's about actively accepting our private experiences: thoughts, feelings, memories, and so on. It is *not* about passively accepting our life situation. ACT advocates that we take action to improve our life situation as much as possible: acceptance *and* commitment! For example, if you were in an abusive relationship, we'd advocate that you make room for all the painful thoughts and feelings showing up (instead of doing self-defeating things such as drinking, smoking, overeating, ruminating, worrying, and so on)—*and* simultaneously act on your values to either improve the relationship or leave it.

GETTING TO ACCEPTANCE

In many protocols, and in the original 1999 ACT textbook, acceptance/willingness follows creative hopelessness/confronting the agenda. If that's where you're coming from, you could segue into it like this: "Okay, so if trying to control how you feel doesn't work too well, then what's the alternative?" The Pushing Against the Clipboard Metaphor (chapter 6) lends itself very nicely to this transition:

Therapist: So let's just do a quick recap. (*The therapist quickly recaps the clipboard metaphor and gets the client pushing against it once more.*) So you're pushing and pushing and pushing, and it's taking up all your time and your energy. Your shoulders are tired, and you're hemmed in, and you can't do anything useful like drive a car or cook dinner or hug someone you love while you're doing this. Now (*pulls the clipboard away*) let it just sit there on your lap. (*Therapist lays the clipboard gently on the client's lap.*) Now how's that? Isn't that a lot less effort?

Client: Well ... yes. It's less effort. But it's still there.

Therapist: Absolutely. Not only is it still there, it's even closer to you than before. But notice the difference: now you're free to do the things that make your life work. You can hug someone you love, cook dinner, or drive a car. It's not draining you, tiring you, tying you up, closing you off. Isn't that easier than this? (*Therapist mimes pushing the clipboard away.*) Now suppose you learned how to do this with your feelings instead of fighting with them or organizing your life around trying to avoid them. How do you think that might benefit you?

To lead into acceptance from defusion, you could say, "So far we've been looking at painful thoughts, but what about feelings?" or "Your mind says this feeling is unbearable. How about we check it out and see if that's the case?"

From values: "So as you talk about these values, what feelings show up for you?"

From committed action: "What feelings are likely to show up for you when you take this action?" or "So as you think about doing this, what're you feeling?" or "What feelings will you need to make room for in order to do this?"

From self-as-context: "So from the perspective of the observing self, let's now take a look at some of these feelings you've been struggling with."

One of our challenges is making acceptance acceptable to our clients. The more experientially avoidant our clients, the more reluctant they'll be to accept unpleasant private experiences. So we'll need to go more slowly and more gently. We'll generally need to do more work around creative hopelessness, and we may well have to go back to it repeatedly.

Work around values is also very important here. We need to make a clear link between acceptance and vitality—that accepting this pain is in the service of something important, meaningful, and life enhancing. The magic wand question is often very useful: "If I waved a magic wand so that these feelings couldn't hold you back in any way, what would you do differently in your life?" Once we know the answer, we can say, "Okay. So if that's what you want to do with your life, let's make it possible. I don't have a magic wand, but we can learn some skills here so that these feelings no longer hold you back."

Of course we also need to keep this work safe. We want to be mindful that we don't lecture or coerce our clients; we always ask permission, always give them a choice, and let them know they can stop at any point.

THE ACCEPTANCE TOOL KIT

As with all six core ACT processes, there's a wide variety of techniques available to you. Some take only a few seconds, and others take up to fifteen or twenty minutes. So, given that I'm about to open up a whole new tool kit, I feel the need to give you a gentle reminder (sorry): acceptance is a process, not a technique. The tools and techniques are used to learn the process.

Acceptance of Emotions

Now we're going to kick off with a long mindfulness exercise, which is constructed from eight different techniques strung together: observe, breathe, expand, allow, objectify, normalize, show self-compassion, and expand awareness. Afterward I'll unpack it. As usual, I'd like you to read it out loud as if talking to a client. (However, I recognize you may not wish to do this if you're in a library!) The ellipses indicate brief pauses of one to three seconds. (Also please note: with my clients, and throughout this book, I use the words "feelings" and "emotions" interchangeably.)

OBSERVE

Therapist: I invite you to sit upright in your chair with your back straight and your feet flat on the floor. Most people find they feel more alert and awake sitting this way, so check it out and see if this is the case for you. And either close your eyes or fix them on a spot, whichever you prefer. And take a few slow, deep breaths, and really notice the breath flowing in and out of your lungs. (*Pause 10 seconds.*) Now quickly scan your body from head to toe, starting at your scalp and moving downward. And notice the sensations you can feel in your head ... throat ... neck ... shoulders ... chest ... abdomen ... arms ... hands ... legs ... and feet. Now zoom in on the part of your body where you're feeling this feeling most intensely. And observe the feeling closely, as if you're a curious scientist who has never encountered anything like this before. (*Pause 5 seconds.*) Observe the sensation carefully ... Let your thoughts come and go like passing cars, and keep your attention on the feeling ... Notice where it starts and where it stops ... Learn as much about it as you can ... If you drew an outline around it, what shape would it have? ... Is it on the surface of the body or inside you, or both? ... How far inside you does it go? ... Where is it most intense? ... Where is it weakest? (*Pause 5 seconds.*) If you drift off into your thoughts, as soon as you realize it, come back and focus on the sensation ... Observe it with curiosity ... How is it different in the center than around the edges? Is there any pulsation or vibration within it? ... Is it light or heavy? ... Moving or still? ...What is its temperature? ... Are there hot spots or cold spots? ... Notice the different elements within it ... Notice that it's not just one sensation—there are sensations within sensations ... Notice the different layers. (*Pause 5 seconds.*)

BREATHE

Therapist: As you're observing this feeling, breathe into it ... Imagine your breath flowing into and around this feeling ... Breathing into and around it ...

EXPAND

Therapist: And as you're breathing into it, it's as if, in some magical way, all this space opens up inside you ... You open up around this feeling ... Make space for it ... Expand around it ... However you make sense of that ... Breathing into it and opening up around it ...

ALLOW

Therapist: And see if you can just allow this feeling to be there. You don't have to like it or want it ... Just allow it ... Just let it be ... Observe it, breathe into it, open up around it, and allow it to be as it is. *(Pause 10 seconds.)* You may feel a strong urge to fight with it or push it away. If so, just acknowledge the urge is there without acting on it. And continue observing the sensation. *(Pause 5 seconds.)* Don't try to get rid of it or alter it. If it changes by itself, that's okay. If it doesn't change, that's okay too. Changing or getting rid of it is not the goal. Your aim is simply to allow it ... to let it to be. *(Pause 5 seconds.)*

OBJECTIFY

Therapist: Imagine this feeling is an object ... As an object, what shape does it have? ... Is it liquid, solid, or gaseous? ... Is it moving or still? ... What color is it? ... Transparent or opaque? ... If you could touch the surface, what would it feel like? ... Wet or dry? ... Rough or smooth? ... Hot or cold? ... Soft or hard? *(Pause 10 seconds.)* Observe this object curiously, breathe into it, and open up around it ... You don't have to like it or want it. Just allow it ... and notice that you are bigger than this object, ... no matter how big it gets, it can never get bigger than you. *(Pause 10 seconds.)*

NORMALIZE

Therapist: This feeling tells you some valuable information ... It tells you that you're a normal human being with a heart ... it tells you that you care ... that there are things in life that matter to you ... And this is what humans feel when there's a gap between what we want and what we've got ... The bigger the gap, the bigger the feeling. *(Pause 5 seconds.)*

SHOW SELF-COMPASSION

Therapist: Take one of your hands and place it on this part of your body ... imagine that this is a healing hand ... the hand of a loving friend or parent or nurse ... and feel the warmth flowing from your hand into your body ... not to get rid of the feeling but to make room for it ... to soften up and loosen up around it. (*Pause 10 seconds.*) Hold it gently, as if it's a crying baby or a frightened puppy. (*Pause 10 seconds.*) And letting your hand fall, once again breathe into the feeling and expand around it. (*Pause 10 seconds.*)

EXPAND AWARENESS

Therapist: Life is like a stage show ... and on that stage are all your thoughts, and all your feelings, and everything that you can see, hear, touch, taste, and smell ... and for the last few minutes, we dimmed the lights on the stage, and we shined a spotlight on this feeling ... and now it's time to bring up the rest of the lights ... So bring up the lights on your body ... notice your arms and legs and head and neck ... and notice that you're in control of your arms and legs, regardless of what you're feeling ... Just move them around a little to check that out for yourself ... and now take a stretch, and notice yourself stretching ... and bring up the lights on the room around you ... Open your eyes, look around, and notice what you can see ... and notice what you can hear... and notice that there's not just a feeling here ... there's a feeling inside a body, inside a room, inside a world full of opportunity ... and welcome back!

Practical Tip   Keep your own eyes open when doing any mindfulness exercise and mindfully observe the client. Look out for signs of distress or nodding off, and intervene as required. When you do these longer exercises with clients, it's a good idea to keep checking in with simple questions such as "How are you doing? Are we okay to keep going with this?"

You can mix and match these eight techniques—observe, breathe, expand, allow, objectify, normalize, show self-compassion, expand awareness—in any way you like. You can stretch them out or cut them down, use any one of them alone, or any number in combination. In the above script, we focused on just one sensation—the most intense one. Often this is enough so that acceptance "spreads" through the whole body. But sometimes there may be other strong sensations in different parts of the body, in which case, we can repeat the procedure with each one.

As we take the client through this exercise, one of two things will happen: either her feelings will change—or they won't. It doesn't matter either way. The aim is not to change or reduce feelings but to accept them—to allow them to be there without a struggle. Why? Because when we aren't investing so much time, energy, and effort in trying to control how we feel, we can invest it instead in acting on our values.

Our clients often find that when they accept a painful emotion or sensation, it reduces significantly or even disappears. When this happens, we need to clarify that (1) this is a bonus, not the goal, and (2) it won't always happen, so don't expect it. We could say, "Here's the reality. When we accept our feelings, they may or may not reduce in intensity. We can't predict it. But we can predict this: when we try to control or avoid our feelings, it's very likely that they'll increase in intensity and cause us more distress."

If we don't explicitly address this issue, then, as with defusion, our clients will start using acceptance techniques to try to control their feelings. And, of course, that will soon backfire. The client will then be disappointed, and come back and complain, "It isn't working." We respond to this as with similar issues around defusion (see chapter 7, It's Not Working!).

Practical Tip   Suppose your client reports something like, "The feeling's gone" or "I can hardly feel it now" or "I feel so much better now." If you smile and say, "That's great!", then you've just reinforced the control agenda, and the chances are the client will now try to turn this into a control technique. So instead, aim for nonchalance: "Enjoy that when it happens. But please don't think this is a magic wand to control your feelings. It's not. What we're aiming for is to let go of the struggle with our feelings so we can put our energy into doing the things that make life meaningful." If your client seems confused or ambivalent, you can go back and revisit creative hopelessness. The Pushing Against the Clipboard Metaphor is a fast and effective way to do this.

Unpacking the Acceptance of Emotions

SECTION 1: OBSERVE

In order to accept a feeling or sensation, we must first notice it. (This is where contacting the present moment overlaps with acceptance.) The metaphor of "observing like a curious scientist" helps to encourage openness and curiosity toward the feeling: approach, instead of avoidance. Simply observing or noticing a feeling with curiosity often leads to acceptance—and if not, it's at least a step in the right direction.

The Ten-Second Version

Therapist: Notice that feeling. Notice where it is. Notice where it's most intense.

SECTION 2. BREATHE

Many clients—but not all—find breathing into a feeling enables them to make room for it. Slow, diaphragmatic breathing seems particularly useful for a lot of people.

The Ten-Second Version

Therapist: Notice that feeling and gently breathe into it.

SECTION 3. EXPAND

Metaphorical talk around making room, creating space, opening up, or expanding is often helpful.

The Ten-Second Version

Therapist: Notice that feeling, and see if you can just open up around it a little—give it some space.

SECTION 4. ALLOW

Again and again and again, we remind our clients that acceptance does not mean liking, wanting, or approving of a thought or feeling: it means *allowing* it.

The Ten-Second Version

Therapist: I know you don't like this feeling, but see if you can just let it sit there for a moment. You don't have to like it—just allow it to be there.

SECTION 5. OBJECTIFY

Quite often our clients, especially those who are very visual, will spontaneously do this when we ask to them observe their feelings. When we turn a feeling into an object, it helps us experience that this feeling is not bigger than we are; we have plenty of room for it.

In some models of therapy, you might try dissolving the object with white light or shrinking it in various ways. In ACT we would *not* do this, as that would reinforce the agenda of control. However, as it happens, the object almost always spontaneously changes. Typically it gets smaller or softer, but sometimes it gets bigger. If the latter, we might say, "No matter how big this feeling gets, it can't get bigger than you. So observe it, breathe into it, and make more room for it."

The point is we don't need to shrink or remove the object; we just need to make room for it. With acute grief work, I often have clients leaving my office with a heavy black rock inside their stomach or a thick plank of wood on their chest. That's only to be expected. Major losses give rise to painful feelings. Let's help our clients to carry those feelings willingly, instead of getting bogged down in a struggle with them, so they can engage fully in life and do what matters.

The Ten-Second Version

Therapist: If this feeling was an object, what would it look like?

SECTION 6. NORMALIZE

If we can recognize that it's normal and natural to have painful feelings—that this is an inevitable part of being human—we're more likely to accept them. In contrast, suppose your client is fused with a story like this: "Normal people don't feel this way. There must be something wrong with me." What effect will that have on his attitude toward his feelings?

Instead of a ten-second version, here are two longer interventions that can help establish a more realistic view of human emotion.

Nine Basic Emotions

Therapist: I'm going to run through a list of the nine basic human emotions. There's debate about this, but most "experts" tend to agree on these basics. As I call them out, I want you to give me the thumbs up or the thumbs down. Thumbs up means it's a "good" or "positive" emotion. Thumbs down means it's a "bad" or "negative" emotion. No hesitation allowed—just thumbs up or thumbs down. Ready? Love … Joy … Curiosity … Anger … Fear … Sadness … Guilt … Shock … Disgust. Now isn't that interesting? You did a thumbs-down for six out of nine of the normal human emotions. Get that: six out of nine. This tells you something about what it is to be human. Two-thirds of the normal human emotions that every human being will repeatedly experience throughout life do not feel good! We live in a feel-good society that tells us we should feel good all the time, but how realistic is that?

The Reality Gap

I coined the phrase "reality gap" in reference to the gap between the reality we have and the reality we desire: the bigger that gap, the more pain we feel.

Therapist: There's a gap here between the reality you want and the reality you have. And it's not just a small gap—it's huge. So let me ask you this: What would you expect any human being to feel when there's such a big gap between what you want and what you have? (*Usually the client will name emotions similar to her own. If not, you can name the emotions yourself.*) That's right. So what you're feeling is a normal human emotion. This is what we feel when there's a reality gap. And the bigger the gap, the bigger and more painful the feeling.

SECTION 7. SELF-COMPASSION

Self-compassion—being kind and caring toward yourself—adds an extra element to acceptance. You'll often notice this clinically: you'll see your client "softening up" facially and easing the tension in his body. When the client lays his hand on a painful feeling, it often promotes acceptance very powerfully. Presumably the warm sensations of the hand and the rich metaphor of "healing hands" contribute to the effectiveness.

The Ten-Second Version

Therapist: Just place a hand where you feel this most intensely—and see if you can open up around it ... Hold it gently.

SECTION 8. EXPAND AWARENESS

At times, we may want to focus on our emotions—such as when we're learning a mindfulness skill or grieving for a loved one. However, much of the time, if we're too intently focused on our feelings, they'll get in the way of living life. At times, clients will leave your session with strong unpleasant feelings or sensations in their body. For example, this is very likely when working with chronic pain syndrome, acute grief due to a sudden loss, or anxiety about some impending major crisis or challenge. We want clients to be able to make room for their feelings *and* engage with the world around them *and* do whatever they need to do to make their life work.

The Stage Show Metaphor assists the concept of narrowing attention and expanding awareness. As we expand awareness, the feeling is no longer in the spotlight; it's simply one of many actors on a well-lit stage. This in itself facilitates acceptance: when it's just "one part of the whole show," the feeling no longer seems so big and threatening.

The Ten-Second Version

Therapist: Notice the feeling. And also notice your breathing ... and notice your body. Also notice the room around you. Notice there's a lot going on.

Enhancing Acceptance

Acceptance is implicit in mindfulness, but you can enhance the acceptance "element" of any mindfulness exercise by adding in simple instructions such as these:

- "Allow your feelings to be as they are. Don't try to change them or control them."

- "If a difficult feeling shows up for you, such as anxiety or backache, simply acknowledge it. Silently say to yourself, *'Here's a feeling of backache'* or *'Here's a feeling of anxiety.'*"

Also remember that acceptance is always in the service of valued action, so we can enhance it by explicitly linking it to values: "Are you willing to make room for this feeling if this will enable you to do what really matters to you?" From an ACT perspective, there's no point in making room for our painful private experiences unless that enables us to take meaningful, life-enriching action. The Wade Through the Swamp Metaphor (Hayes et al., 1999) illustrates this.

WADE THROUGH THE SWAMP METAPHOR

Therapist: Suppose you love mountain climbing. It's something you're absolutely passionate about. And one day you set out to climb this mountain that you've heard great things about. But when you get close to the mountain, you discover that a swamp runs all the way around it. It's a big surprise. No one told you about it. But now the only way you'll get to climb that mountain is to wade through the swamp. So that's what you do. You wade through the swamp. You don't wallow in it, just for the sake it. You wade through the swamp because climbing that mountain matters.

DEFUSION AND ACCEPTANCE: HAND IN HAND

Defusion and acceptance are both about opening up and making room. When we accept a thought—notice it and make room for it—that involves defusion. When we defuse from a thought—see it for what it is (words or pictures) and allow it to be there—that involves acceptance. We tend to reserve the term "defusion" for dealing with thoughts, images, and memories, and we tend to talk about acceptance when dealing with emotions, sensations, and urges. Colloquially we can lump them both together as "opening up".

You'll generally find it much easier to facilitate acceptance if you've previously done some work around defusion. For example, suppose your client, while breathing into feelings of anxiety, protests, "It's too hard. I can't do it." You might say, "Okay, so your mind's telling you it's too hard. Is it okay if we let your mind say that, and we stick with the exercise a little longer?"

PSYCHOEDUCATION

Psychoeducation about emotions can play a big role in acceptance. We often talk to clients about the evolutionary origins of emotions, and how they may be beneficial in some contexts and a nuisance in others. For example, we often talk about the fight-or-flight response: how it's triggered by perceived threats or challenges; how that leads to fear, anxiety, and stress; and how, in some situations, anxiety can enhance performance or provide useful motivation.

Almost every client we see is likely to be somewhat avoidant of anxiety. (Aren't you? I know I am!) So one thing we want to emphasize is that change almost always brings anxiety, and if we're not willing to make room for it, we're going to have difficulty making changes. The question we ask is this: "Are you willing to make room for this anxiety in order to make the changes that will enrich your life?" We can accentuate this by asking the client to keep a journal of everything she gives up or misses out on because she's unwilling to make room for anxiety.

Another important insight for all our clients is that our feelings do not *control* our actions. Influence, yes—control, no. For this, we can use the exercises mentioned in chapter 7: If Our Thoughts and Feelings Controlled Our Actions and Have You Ever Had Thoughts and Feelings You Didn't Act On? Far more powerful, though, is to work with strong feelings in session. If your client is feeling strong anger, fear, sadness, or other emotions, you might say, "Notice these emotions showing up—and notice that even though they're intense, you have control of your arms and legs and mouth. Don't take my word for it—check it out. Move your arms and legs around, play around with your hands, make some gestures. Notice that you can't control your feelings, but you can control your actions." If a client is feeling strong anger, you might ask him to tell you in a whisper how angry he is—to show him he has control over whether he yells or not. If a client has strong anxiety, you might ask her to walk to different parts of the room, and even to leave and return, to demonstrate she can control where she goes and what she does.

And one last component to consider here: if a client has limited awareness of his own emotions, we can teach him to recognize and label them. This is an essential skill for emotional intelligence.

COMMON ACCEPTANCE TECHNIQUES

Figure 8.1 below encapsulates many common acceptance techniques. We've covered most of them already. In finishing off this chapter, I want to briefly touch on three boxes (from figure 8.1): the Observing Self, the Choice to Feel, and Metaphors.

The Observing Self

Once we've done some work around self-as-context—we'll look at this in detail in chapter 10—we have yet another pathway to acceptance. We could say, "See if you can go into the psychological space of your observing self—and from that spacious awareness, look at this feeling, notice where it is, and what it's made of." Or more simply, "Look at this feeling from the observing self."

HEALING HAND

Lay a hand on the part of your body where you feel this most intensely. Imagine this is a healing hand--the hand of a loving nurse or parent or partner. Send some warmth into this area--not to get rid of the feeling, but to open up around it, make room for it, hold it gently.

SOFTENING

See if you can soften up around the feeling, loosen up, and hold it gently.

ALLOWING

See if you can allow this feeling to be there. You don't have to like it or want it--just allow it.

EXPANSION

See if you can open up and expand around the feeling. It's as if, in some magical way, all this space opens up inside you.

THE OBSERVING SELF

Take a step back and look at this feeling from your observing self.

THE CURIOUS SCIENTIST

Notice where this feeling is in your body. Zoom in on it. Observe it as if you are a curious scientist who has never encountered anything like this. Where are the edges? Where does it start and stop? Is it moving or still? Is it at the surface or inside you? Hot or cold? Light or heavy?

THE CHOICE TO FEEL

Suppose I could give you a choice:
(a) you never have to have this feeling ever again, but it means you lose all capacity to love and care, or
(b) you get to love and care, but when there's a gap between what you want and what you've got, feelings like this one show up.
Which do you choose?

FEELINGS

PHYSICALIZING

Imagine this feeling is an object. Is it liquid, solid, or gaseous? How big is it? Is it light or heavy? What temperature is it? Is it at the surface or inside you? What shape does it have? What color? Is it transparent or opaque? What does the surface feel like--hot or cold, rough or smooth, wet or dry?

COMPASSION

Hold this feeling gently as if it's a crying baby or a whimpering puppy.

THE STRUGGLE SWITCH

Is the struggle switch on, off, or at the halfway point we call "tolerating it"?
If the switch was like a dial with a scale of 0 to 10, and 10 is full on struggle, and 0 no struggle at all, then right now, what level are you? Are you willing to see if we can bring it down a notch or two?

NORMALIZING

This feeling tells you that you're a normal human being who has a heart and who cares. This is what humans feel when there's a gap between what we want and what we've got.

METAPHORS

Quicksand
Passengers on the Bus
Demons on the Boat
Wade Through the Swamp
Pushing Against a Clipboard

BREATHE INTO IT

Breathe into this feeling. It's as if your breath flows into and around it.

NOTICING

Notice where this feeling is.
Notice where it's most intense.
Notice the hot spots and cold spots.
Notice the different sensations within the feeling.

Figure 8.1 **Common Acceptance Techniques**

The Choice to Feel

This is a very powerful question, adapted from the workshops of Kelly Wilson: "Suppose I could give you a choice. Option A: you never have to feel this painful feeling ever again—ever. But it means you lose all capacity to love and care. You care about nothing and no one. Nothing matters. No one matters. Life becomes meaningless because you don't care about anything whatsoever. Option B: You get to love and care. People matter to you. Life matters. You care about what you do, and what happens. You care about friends and family. You get to build loving relationships. Life becomes meaningful. And when there's a gap between what you want and what you've got, painful feelings like this one will show up. Which option do you choose?"

This question confronts us with the human condition: if we're going to love and care, then we're going to feel pain. Love and pain are intimate dance partners; they always go hand in hand. In order to avoid pain, some people try desperately hard not to care or love or want. They may try to do this in a myriad of different ways, from drugs and alcohol to social withdrawal to proclaiming "Nothing matters" or "I don't care about anything." Obviously such attempts are doomed to failure: they paradoxically end up creating more pain, not less.

Almost all clients choose option B, but once in a blue moon, someone will pick option A. If so, you could reply, "Of course, that's what you would choose now because your pain seems so unbearable. But in the ideal world, which option would you like to choose?" At that point, the client almost always chooses option B, and then therapy becomes about making that choice possible. This question is particularly useful in grief work and naturally flows into values, as we'll see in chapter 11.

If the client still chooses option A, we can turn this into a brief creative hopelessness intervention. We could say, "I completely understand why you'd choose that. Life is so painful right now, you'd do anything to stop the pain, no matter what the cost. So let me ask you: isn't this what you've been trying to do? When you take drugs/get drunk/take an overdose/stay in bed all day/withdraw from your friends/cut yourself with a knife—aren't those all just ways of trying to stop the pain? And how is that actually working? In the long run, are these strategies actually making your life less painful or more painful?"

Metaphors

There are a huge number of metaphors for acceptance, and the ones in this box are a mere sprinkling. Passengers on the Bus (Hayes et al., 1999) and Demons on the Boat (Harris, 2007) are very versatile in that they encapsulate the entire hexaflex in one metaphor, and can therefore be used to accentuate any process in any session. Both metaphors are essentially the same. I changed Passengers on the Bus to Demons on the Boat for three reasons: (1) demons and boats have a much richer cultural heritage than passengers and buses; (2) just about every single book on ACT has Passengers on the Bus as a key metaphor and I felt like a change; and (3) that's just the kind of guy I am.

DEMONS ON THE BOAT METAPHOR

Therapist: Imagine you're steering a boat out at sea. And there are all these big, scary, ugly demons that live beneath the deck. And they've made a deal with you. As long as you drift aimlessly out at sea, they'll stay beneath the deck so you don't have to look at them. So this is okay for a while. But then you see all these other boats, heading toward the shore. And you know that's where you really want to go. You've got maps and plans—there are places you want to see. So you pluck up courage and you turn the tiller and head toward the shore. But the instant the boat changes direction, all the demons rush up from below the decks and threaten to tear you to pieces. And they look mean. And they're huge. Razor-sharp teeth. Massive horns. Enormous claws. And they say, "We're going to tear you to shreds. We're going to rip you to pieces." So you're terrified. And you go, "Whoa! Sorry, demons!" And you turn the boat around and head back out to sea. As soon as the boat is drifting aimlessly once more, the demons disappear. You go "Phew!" and breathe a sigh of relief. And for a while, it's okay—drifting without any direction. But then you see all those other boats heading toward the shore. And you look down at your maps and your plans. And you know where you really want to go. So you pluck up courage, turn the tiller, and the instant the boat changes direction, the demons are back. Huge teeth, huge claws: "We're gonna kill you!" Now here's the thing: although these demons have been threatening to kill you your whole life, they've never actually harmed you. That's because they can't. They have no capacity to harm you. All they can do is threaten you. And as long as you believe that they're going to do the things they say they're going to do, they've got control of the boat. So—armed with this knowledge—if heading toward the shore really matters, what do you need to do? (*Elicit response from the client.*) That's right; you need to keep your hands on the tiller and keep heading toward the shore. The demons will then gather round and try to intimidate you. But that's all they can do. And as you let them gather around, you'll be able to get a good look at them in direct sunlight. And you'll realize that they're nowhere near as big and nasty as they appeared; they were using special effects to make themselves seem ten times their real size. And as you keep your hands on that tiller, heading toward the shore, you notice that there's an entire boat here. And there's the sky, and the sea, and the sun, and the wind—and fish, and birds, and other ships; there's a whole world out there to explore and appreciate, not just these demons. And notice that no matter how far you are from the shore, the instant you turn that tiller, you're on an adventure; you're instantly moving in the direction you want to go, instead of drifting aimlessly.

If the client suggests throwing the demons overboard, we reply:

Therapist: But there's an infinite number of demons. No matter how many you throw overboard, more will come. And while you're trying to get rid of them, who's steering the boat? It could crash on the rocks or capsize.

If the client suggests jumping overboard, we reply:

Therapist: Unfortunately you can't. The sea is full of killer sharks.

You can now use this metaphor to assist with creative hopelessness (trying to throw the demons overboard); acceptance (allowing the demons to gather around); defusion (seeing them in broad daylight, seeing through the special effects); valued directions (heading to shore); committed action (keeping your hands on the tiller); contacting the present moment (noticing the sea, sky, wind, sun, and so on); and even the observing self (you are not the boat or the demons).

Thus, for a defusion technique, you might name the demons—for example, the "I can't do it" demon, the "I've wasted my life, and now it's too late" demon, or the "you won't like it when you get there" demon. For acceptance, you can ask the client, "If heading toward the shore is what matters, are you willing to let the demons gather around?" Or you might say, "Which demon is controlling the boat now?" Once it has been named, you could say, "So how about we take a look at this demon in broad daylight?" and then lead into a defusion or acceptance exercise.

THE STRUGGLE SWITCH

The Struggle Switch (Harris, 2007, adapted from Two Scales, Hayes et al., 1999) is an extended metaphor that covers both creative hopelessness and acceptance; once introduced, it becomes a powerful interactive tool for acceptance work.

Therapist: Imagine that at the back of our mind is a "struggle switch." When it's switched on, it means we're going to struggle against any physical or emotional pain that comes our way; whatever discomfort shows up, we'll try our best to get rid of it or avoid it. Suppose what shows up is anxiety. (*This is adapted to the client's issue: anger, sadness, painful memories, urges to drink, and so on.*) If my struggle switch is on, then I absolutely have to get rid of that feeling! It's like, "Oh no! Here's that horrible feeling again. Why does it keep coming back? How do I get rid of it?" So now I've got anxiety about my anxiety. In other words, my anxiety just got worse. "Oh, no! It's getting worse! Why does it do that?" Now I'm even more anxious. Then I might get angry about my anxiety: "It's not fair. Why does this keep happening?" Or I might get depressed about my anxiety: "Not again. Why do I always feel like this?" And all these secondary emotions are useless, unpleasant, unhelpful, and a drain on my energy and vitality. And then—guess what? I get anxious or depressed about that! Spot the vicious cycle?

But now suppose my struggle switch is off. In that case, whatever feeling shows up, no matter how unpleasant, I don't struggle with it. So anxiety shows up, but this time I don't struggle. It's like, "Okay, here's a knot in my stomach. Here's tightness in my chest. Here's sweaty palms and shaking legs. Here's my mind telling me a bunch of scary stories." And it's not that I like it or want it. It's still unpleasant. But I'm not going to waste my time and energy struggling with it. Instead I'm going to take control of my arms and legs and put my energy into doing something that's meaningful and life enhancing.

So with the struggle switch off, our anxiety levels are free to rise and fall as the situation dictates. Sometimes they'll be high, sometimes low, and sometimes there will be no anxiety at all. Far more importantly, we're not wasting our time and energy struggling with it. But switch it on, and it's like an emotional amplifier—we can have anger about our anger, anxiety about our anxiety, depression about our depression, or guilt about our guilt. (*At this point, check in with the client:* "*Can you relate to this?*")

Without struggle, we get a natural level of physical and emotional discomfort, which depends on who we are and what we're doing. In ACT, we call this "clean discomfort." There's no avoiding "clean discomfort." Life serves it up to all of us in one way or another. However, once we start struggling with it, our discomfort levels increase rapidly. We call this additional suffering "dirty discomfort." We can't do anything about the clean discomfort, but we can reduce the dirty discomfort. Guess how? (*Wait for client's reply.*) That's right: we learn how to turn off the struggle switch. And what I'd like to do next, if you're willing, is to show you how to do that.

The next step is to work with a painful emotion and practice turning off the struggle switch. The following transcript illustrates this.

WORKING WITH THE STRUGGLE SWITCH

The therapist has just finished asking the client to scan her body and identify where she's feeling her anxiety most intensely.

Therapist: (*summarizing*) Okay, so there's a lump in your throat, tightness in your chest, and churning in your stomach. And which of these bothers you the most?

Client: Here. (*The client touches her throat.*)

Therapist: Okay. And on a scale of 0 to 10, if 0 is no anxiety at all and 10 is sheer terror, how would you rate this?

Client: About an 8.

Therapist: Okay. So remember that struggle switch we talked about? (*Client nods.*) Well, right now would you say it's on or off?

Client: On!

Therapist: Okay. Suppose we turned it into a dial. On a scale of 0 to 10 if 10 is full on, out and out struggle—"I have to get rid of this feeling no matter what"—and 0 is no struggle at all—"I don't like this feeling, but I'm not going to struggle with it"—and 5 is the halfway point, what we might call tolerance or putting up with it. On that scale, how much are you struggling with this feeling right now?

Client: About a 9.

Therapist: Okay. So a lot of struggle going on right now. Let's see if we can bring it down a couple of notches. We may or may not be able to, but let's give it a go.

The therapist now takes the client through sections 1–4 of the Acceptance of Emotions Exercise: observe, breathe, expand, allow. Then he checks in with the client to see what's happening.

Therapist: So what's happening now with the struggle switch?

Client: Well, I feel less anxious.

Therapist: Okay, well we'll come to that in a moment. What I'm interested in now is the struggle. On a scale of 0 to 10, how much are you struggling with this feeling?

Client: Oh, about a 3.

Therapist: About a 3. Okay. Now you mentioned that your anxiety is less. On a scale of 0 to 10, what is it now?

Client: About a 6.

Therapist: Okay, so enjoy that when it happens; at times, when you drop the struggle with anxiety, it will reduce, but that's not what we're trying to achieve here. Our aim is to drop the struggle. Would you be willing to keep going? Let's see if we can get the struggle switch down another notch or two?

Practical Tip   Be on the alert for pseudoacceptance. When your client experiences a reduction in the intensity of his feelings, he often ignores or misunderstands that "it's a bonus, not the goal." He leaves the session thinking, *Now I know a way to reduce my anxiety,* and starts practicing "acceptance" in order to get rid of his unpleasant feelings. However, that is not true acceptance. True acceptance is willingness to have the feelings, regardless of whether they increase or decrease. This one of the most common places you and your clients will get stuck.

Common Pitfalls for Therapists

In working with defusion and acceptance, be alert for several common pitfalls: too much talk, not enough action; reinforcing avoidance; insensitivity; failing to link acceptance to values; and being too pushy. Let's take a quick look at each of these now.

Too much talk, not enough action. Trying to explain defusion and acceptance didactically is largely a waste of time, so do it experientially. We can easily feed fusion and avoidance by getting into "analysis paralysis"—that is, discussing, analyzing, and intellectualizing instead of doing experiential work.

Reinforcing avoidance. As mentioned already, if we get excited whenever painful feelings reduce and thoughts disappear, then we reinforce avoidance (or pseudoacceptance).

Insensitivity. If we don't validate and empathize with our clients, if we insensitively rush in with all our clever tools and techniques, we'll damage the therapeutic relationship.

Failing to link acceptance to values. If we fail to draw the connection between valued-living and acceptance, our clients are likely to resist.

Being too pushy. If we push our clients into intense experiential exercises before they're ready, we're doing them a major disservice, and they may drop out of therapy.

HOMEWORK AND THE NEXT SESSION

One form of homework is to formally practice a mindfulness exercise centered around acceptance of emotions. This is particularly useful for anxiety disorders and grief work. The ideal thing is to do such exercises in session and record them as you go, and then give your client the recording to take home. Or you can give them a prerecorded CD to practice with—your own or a commercially available one. (My CD *Mindfulness Skills: Volume 1* has a recording on track 3 very similar to the main exercise in this chapter.) At www.actmadesimple.com, you can also download the Expansion Practice Sheet (at end of this chapter) and use it as an adjunct to encourage practice.

A second thing you can do is ask your client this question: "Between now and next session, I wonder if you'd be willing to practice making room for your feelings, as we've done today. As soon as you realize you're struggling, just run through the exercise." Then, so she doesn't forget, write down the key steps you want her to practice—for example, "observe, breathe, expand" or "make it into an object and breathe into it."

A third option is this: "Over the next week, notice when you're struggling with your feelings, and notice when you're opening up and making room for them. And notice what effects it has when you respond in each way." You could also download from www.actmadesimple.com a copy of the Struggling vs. Opening Up Worksheet (at the end of this chapter) and ask the client to fill it in.

Traditionally after defusion and acceptance, we move on to contacting the present moment and self-as-context—but of course we can move to any part of the hexaflex with any client in any session. So, in the next session, ideally after a brief check-in and mindfulness exercise, we review the homework and see what happened. If our client is open to the idea of acceptance but is struggling to put it into practice, we could do more work on acceptance skills and perhaps bring in defusion or self-as-context interventions to assist. If he's fallen back into the control agenda, we can either revisit creative hopelessness (What is it costing you to struggle with these feelings? How is it working for you?) or turn to values (What's important to you in life? Are you willing to make room for these feelings in order to do what matters?).

HOMEWORK FOR YOU

Try these techniques and worksheets on yourself. Pick some painful issue in your life right now.

- Practice opening up and making room for those feelings. Try this when you have a difficult therapy session—both during and after—because one of the abilities of a good therapist is being able to accept your own emotional reactions.

- Read all the exercises, metaphors, and psychoeducation components out loud, as if you're taking a client through them.

- Review the cases of two or three clients, and identify key feelings that they are fighting with or trying to avoid. Then consider which acceptance techniques you might try with them.

SUMMARY

Acceptance is the process of actively making room for unwanted private experiences (including thoughts, memories, feelings, urges, and sensations). Acceptance and defusion go hand in hand: in acceptance, as we make direct contact with our private experiences, we defuse from our thoughts about them. Defusion and acceptance also go hand in hand: defusion, as we notice our thoughts and allow them to be as they are, is an act of acceptance. So hopefully now you're starting to see what I meant when I said the different parts of the hexaflex are all interconnected like six facets of a diamond. The diamond itself is psychological flexibility: the capacity to "be present, open up, and do what matters." And thus, when we talk of "opening up," that includes both defusion and acceptance. In the next two chapters, we will focus on "being present."

EXPANSION PRACTICE SHEET

Expansion means opening up and making room for difficult feelings, urges, and sensations, thereby allowing them to "flow through" you without a struggle. You don't have to like or want these feelings—you just make room for them and allow them to be there even though they are unpleasant. Once you learn this skill, if these feelings should resurface, you can rapidly make room for them and let them "flow on by" so you can invest your time and energy in doing meaningful life-enhancing activities instead of struggling. Aim to practice at least once a day breathing into and making room for difficult feelings and sensations.

Expansion Practice Sheet			
Day/Date/Time Feelings/Sensations	How long I practiced (in minutes) What struggle switch rating (0–10)? 10 = switch on, 0 = switch off, 5 = halfway point (tolerance)	Used a CD or MP3 to assist? yes/ no	Benefits and/or Difficulties

STRUGGLING VS. OPENING UP

Fill in this worksheet once a day to help keep track of what happens when you struggle with your emotions and what happens when you open up and make room for them.

Struggling vs. Opening Up Worksheet			
Day/Date/Time Feelings/Sensations What events triggered this?	How much did you struggle with these feelings? 0 = no struggle, 10 = maximum struggle. What did you actually do during the struggle?	Did you open up and make room for these feelings, allowing them to be there even though they were unpleasant? If so, how did you do that?	What was the long-term effect of the way you responded to your feelings? Did it enhance life or worsen it?

CHAPTER 9

Be Here Now

CONTACT WITH THE PRESENT MOMENT IN A NUTSHELL

In Plain Language: *Contact with the present moment* means being in the here and now, fully conscious of our experience, instead of being lost in our thoughts. It involves flexibly paying attention to both the inner psychological world and the outer material world.

Aim: To enhance conscious awareness of our experience in the present moment, so we can perceive accurately what's happening, and gather important information about whether to change or persist in behavior. To engage fully in whatever we're doing for increased effectiveness and fulfillment.

Synonyms: Being psychologically present, consciousness, awareness, flexible attention.

Method: Notice what is happening here and now; discriminate between noticing and thinking; pay attention flexibly to both the inner world and the outer world.

When to Use: When clients are overly preoccupied with the past or future, acting impulsively or mindlessly, "disconnected" in their relationships, lacking in self-awareness, or otherwise out of contact with their here and now experience.

The Only Time Is Now

As Leo Tolstoy once put it, "There is only one time that is important—NOW! It is the most important time because it is the only time that we have any power." Tolstoy's famous quote reminds us that life happens now—in *this* moment. The past and future only exist as thoughts occurring in the present. We can plan for the future, but that planning happens here and now. We can reflect on and learn from the past, but that reflection happens in the present. This moment is all we ever have.

In popular usage, the word "mindfulness" has become synonymous with "being in the moment," "being present," or "living in the now." Why? Because contacting the present moment lies at the heart of all mindfulness. For example, the starting point for all defusion and acceptance techniques is to consciously notice the thoughts and feelings that are present in this moment.

Being present plays a major role in values-congruent living. If you're acting on your values but not fully engaged in what you're doing, then you're "missing out." Being present adds richness and fullness to your experience. It also enables effective action: it's hard to act effectively when you don't pay attention to what you're doing.

When doing values work, many clients will mention something like "living in the moment," "appreciating what I've got," or "stopping and smelling the roses," and almost everyone will talk about wanting to cultivate loving or caring relationships. These activities all require us to be present. And, of course, to know whether or not we're living by our values, and whether our behavior is workable or not, we need to be aware of what we're doing and notice the consequences of our actions.

Contacting the present moment is also essential for self-awareness and self-knowledge. The more in touch we are with our own thoughts and feelings, the better we're able to regulate our behavior and make wise choices that take our life in the direction we want to go.

GETTING TO CONTACT WITH THE PRESENT MOMENT

At times in every session, we'll ask the client to notice what's happening in this moment: "Notice what your mind is telling you right now," "Notice what's happening in your body right now," "What are you feeling? Where do you notice that feeling most intensely?", "As you make that commitment, what's showing up for you?", and so on.

In some ACT protocols, right from the very first session, even before creative hopelessness, clients are asked to do short exercises around noticing their breath or noticing the sounds in the room, and are asked to practice these for homework (for example, see Walser & Westrup, 2007). However, typically it's not until after defusion and acceptance that therapists start explicitly talking about living in the moment and making that the central focus of a session.

On the other hand, if you've started therapy with work around values and committed action, you can segue into this by drawing the link between being present and building resonant relationships, acting effectively, performing skillfully, or getting the most fulfillment out of whatever it is you're doing.

At times, you may even start therapy by explicitly focusing on this process, especially with clients who dissociate easily or who get so swept away by their emotions that it's difficult to do any constructive work.

The Mindful Therapist

Obviously in order to do effective therapy, we ourselves need to be fully present: attuned to our clients, noticing both their physical and verbal responses. (Indeed, this is essential for any relationship we wish to enhance. Building resonant relationships requires emotional intelligence: awareness of our own emotional reactions as well as those of the people with whom we interact.) Of course, being fully present as a therapist is easier said than done. Have you ever been in a session and suddenly realized that you haven't heard a word your client's been saying for the last two minutes? And then you tried to hide the fact by saying something like, "Hmmm. Can you tell me a bit more about that?"

A gutsier and more useful response at those embarrassing moments is simply to come clean: "I'm very sorry about this. I just got all caught up in my mind for a moment there, and I wasn't really listening to you. If we were at a social function, I'd try to cover that up and pretend it hadn't happened, but here it's a good opportunity to demonstrate that we're all in the same boat. Our minds just pull us out of our experience. So I hope you'll forgive me, and could you please repeat what you just said?"

While responding in this way is likely to bring up some anxiety for you, it builds a more open, honest, and equal relationship, and it powerfully models both self-acceptance and being present. It also brings home the reality that being present is simple but not easy. While it is easy to *get* present—we simply notice our experience—it's very difficult to *stay* present. Our mind all too easily carries us off. We need to be up front with our clients on this issue. We need to let them know that we can get better at being present—like any skill, the more we practice, the better we get—but we can't get perfect. Even Zen masters get hooked by their minds at times.

Introducing the Present Moment

When explicitly introducing this element, it's often good to start with a metaphor that conveys the difficulties of being present. For example, if we've introduced the mind as a problem-solving machine (as in chapter 1), we can refer back to it: "We've talked before about how our mind is like a problem-solving machine. And it's very, very good at its job. It's always looking out for problems. And unfortunately when we get caught up in problem solving, we often miss out on enjoying or appreciating life. It's hard to appreciate what we have right now when we're focused on all the things that are bad or wrong, or not quite right, or need to be fixed and sorted. So one important part of our work here is learning how to do that—to shift from problem-solving mode to appreciating what's here and now." Other good candidates for introducing this notion include these metaphors: Hands As Thoughts (see chapter 2), section 1 of ACT in a Nutshell (see chapter 1), or the Time Machine (see below). With depressed or anxious clients, you can directly and explicitly link these metaphors to dwelling on the past or worrying about the future.

THE TIME MACHINE METAPHOR

Therapist: It's lucky for us that our mind can conceptualize the past and the future. It's a hugely useful ability. It allows us to reflect on and learn from the past, and to predict and plan for the future. As we grow older, our mind gets better and better at doing these tricks: conjuring up the past and the future. But unfortunately, this starts to create problems. As children, we can easily live in the present, but by adulthood our mind is like an out-of-control time machine that constantly pulls us back into the past or forward into the future. As a result, we spend a lot of time in the past reliving old hurts, failures, rejections, and mistakes, or a lot of time in the future, worrying about everything that could go wrong. And meanwhile we're missing out on life in the present. It's hard to get any satisfaction or fulfillment from your life if you're not actually present to appreciate it.

Once you've used a metaphor to introduce this process and convey why it's relevant to the client, there are a vast number of exercises you can turn to—and they all boil down to one basic instruction.

THE BASIC MINDFULNESS INSTRUCTION

The basic instruction that you'll find at the core of every single mindfulness exercise—from a ten-second ACT technique to a ten-day silent meditation retreat—is this: "Notice X." (Common alternatives to "notice" include observe, pay attention to, focus on, be aware of, or bring your awareness to.) The "X" that we're noticing can be anything that's present in this moment: a thought, a feeling, a sensation, a memory—or anything that we can see, hear, touch, taste, or smell. X might be the view from a window, the expression on the face of a loved one, the sensations of a hot shower, the taste of a piece of chocolate in our mouth, the action of tying our shoelaces, the movement of our lungs, or the sounds we can hear in the room around us.

At times, we may want a very broad awareness of the present: for example, if we're walking in the countryside and we want to take in all the sights and sounds and smells. At other times, we may want a much more focused attention: if we're driving in pouring rain, we want to be absolutely focused on the road, not tuning in to the radio or chatting with the passengers. At times, we may want to direct our attention inward to the world of thoughts, feelings, and sensations; at other times, outward to the world around us; and much of the time, to both worlds at once—freely moving from one event to another, as required by the demands of the situation. A useful term for this ability is *flexible attention*.

Construct Your Own Mindfulness Exercises

In this and every other book on ACT, you'll find plenty of scripts for mindfulness exercises, but once you know the "basic formula," you can easily construct your own. All exercises basically boil down to some combination of these three instructions:

1. Notice X.

2. Let go of your thoughts.

3. Let your feelings be.

All mindfulness exercises include instruction 1: noticing your experience is the very core of mindfulness. Most exercises also include instruction 2, defusion. Instruction 3, acceptance, is less commonly given (but always implied).

Read through some of the longer scripts in this book or any other mindfulness book you may have, and you'll see they're all constructed around some combination of these basic instructions. For example, the first section of the Acceptance of Emotions Exercise (see chapter 8) is simply an extended riff on "notice X," where X is an intense sensation in the body. The Leaves on a Stream Exercise (see chapter 7) is built around both "notice X" and "let go of your thoughts," as is the common mindfulness instruction, "When you notice that you've drifted off into your thoughts, gently acknowledge it and bring your attention back to X."

To construct an exercise around contacting the present moment is simple. All you need to do is direct your client's attention to "X"—for example, breath, body posture, feelings, sounds in the room, and so on—and then ask her to observe "X" with openness and curiosity. If you wish to add in elements of defusion or acceptance then simply add instructions 2 or 3 from above.

One of the most popular exercises to start off with is Mindfulness of the Breath (below). I ask clients initially to practice this for five minutes once or twice a day, then increase the duration by two or three minutes every few days until they can do this for fifteen to twenty minutes at a time. (Of course, not all clients will agree to this or follow through with it, but those who do usually derive significant benefits.)

MINDFULNESS OF THE BREATH

Therapist: I invite you to sit with your feet flat on the floor and your back straight, and either fix your eyes on a spot or close your eyes. Bring your attention to your breathing, and observe it as if you're a curious scientist who has never encountered breathing before. (*Pause 5 seconds.*) Notice the air as it comes in through your nostrils ... and goes down to the bottom of your lungs. (*Pause 5 seconds.*) And notice it as it flows back out again. (*Pause 5 seconds.*) Notice the air moving in and out of your nostrils ... how it's slightly warmer as it comes out ... and slightly cooler as it goes in. Notice the subtle rise and fall of your shoulders ... (*Pause 5 seconds.*) and the gentle rise and fall of your rib cage ... (*Pause 5 seconds.*) and the soothing rise and fall of your abdomen. (*Pause 5 seconds.*) Fix your attention on one of these areas, whichever you prefer: on the breath moving in and out of the nostrils, on the rising and falling of the rib cage, or the abdomen. (*Pause 5 seconds.*)

Keep your attention on this spot, noticing the movement—in and out—of the breath. (*Pause 20 seconds.*) Whatever feelings, urges, or sensations arise, whether pleasant or unpleasant, gently acknowledge them, as if nodding your head at people passing by you on the street. (*Pause 5 seconds.*) Gently acknowledge their presence and let them be. (*Pause 5 seconds.*) Allow them to come and go as they please, and keep your attention on the breath. (*Pause 20 seconds.*) Whatever thoughts, images, or memories arise, whether comfortable or uncomfortable, simply acknowledge them and allow them to be ... Let them come and go as they please, and keep your attention on the breath. (*Pause 20 seconds.*) From time to time, your attention will wander as you get caught up in your thoughts. Each time this happens, notice what distracted you, then bring your attention back to the breath. (*Pause 20 seconds.*) No matter how often you drift off, whether a hundred times or a thousand—your aim is simply to note what distracted you and to refocus on your breath. (*Pause 10 seconds.*) Again and again and again, you'll drift off into your thoughts. This is normal and natural and happens to everyone. Our minds naturally distract us from what we're doing. So each time you realize your attention has wandered, gently acknowledge it, notice what distracted you, and return your attention to the breath. (*Pause 20 seconds.*) If frustration, boredom, anxiety, impatience, or other feelings arise, simply acknowledge them, and maintain your focus on the breath. (*Pause 20 seconds.*) No matter how often your attention wanders, gently acknowledge it, note what distracted you, and then refocus on your breath. (*Pause 10 seconds.*) And when you are ready, bring yourself back to the room and open your eyes.

MINDFULNESS OF YOUR HAND

The exercise that follows is my personal favorite, and was inspired by my son, Max. Once, when Max was about ten months old, I watched him discovering his hands. He held one tiny little hand up in front of his face, wiggling his tiny little fingers around, utterly fascinated by their movements—as was I! And I thought, "Wow. That would make a good mindfulness exercise." (I don't mean looking at Max's hands—I mean looking at your own!) It's impossible to appreciate the beauty and simplicity of this exercise purely through reading, so I've also recorded a version as an MP3, which you can download for free from www.actmadesimple.com.

Therapist:	In a moment, I'm going to ask you to notice your hand. And I mean, *really* notice it. In fact, I'm going to ask you to look at it for five minutes. But before we do that, I'd like to know, what's your mind predicting about the next five minutes?
Client:	Seems like a long time.
Therapist:	Yeah. And—just guessing here—is your mind predicting it's going to be boring, tedious, difficult—something like that?
Client:	(*laughs*) Yeah, it sounds pretty boring.
Therapist:	Okay. So let's check it out and see if that's the case. Sometimes our mind is right on at predicting things. Gets it absolutely right. But very often, its predictions are a bit off mark. So let's see what happens—see if it really is slow, tedious, and boooooring.

In the following transcript, the ellipses indicate pauses of about three seconds.

Therapist: I invite you to get into a comfortable position. And just turn one of your hands palm upward, and hold it a comfortable distance from your face. For the next few minutes, I'd like you to observe your hand as if you're a curious scientist who has never seen a hand before. And from that perspective, first notice the outline. Mentally trace the outline of your hand, starting at the base of the thumb, and tracing around all the fingers … and notice the shapes of the spaces in between the fingers … and notice where your hand tapers in at the wrist. And now, notice the color of your skin … notice it's not just one color … there are different tones and shades, and dappled areas … and ever so slowly, stretch your fingers out, and push them as far back as they will go, and notice how the color changes in your skin … and then slowly release the tension, and notice how the color returns … and do that once more, ever so slowly, noticing the color disappear … and then return … and now notice the large lines on your palm … notice the shapes they make where they come together or diverge or intersect … and zoom in one of those lines and notice how there are many, smaller lines feeding into it and branching out of it … and now shift your attention to one of your fingertips … and notice the spiral pattern there … the pattern that you always see on fingerprints … and notice how the pattern doesn't stop in your finger tip … it carries on down your finger … and trace it right on down and notice how it continues into your palm … and now ever so slowly, bring your little finger toward your thumb … and notice the flesh in your palm scrunches up …and now slowly release … and notice the flesh resume its normal contours …and now turn your hand to the karate-chop position … and notice the difference between the skin on the palm and the skin on the back … and look at your index finger, and notice there's a sort of dividing line, where those two types of skin meet each other… and ever so slowly turn your hand over … and notice the skin on the back … and notice any criticisms or judgments your mind makes … notice any scars, sunspots, blemishes … and notice the different colors in the skin … where it passes over a vein … or over your knuckles … and ever so slowly, curly your hand into a gentle fist … and notice how the texture of your skin changes … and notice any comments your mind makes about that … and focus in on your knuckles …and gently rotate your fist, and notice the contours and valleys of your knuckles … and now tighten your fist, and notice what happens to the knuckles … to their color and their prominence … and then ever so slowly open your hand up, straighten your fingers, and notice how your knuckles just disappear … and now bring your attention to one of your fingernails … and notice the texture of the nail … and the different shades of color … and notice where it disappears under the skin … and the cuticle that seals it in there … and now ever so slowly, ever so gently, wiggle your fingers up and down … and notice the tendons moving under the skin … pumping up and down like pistons and rods … and that brings us to just over five minutes.

Client: (*Amazed*) You're kidding? That was five minutes?

Therapist: Sure was. And was it slow, tedious, boring?

Client: No. It was really interesting.

Almost everybody who does that exercise is amazed not only at how quickly time passes —it seems like the blink of an eye—but also at just how fascinating their hand is. We now debrief the exercise: "What did you discover? What interested you most?" Then we can ask, "So what is the relevance of this exercise to your life?" Through questioning our client—and providing the answers if he doesn't come up with any—we now draw out (a) how we take things for granted and fail to appreciate them, and (b) how, when we really pay attention, life is so much more interesting and fulfilling.

Useful questions to ask include these: "What might happen in your closest relationships if you paid attention to your loved ones in the same way you just did to your hand? Would you be willing to give it a go?" "Next time you're feeling bored, stressed, anxious, or otherwise caught up in your head, would you be willing to really engage in whatever it is you're doing, like you just did with your hand, and notice what happens?"

BEING PRESENT AND LIFE SATISFACTION

We like to draw the connection between being entangled in your mind and missing out on your life. We can ask clients questions such as these: "What's it like for you, spending so much time caught up in worries about the future or pain from the past?" "Is that really where you want to spend your time?" "What do you miss out on, when you're trapped inside your mind?" We can point out that although we can't stop our mind from bringing up painful memories or telling us scary stories about the future, we *can* learn to let those thoughts come and go instead of latching on to them (that is, instead of worrying or ruminating). Leaves on a Stream (see chapter 7) is an excellent exercise for this purpose.

Also establish that fully engaging in your experience leads to increased satisfaction and fulfillment. The exercise that follows, Mindfully Eating a Raisin (Kabat-Zinn, 1990), makes this point very powerfully. (If your client doesn't like raisins, a peanut or a small piece of chocolate will do nicely.)

MINDFULLY EATING A RAISIN

The ellipses represent pauses of five seconds.

Therapist: Throughout this exercise, all sorts of thoughts and feelings will arise. Let them come and go, and keep your attention on the exercise. And whenever you notice that your attention has wandered, briefly note what distracted you, and then bring your attention back to the raisin.

Now take hold of the raisin, and observe it as if you're a curious scientist who has never seen a raisin before ... Notice the shape, the colors, the contours ... Notice that it's not just one color—there are many different shades to it ... Notice the weight of it in your hand ... and the feel of its skin against your fingers ... Gently squish it and notice its texture ... Hold it up to the light, and notice how it glows ... Now raise it to your nose and smell it ... and really notice the aroma ... And now raise it to your mouth, rest it against your lips, and pause for a moment before biting into it ... And notice what's happening inside your mouth ... Notice the salivation ... Notice the urge to bite ... And in a moment—don't do it yet—I'm going to ask you to bite it in half, keeping hold of one half and letting the other half drop onto your tongue ... And so now, in ultraslow motion, bite the raisin in half, and notice what your teeth do ... and let the raisin sit there on your tongue for a moment ... and I invite you to close your eyes now, to enhance the experience ... And just notice any urges arising ... And then gently explore the raisin with your tongue, noticing the taste and the texture ... And now, in ultraslow motion, eat the raisin and notice what your teeth do ... and your tongue ... and your jaws ... and notice the changing taste and texture of the raisin ... and the sounds of chewing ... and notice where you can taste the sweetness on your tongue ... and when the urge to swallow arises, just notice it for a moment before acting on it ... and when you do swallow, notice the movement and the sound in your gullet ... and then notice where your tongue goes and what it does ... and after you've swallowed, pause ... and notice the way the taste gradually fades ... but still faintly remains ... and then, in your own time, eat the other half in the same way.

Afterward debrief the exercise much as for the Mindfulness of Your Hand Exercise. Clients commonly comment with amazement on how much taste and flavor there is in one raisin, and how much activity goes on in the mouth. Ask your client how she usually eats raisins, and she'll usually mime chucking a whole handful into her mouth. Use this exercise as a metaphor for life: how much richer it is when we're mindful. This exercise can be very useful for depressed or dysphoric clients who complain they get no pleasure from previously enjoyable activities; it's hard to get pleasure or enjoyment from an activity if you are not psychologically present (that is, if you're fused with an ongoing stream of negative thoughts).

NOTICING SELF-DEFEATING BEHAVIOR

Most impulsive, self-defeating, or self-destructive behaviors are motivated by fusion and avoidance. Mindfulness exercises can be designed to enhance your client's self-awareness around what they're fusing with and what they're trying to avoid. For example, you can ask your clients to notice their thoughts and feelings *before* they actually start doing the problem behavior (drinking, binge eating, self-harming, gambling, and so on). You might say, "Next time you're about to start [doing the problem behavior], stop for a moment, take a deep breath, and notice your thoughts/feelings/sensations. Notice any thoughts or feelings you're trying to push away/escape from/get rid of. Notice any urges. Notice what your mind is telling you to do."

Mindfulness exercises can also disrupt problematic behaviors. Clients can be assigned to mindfully observe the way they do the problematic behavior, to notice every aspect of it in great detail, and, in particular, to notice what thoughts and feelings are present while they're doing so. Often simply bringing full awareness to the behavior disrupts it.

NARROW FOCUS VS. BROAD FOCUS

Think about whether the clinical problem warrants a broader focus or a narrower focus for mindfulness. For example, if clients are prone to worry and rumination, you may want to encourage a narrower focus: have them engage in some valued activity and focus their attention primarily on that activity. They can let thoughts come and go in peripheral awareness while repeatedly bringing their attention back to the activity itself. In contrast, if the problem is chronic pain, you may want to encourage a broader focus. While pain is acknowledged and accepted, awareness is broadened to encompass the five senses, the surrounding environment, and the current activity. Thus pain becomes only one aspect of a much broader experience.

In session, we often ask clients to focus primarily on one aspect of their private experience—for example, on their thoughts, feelings, or sensations. It's important that they realize this is simply to teach them a skill. In the world of everyday living, the idea is that when distressing thoughts and feelings arise, they can be accepted as just one aspect of awareness (one performer among many on a well-lit stage) rather than completely dominating awareness (one performer standing in a spotlight on a darkened stage).

Keeping Clients Present

When working with people that dissociate easily, or those at the extreme end of the experiential avoidance spectrum (for example, clients with borderline personality disorder or eating disorders), it's generally best to start with exercises focused on the external world: we ask them to notice what they can see and hear and touch. And if our client is very drowsy or dissociates easily, we keep these exercises short, and they do them with their eyes open.

If our client "drifts off" in a session, we bring him back: "I seem to have lost you. Where are you?" or "I may be wrong about this, but I get a sense that you're not fully present right now. You seem a bit distant or preoccupied." Or "Can I just check in with you for a moment? I notice you're staring down at the floor and I think you may have gotten caught up in a story. Am I right?" Once our client is present again, we could ask "Where did your mind take you just then?" or "So how did it hook you?" We can take these opportunities to point out—compassionately and respectfully— how easily our mind pulls us out of our experience.

When our client keeps drifting into the past or the future—rehashing a story we've already heard several times—we can respectfully point out what's happening and interrupt it. If we just sit back, say nothing, allow him to ramble on, we're not helping him, or ourselves; he's uselessly fused with his worries or memories, and he's missing out on the present—plus we're getting bored or frustrated, and we're missing the opportunity to help him develop a useful mindfulness skill. Here's an example:

Client: That bitch! I'm tellin' ya. I still can't believe it. I can't believe—ten f****ing years, there I am working like a dog, morning, noon, and night—while she's at home f****ing the next-door neighbor. And then—then she has the balls to ask for half the house.

Therapist: I'm sorry to interrupt you. I can see how painful this is for you, and I can only begin to imagine what that must feel like. At the same time, I'm wondering if you've noticed what's happening here. You've already told me about this several times now in quite some detail. Is there anything helpful or useful in going over it again?

Client: (long pause) Not really. No.

Therapist: Can you notice how your mind keeps hooking you here? Pulling you back into the past, back into all that pain. Is that really where you want to be right now?

Client: No. But—I can't stop thinking about it.

Therapist: I'm not surprised. This is very painful for you. It's not like you can just put on a happy face and pretend it never happened.

Client: That's right. My friends say I should get over it, but I'd like to see them try it.

Therapist: So how about this: rather than trying to stop the thoughts, how about we practice letting them come and go instead of holding on to them?

DROPPING ANCHOR

At any point in a session where our client seems to be experiencing emotional distress, it's useful to bring her into contact with the present. For example, we could say, "I can see you're distressed. What are you feeling right now? Where are you feeling it?" We could then go into her physical sensations and do some work with acceptance. Or we could move to defusion: ask her to notice what she's thinking. Or we could ask him to contact the external world: "Can you have this feeling and also stay present in the room? See if you can allow the feeling to be there, and also notice what you can see and hear around you. See if you can really be present with me—fully here with me—even while you're having this feeling."

A useful metaphor/mindfulness technique/exercise for working with distressed clients is Dropping Anchor. In the transcript below, the client has been talking feverishly about her partner's intention to leave her, and is clearly very distressed.

Therapist: This is clearly a very stressful situation, so it's hardly surprising that you're feeling distraught. The thing is, right now you're caught in an emotional storm. All these thoughts and feelings are whirling around your body, dragging you here, there, and everywhere. And you can't do anything useful until you drop an anchor.

Client:	*(talking very fast)* What d'you mean? There's nothing I can do. He's going to leave me. He's not going to change his mind now. He's got someone else. He's already taken most of his stuff. And there's no way I can pay the rent by myself. Plus everything's in his name—the gas, the electricity, the phone, the …
Therapist:	Please excuse me for interrupting you, but it's important to notice what's happening here. Your mind's pulling you all over the place. You're being tossed around in a storm of thoughts and feelings and while that's going on, you can't think effectively or act effectively. There's one thing you need to do before anything else: you need to drop an anchor.
Client:	What do you mean?
Therapist:	Okay. Push your feet hard into the floor. Feel the ground beneath you. Now sit up in your chair, and notice how you're sitting. And look around the room, and notice what you can see. Notice what you can hear. Notice what you're doing right now—notice that you and I are in this room, talking to each other. Now take a few deep breaths, and see if you can breathe down into your feet. And keep them firmly pressed into the floor. And notice how your mind keeps trying to pull you somewhere else, and see if you can stay present. Notice the room around you. Notice what we're doing here, right now.

When a client attends in crisis mode or becomes highly emotionally aroused during a session, these are valuable opportunities for teaching him how to ground himself: an essential first step in responding effectively to the challenge at hand.

HOMEWORK AND THE NEXT SESSION

Homework is to practice being present. You can ask your client to mindfully do any activity: wash the dishes, play with her kids, drive the car, do the gardening, work out at the gym, take a shower, iron shirts, brush teeth, put the garbage out, cook dinner, listen to music, stretch, walk, run, dance, sing, eat, drink, talk, shave, make love, make a cup of tea, and so on. Here are a few of the things I often ask clients to do:

- Practice ten to twenty minutes of mindful breathing each day. (This is much easier for your client if he has a CD to practice with. Naturally I recommend my own CDs, but there are many others out there. In fact, you can easily record your own: a simple MP3 recorder and a CD burner on your computer are all you need. It may not have the same sound quality as a professionally recorded CD, but your clients won't care a bit. The sound of your voice will have special significance for them.)

- Practice five to ten mindful, slow, deep breaths at every opportunity throughout the day (for example, at traffic lights, in supermarket lines, during commercial breaks on TV).

- Practice a brief centering technique (a) whenever you feel yourself starting to "zone out"/ dissociate/"flip out"; (b) whenever you're entering a stressful situation; (c) the moment you realize that you have been "zoning out"/"flipping out"/dissociating, and so on; (d) at every opportunity throughout the day (for example, at traffic lights, in supermarket lines, during commercial breaks on TV).

You could also give your clients a copy of Informal Mindfulness Practice, Simple Ways to Get Present, or the Mindful Breathing Practice Sheet, which you'll find at the end of this chapter. These worksheets can also be downloaded from www.actmadesimple.com.

In traditional protocols, work around being present segues into self-as-context. In others, it segues into more explicit work around values and committed action. Being present is, of course, essential for valued actions such as connecting and caring, loving and nurturing, appreciation and gratitude, and peak performance.

HOMEWORK FOR YOU

- Read all the exercises, metaphors, and psychoeducation components out loud as if taking a client through them.

- Review the cases of two or three clients, and identify when and how they're losing touch with the present moment: worrying, ruminating, dissociating, using drugs and alcohol, and so on. Then do the same for yourself. In particular, notice how you "drift off" during your therapy sessions: How does your mind pull you away from your client? How often do you get caught up in thinking about what to do next or in judging yourself or your client?

- Practice the activities described in Informal Mindfulness Practice (below) and notice what happens. This is invaluable information for you because whatever you struggle with, your clients will also struggle with. And if you don't do the exercises, notice how your mind stopped you: What stories did it get you to buy into? Was it perhaps one of these—too busy, too tired, can't be bothered, not important, do it later, why should I, it's too hard, I already know this stuff?

- Invent a few mindfulness practices of your own. What do you have in your therapy room that could become an "X" to notice?

SUMMARY

Contact with the present moment is at the very core of mindfulness and naturally plays an important role in every session of ACT. To facilitate this process, the basic instruction we give to our clients is "notice X," where X is anything that is here in this moment. Contact with the present moment is implicit in both defusion and acceptance: the first step in defusing from a thought or accepting a feeling is to notice it.

Of course, at times we find it life enhancing to "escape from the present moment" through daydreams, fantasies, novels, and movies. However, in general, the more fully we can contact our here and now experience, the more effectively we can act and the more fulfilling life becomes.

INFORMAL MINDFULNESS PRACTICE

1. *Mindfulness in Your Morning Routine*

   Pick an activity that constitutes part of your daily morning routine, such as brushing your teeth, shaving, making the bed, or taking a shower. When you do it, totally focus attention on what you're doing: the body movements, the taste, the touch, the smell, the sight, the sound, and so on. Notice what's happening with an attitude of openness and curiosity. For example, when you're in the shower, notice the sounds of the water as it sprays out of the nozzle, as it hits your body, and as it gurgles down the drain. Notice the temperature of the water, and the feel of it in your hair, and on your shoulders, and running down your legs. Notice the smell of the soap and shampoo, and the feel of them against your skin. Notice the sight of the water droplets on the walls or shower curtain, the water dripping down your body and the steam rising upward. Notice the movements of your arms as you wash or scrub or shampoo.

   When thoughts arise, acknowledge them, and let them come and go like passing cars. Again and again, you'll get caught up in your thoughts. As soon as you realize this has happened, gently acknowledge it, note what the thought was that distracted you, and bring your attention back to the shower.

2. *Mindfulness of Domestic Chores*

   Pick an activity such as ironing clothes, washing dishes, vacuuming floors—something mundane that you have to do to make your life work—and do it mindfully. For example, when ironing clothes, notice the color and shape of the clothing, and the pattern made by the creases, and the new pattern as the creases disappear. Notice the hiss of the steam, the creak of the ironing board, the faint sound of the iron moving over the material. Notice the grip of your hand on the iron, and the movement of your arm and your shoulder.

   If boredom or frustration arises, simply acknowledge it, and bring your attention back to the task at hand. When thoughts arise, acknowledge them, let them be, and bring your attention back to what you're doing. Again and again, your attention will wander. As soon as you realize this has happened, gently acknowledge it, note what distracted you, and bring your attention back to your current activity.

3. *Mindfulness of Pleasant Activities*

   Pick an activity you enjoy such as cuddling with a loved one, eating lunch, stroking the cat, playing with the dog, walking in the park, listening to music, having a soothing hot bath, and so on. Do this activity mindfully: engage in it fully, using all five of your senses, and savor every moment. If and when your attention wanders, as soon as you realize it, note what distracted you, and re-engage in whatever you're doing.

SIMPLE WAYS TO GET PRESENT

Take Ten Breaths

This is a simple exercise to center yourself and connect with your environment. Practice it throughout the day, especially any time you find yourself getting caught up in your thoughts and feelings:

1. Take ten slow, deep breaths. Focus on breathing out as slowly as possible until your lungs are completely empty—and then allow them to refill by themselves.

2. Notice the sensations of your lungs emptying. Notice them refilling. Notice your rib cage rising and falling. Notice the gentle rise and fall of your shoulders.

3. See if you can let your thoughts come and go as if they're just passing cars, driving past outside your house.

4. Expand your awareness: simultaneously notice your breathing and your body. Then look around the room and notice what you can see, hear, smell, touch, and feel.

Dropping Anchor

This is another simple exercise to center yourself and connect with the world around you. Practice it throughout the day, especially any time you find yourself getting caught up in your thoughts and feelings:

1. Plant your feet into the floor.

2. Push them down—notice the floor beneath you, supporting you.

3. Notice the muscle tension in your legs as you push your feet down.

4. Notice your entire body—and the feeling of gravity flowing down through your head, spine, and legs into your feet.

5. Now look around and notice what you can see and hear around you. Notice where you are and what you're doing.

Notice Five Things

This is yet another simple exercise to center yourself and engage with your environment. Practice it throughout the day, especially any time you find yourself getting caught up in your thoughts and feelings:

1. Pause for a moment.

2. Look around and notice five things that you can see.

3. Listen carefully and notice five things that you can hear.

4. Notice five things that you can feel in contact with your body (for example, your watch against your wrist, your trousers against your legs, the air on your face, your feet upon the floor, your back against the chair).

5. Finally, do all of the above simultaneously.

THE MINDFUL BREATHING PRACTICE SHEET

Mindful breathing practice enables you to develop several skills: the ability to focus and engage in what you are doing; the ability to let thoughts come and go without getting caught up in them; the ability to refocus when you realize you're distracted; and the ability to let your feelings be as they are without trying to control them. Even five minutes of practice a day can make a difference over time. Ten minutes twice a day or twenty minutes once a day is even better.

Mindful Breathing Practice Sheet			
Day/Date/Time(s) How long I practiced (in minutes)	Difficult thoughts and feelings that showed up	Used CD yes/no	Benefits and/or difficulties

CHAPTER 10

Pure Awareness

SELF-AS-CONTEXT IN A NUTSHELL

In Plain Language: Self-as-context is not a thought or a feeling but a "viewpoint" from which we can observe thoughts and feelings, and a "space" in which those thoughts and feelings can move. We access this "psychological space" through noticing that we are noticing, or becoming conscious of our own consciousness. It is a "place" from which we can observe our experience without being caught up in it. "Pure awareness" is a good alternative term because that's all it is: awareness of our own awareness.

Aim: To connect with a transcendent sense of self that is separate from thoughts and feelings, and that provides a safe and constant viewpoint from which to observe and accept them. To help people stop running from their pain, we help them experience that there is a "place inside" where, no matter how great the pain is, it cannot harm them.

Synonyms: Self-as-perspective, the observing self, the noticing self, the silent self, pure consciousness, pure awareness, the transcendent self.

Method: Any ongoing mindfulness practice generally leads to a sense of self-as-context. This is enhanced by exercises that explicitly direct attention to one's own consciousness.

When to Use: To facilitate acceptance, when the client is afraid of being harmed by his own inner experiences; to facilitate defusion when the client is overly attached to the conceptualized self; to facilitate conscious choice and effective action by providing a space in which thoughts and feelings don't control actions.

Three Senses of Self

While there are many ways in which we can talk about self, ACT traditionally focuses on three senses of self: the conceptualized self, self-as-awareness, and self-as-context. (These are not terms we use with clients. When you read ACT textbooks, you may become a bit confused as different authors use different terminology, so here I've stuck with the most commonly used terms.)

- **The conceptualized self:** all the beliefs, thoughts, ideas, facts, images, judgments, memories, and so on that form my self-concept, that describe "who I am" as a person: my self-description. Fusion with these thoughts leads to a sense of self-as-description: I am my thoughts!

- **Self-as-awareness:** the ongoing process of noticing our experience, contacting the present moment.

- **Self-as-context:** the locus/space from where noticing happens; the perspective/viewpoint from which noticing happens; the "I" that notices whatever is being noticed in any moment.

THE SLIT LAMP METAPHOR

A metaphor adapted from Buddhism illuminates these three senses of self. Imagine walking into a pitch-black room. In your hands is a slit lamp. You open the slit, and a beam of light shoots out and illuminates part of the room, revealing a chair, a bed, and a table. The furniture is like your conceptualized self. The beam of light is like the ongoing process of noticing (self-as-awareness). When the light shines on different parts of the room, different pieces of furniture are revealed: a desk, a wardrobe, a chest of drawers. But wherever the light shines, whatever it illuminates and reveals, the light beam is always coming from the same source, the same locus: the lamp itself. The lamp is like self-as-context.

The Observing Self Is Implicit in Mindfulness

René Descartes, in his famous declaration, said, "I think, therefore I am," but who is the "I" that notices all that thinking? In ACT, we often refer to this "I" as the "observing self," and the observing self is implicit in all mindfulness. If the basic mindfulness instruction is "notice X," that implies there's a locus or perspective from which X is noticed. And this locus or perspective never changes. I notice my thoughts, I notice my feelings, I notice my body, I notice the world outside my body—and I even notice my own noticing. So that which is being noticed—X—changes continually. But the locus or perspective from which the noticing happens, in and of itself, never changes: throughout life, everything is always noticed from a locus or perspective of I/here/now.

If you're struggling to make sense of this, it's not surprising, because the observing self is an experience beyond all words. Whatever words we use to describe it, whatever images we create of it, whatever beliefs or concepts we formulate about it—they're not it! It's the aspect of us that notices or observes all those words, images, beliefs, and concepts that we use to try and describe it. Even calling it "it" is a problem, because when you label something "it," you're treating "it" as an object. And yet this observing self cannot be an object as "it" has no physical properties.

The closest we can get to this experience in language is via metaphor. Metaphors usually refer to it as a "space" in which thoughts and feelings move, or a "perspective" from which thoughts and feelings are observed. One excellent metaphor (which can be found in Buddhism, Taoism, and Hinduism) compares the observing self to the sky. You can use this metaphor conversationally with your clients, but I prefer to deliver it at the end of a mindfulness exercise, as written below:

THE SKY AND THE WEATHER METAPHOR

Therapist: Your observing self is like the sky. Thoughts and feelings are like the weather. The weather changes continually, but no matter how bad it gets, it cannot harm the sky in any way. The mightiest thunderstorm, the most turbulent hurricane, the most severe winter blizzard—these things cannot hurt or harm the sky. And no matter how bad the weather, the sky always has room for it—and sooner or later the weather always changes.

Now sometimes we forget the sky is there, but it's still there. And sometimes we can't see the sky—it's obscured by clouds. But if we rise high enough above those clouds—even the thickest, darkest, thunderclouds—sooner or later we'll reach clear sky, stretching in all directions, boundless and pure. More and more, you can learn to access this part of you: a safe space inside from which to observe and make room for difficult thoughts and feelings.

GETTING TO SELF-AS-CONTEXT

In traditional ACT protocols, the observing self is introduced after several sessions on defusion, acceptance, and the present moment. However, as with all six core processes, we can bring self-as-context into any session. In recent years, I've increasingly introduced this concept right from the very beginning of active therapy, using the concept of the thinking self and the observing self (Harris, 2007). Before reading on, please refresh your memory of this concept by turning back to chapter 4 and rereading the section entitled The Thinking Self and the Observing Self.

If we follow a traditional ACT protocol, then we bring in self-as-context after several sessions focused on defusion, acceptance, and being present. We might say, "So you've been doing all these mindfulness exercises—noticing thoughts, noticing feelings, noticing your breath, and so on. What is this part of you that does all the noticing? We don't have a name for it in everyday language. In

ACT, we call it the noticing self or the observing self. And if you're open to it, I'd like to take you through an exercise now to have a deeper connection with this part of you."

Another useful metaphor for introducing self-as-context is the Chessboard (Hayes et al., 1999).

THE CHESSBOARD METAPHOR

Therapist: Imagine a chessboard, where the white pieces are all your positive thoughts and feelings, and the black pieces are all your negative ones. We go through life desperately trying to move our white pieces across and wipe off all the black pieces. But the problem is—there are an infinite number of white and black pieces. No matter how many black pieces you wipe off, more will appear. Also, the white pieces attract black pieces. You move forward the white piece, "I'm a good parent," and it immediately attracts the black piece, "No, you're not. What about the way you yelled at your kids last night." So we can go through life, wasting a lot of time and energy, trying to win this battle that can never be won. Or we can learn how to be more like the chessboard. The board is in intimate contact with all the pieces, but it's not involved in the battle. There's a part of us that operates like this chessboard. In ACT, we call it the observing self. It enables us to step out of the battle with our thoughts and feelings while giving them plenty of space to move around.

Experiential Exercises

Once we've introduced self-as-context by metaphor, there are many experiential exercises we can use. Remember the basic mindfulness instruction—"notice X"? To facilitate self-as-context, X becomes your own awareness or consciousness—that is, you notice your noticing, or notice your awareness, or notice your consciousness. We can facilitate this by adding simple instructions to any mindfulness exercise such as "notice who is noticing" or "be aware that you're noticing." The following exercise illustrates this.

THERE GO YOUR THOUGHTS ...

This exercise is simply an extension of Watch Your Thoughts, the defusion technique introduced in chapter 7.

Therapist: Find a comfortable position, and close your eyes. Now notice: where are your thoughts? ... Where do they seem to be located: above you, behind you, in front of you, to one side? (*Pause 5 seconds.*) And notice the form of those thoughts: are they pictures, words, or sounds? (*Pause 5 seconds.*) And notice—are they moving or still? ... And if moving, what speed and what direction? (*Pause 10 seconds.*) Notice there are two separate processes going on here: there's a process of thinking—your thinking self is throwing up all sorts of words and pictures—and there's a process of noticing—your observing self is noticing all those thoughts. (*Pause 5 seconds.*)

Now this gets your mind whirring, debating, and analyzing, so let's do it again. Notice: where are your thoughts? … Are they pictures or words, moving or still? (*Pause 10 seconds.*) There go your thoughts—and there "you" are, observing those thoughts. Your thoughts keep changing. The "you" that observes them does not change.

Now once again, this gets your mind whirring, debating, and analyzing, so let's just do that one last time. Notice: where are your thoughts? … Are they pictures or words, moving or still? … (*Pause 10 seconds.*) There go your thoughts—and there "you" are, observing them. Your thoughts change; you don't.

NOTICING THE STAGE SHOW

Another useful exercise is Noticing the Stage Show. I won't reproduce it here as it is comprised of sections 1 and 2 of the Hexaflexercise, exactly as transcribed in chapter 4. Please go back and reread it now before continuing.

You can use Noticing the Stage Show as the introduction to any mindfulness exercise, such as Mindfulness of the Breath, Leaves on a Stream, or Mindfully Eating a Raisin. This lays the groundwork for deeper exploration later. The Stage Show Metaphor also provides a useful conclusion to any mindfulness exercise, as in section 8 of the Acceptance of Emotions Exercise (see chapter 8). Again, please go back and reread it now before continuing.

You can also tie this metaphor into earlier defusion and acceptance work: thoughts and feelings are like performers in the show, trying their hardest to get your full attention—and if you're not careful, they grab hold of you and pull you up onto the stage (fusion). Defusion and acceptance are like stepping back from the stage so you can take in the whole show.

NOTICE WHO'S NOTICING

A simple way of bringing self-as-context into any mindfulness exercise is to slip in an instruction such as "And as you notice your breath/your thoughts/this sensation in your chest/the taste of the raisin on your tongue, take a moment to notice who is noticing." Variants on this include "Be aware that you're noticing" or "Recognize that there's a 'you' in there—a 'you' behind your eyes who is noticing all this" or "There is X, and there you are, noticing X."

TALKING AND LISTENING

Here's another ultraquick exercise.

Therapist: For the next thirty seconds, silently listen in to what your mind is saying. And if your thoughts stop, just keep listening until they start again. (*Pause 30 seconds.*) So there you have it: there's a part of your mind that talks—the thinking self—and a part of your mind that listens—the observing self.

> **Practical Tip** Suppose your client says, "I don't get it. I don't seem to have an observing self. I just keep thinking." You can reply (with suitable pauses in between each question):, "So can you notice yourself telling me this? … Can you notice your feelings of confusion? … Can you notice the sensations of that frown upon your forehead? … Can you notice all your thoughts about not getting it? … Can you notice me talking to you? … Can you notice what you're thinking now about my replies? Okay, so there's a part of you in there that notices everything. That's it—that's the observing self."

THE CONTINUOUS YOU

What follows is a much-shortened version of the "classic" observer exercise from Hayes and colleagues (1999), often known as the "continuous you" exercise (for reasons that will soon be obvious). The exercise may at first seem complex, but it's basically comprised of only four instructions:

1. Notice X.

2. There's X—and there you are noticing X.

3. If you can notice X, you cannot be X.

4. X changes continually; the you who notices X does not change.

X can include some or all of the following: your breath, your thoughts, your feelings, your physical body, the roles you play. With most clients, I run through the entire exercise in one go, which takes about fifteen minutes, but you can break it up into smaller sections and debrief them as you go. I always conclude this exercise with the Sky and the Weather Metaphor, which usually has a strong impact.

Therapist: I invite you to sit up straight, with your feet flat on the floor, and either fix your eyes on a spot or close them … Notice the breath flowing in and out of your lungs … notice it coming in through the nostrils … down into the lungs … and back out again … And as you do that, be aware you're noticing … there goes your breath … and there you are noticing it. (*Pause 5 seconds.*) If you can notice your breath, you cannot be your breath. (*Pause 5 seconds.*) Your breath changes continually … sometimes shallow, sometimes deep … sometimes fast, sometimes slow … but the part of you that notices your breath does not change. (*Pause 5 seconds.*) And when you were a child, your lungs were so much smaller … but the you who could notice your breathing as a child is the same you who can notice it as an adult.

Now that gets your mind whirring, analyzing, philosophizing, debating … So take a step back and notice, where are your thoughts? … Where do they seem to be located? .... Are they moving or still? ... Are they pictures or words? ... (*Pause 5 seconds.*) And as you do notice your thoughts, be aware you're noticing ... there go your thoughts ... and there you are noticing them. (*Pause 5 seconds.*) If you can notice your thoughts, you cannot be your thoughts. (*Pause 5 seconds.*) Your thoughts change continually ... sometimes true, sometimes false ... sometimes positive, sometimes negative ... sometimes happy, sometimes sad ... but the part of you that notices your thoughts does not change. (*Pause 5 seconds.*) And when you were a child, your thoughts were so very different than they are today ... but the you who could notice your thoughts as a child is the same you who notices them as an adult. (*Pause 5 seconds.*)

Now I don't expect your mind to agree to this. In fact, I expect throughout the rest of this exercise your mind will debate, analyze, attack, or intellectualize whatever I say, so see if you can let those thoughts come and go like passing cars, and engage in the exercise no matter how hard your mind tries to pull you away. (*Pause 5 seconds.*)

Now notice your body in the chair ... (*Pause 5 seconds.*) And as you do that, be aware you're noticing ... there is your body ... and there you are noticing it. (*Pause 5 seconds.*) It's not the same body you had as a baby, as a child, or as a teenager ... You may have had bits put into it or bits cut out of it ... You have scars, and wrinkles, and moles and blemishes, and sunspots ... it's not the same skin you had in your youth, that's for sure ... But the part of you that can notice your body never changes. (*Pause 5 seconds.*) As a child, when you looked in the mirror, your reflection was very different than it is today ... but the you who could notice your reflection is the same you that notices your reflection today. (*Pause 5 seconds.*)

Now quickly scan your body from head to toe, and notice the different feelings and sensations ... and pick any feeling or sensation that captures your interest ... and observe it with curiosity ... noticing where it starts and stops ... and how deep in it goes ... and what its shape is ... and its temperature ... And as you notice this feeling or sensation ... just be aware you're noticing ... there is the feeling ... and there you are noticing it. (*Pause 5 seconds.*) If you can notice this feeling or sensation, you cannot be this feeling or sensation. (*Pause 5 seconds.*) Your feelings and sensations change continually ... sometimes you feel happy, sometimes you feel sad ... sometimes you feel healthy, sometimes you feel sick ... sometimes you feel stressed, sometimes relaxed ... but the part of you that notices your feelings does not change. (*Pause 5 seconds.*) And when you're frightened, angry, or sad in your life today ... the you who can notice those feelings is the same you that could notice your feelings as a child.

Now notice the role you're playing in this moment ... and as you do that, be aware you're noticing ... right now, you're playing the role of a client ... but your roles change continuously ... at times, you're in the role of a mother/father, son/daughter, brother/sister, friend, enemy, neighbor, rival, student, teacher, citizen, customer, worker, employer, employee, and so on.

(*Pause 5 seconds.*) If you can notice those roles, you cannot be those roles. (*Pause 5 seconds.*) And there are some roles that you will never have again ... like the role of a young child ... (*Pause 5 seconds.*) But the you who notices your roles does not change ... It's the same you that could notice your roles even when you were very young.

We don't have a good name in everyday language for this part of you ... I'm going to call it the observing self, but you don't have to call it that ... you can call it whatever you like ... and this observing self is like the sky. (*Finish the exercise with the Sky and the Weather Metaphor.*)

Longer versions of the exercise take the client back through several memories from different periods of her life and have her recognize that in each case, the observing self was present when the memory was "recorded."

Many clients find this exercise a profoundly moving spiritual experience. It's better not to analyze it afterward or you run the risk of intellectualizing it.

Accentuating Defusion and Acceptance

As mentioned in chapters 7 and 8, once you've introduced the observing self, you can bring it into sessions as a brief intervention to enhance defusion and acceptance: "See if you can take a step back and look at this thought/feeling from the observing self." You can see this play out in the following transcript, from a fourth session, following work on defusion, acceptance, and self-as-context. The client, a middle-aged woman, wants to tell her twenty-six-year-old son to move out of her home.

Client: (*looking pale, tense, agitated, and anxious*) I don't know if I can do it. I want to, I mean, I want him to go ... I've had enough of him ... but ... I feel so ... well, I'm his mother, aren't I? Oh, God. I can't stand this feeling.

Therapist: Take a step back for a moment and see if you can look at this from the observing self ... Notice all those thoughts whizzing through your head ... and all those feelings whirling around in your body ... and notice your body sitting in the chair ... and notice the room around you ... what you can see and hear ... including little old me, sitting over here ... There's a whole stage show going on here—and there's a part of you, an observing self, that's able to notice that show ... From that perspective, notice this feeling in your body ... and recognize that it's only one actor on the stage. Now your mind says you can't stand this feeling, but when you look at it from the observing self, is that really the case?

Client: No. It's—when I look at it like that, it's a bit easier.

Therapist: Easier to make room for?

Client: Yeah.

The session now turns to an exploration of the mother's values. This reveals that asking her son to leave home is in the service of encouraging his independence, helping him to "grow up," and creating a home atmosphere conducive to greater intimacy with her husband. About ten minutes later, the therapist returns to the observing self.

Therapist: For just a moment, can I get you back into contact with your observing self? (*Client nods yes.*) Then once again from that perspective, just notice the thoughts passing though your mind … and notice the feelings surging through your body … and notice that the stage show has changed from a few minutes ago … but the you who notices the stage show has not changed.

The therapist goes through this brief exercise one more time near the end of the session then asks the client:

Therapist: I wonder if you'd be willing to do this exercise two or three times a day—just take a moment to step back and notice the stage show. Notice that it changes all the time—there's a never-ending procession of new thoughts and feelings strutting their stuff on the stage. And as you do that, notice that the part of you noticing the show—the observing self—never changes.

LET YOUR SELF GO

Clients will often say, "I have no self-esteem" or "I want more self-esteem." While there are different constructs of self-esteem, far and away the most popular concept is this: Self-Esteem = Thinking Positively About Yourself. Certainly the majority of self-esteem programs place huge emphasis on trying to judge yourself positively, focusing on your strong points, and trying to reduce or eliminate negative self-judgments. However, from an ACT perspective, fusion with a self-description is likely to create problems whether it is positive or negative. The following transcript makes this clear.

THE GOOD SELF/BAD SELF EXERCISE

Client: But high self-esteem is good, isn't it?

Therapist: Well, you have three young kids, right?

Client: Yeah.

Therapist: So suppose you have the thought *I am a wonderful mother. I do a brilliant job.* Now if you hold on tightly to that thought, there's no doubt it will give you very positive self-esteem. But what might be the danger of fusing with it? Going through your day convinced you're a wonderful mom, doing a brilliant job with no need for improvement?

Client: (*chuckles*) Well, it's not true for a start.

Therapist:	Okay, so one cost is you lose touch with reality. What else? What might happen to your relationship with your kids if you 100 percent believed that everything you did was wonderful?
Client:	I guess I might not realize when I was doing things wrong.
Therapist:	Sure. You would lack self-awareness, and you'd probably become insensitive. And then you wouldn't grow and develop into a better mom because that only happens when you can see your mistakes and learn from them. Now let me ask you: at your funeral, which of these do you want your kids to be saying, "Mom had a really high opinion of herself" or "Mom was really there for me when I needed her?"
Client:	(laughs) The second one. (confused) But can't self-esteem help me to be a better mom?
Therapist:	Okay. Let's check this out. (Therapist pulls out an index card.) When your mind wants to beat you up, what are some of the nastiest things it says to you?
Client:	(sighs) Same old stuff. I'm fat. And I'm dumb.
Therapist:	Okay. So this is the "bad self": "I'm fat" and "I'm dumb." (Therapist writes "I'm fat" and "I'm dumb" on one side of the index card, then turns the card over.) Now on those rare occasions when your mind is being nice to you, what are some of the nice things it says about you?
Client:	Um. I'm a good person. I'm kind to others.
Therapist:	Okay. So this is the "good self." "I'm a good person" and "I'm kind." (Therapist writes these down on the flip side of the card.) This is a bit like that exercise we did a couple of sessions back. So if you're willing to, I'd like you to hold the card up in front of your face so you can read all the negative stuff. That's it—hold it right up in front of you so that's all you can see. (Client holds the card in front of her face, cutting off the therapist from her view.) Hold it tightly. Get all caught up in your "bad self." Now, that's very low self-esteem, isn't it?
Client:	Yeah.
Therapist:	And notice—while you're all caught up in this, what happens to your relationship with me? Do you feel engaged, connected?
Client:	No. I can't see you.
Therapist:	Okay. Now turn it around, so you're looking at all the positive stuff. That's it—and keep it up there right in front of you. (Client turns the card around and continues to hold it up in front of her face.) Now get all caught up in your "good self." Hold it tightly—all those lovely positive thoughts. And now you've got really high self-esteem. But what's your relationship with me like? Do you feel engaged, connected?

Client: (chuckling) No.

Therapist: Okay. Now put the card down on your lap. (Client does so.) Now, what's your relationship like with me?

Client: (Client looks at the therapist. He grins, and she grins back.) Much better.

Therapist: Engaged? Connected?

Client: Yes.

Therapist: And notice, as long as you let it sit there in your lap, it doesn't matter which way up the card is—good self, bad self doesn't matter—if you're not holding on to it or getting absorbed in it, it doesn't stop you from doing what you want to do. So in terms of being a good mom, what's more important? Trying to hold on to tightly to all these thoughts about how good you are, or engaging and connecting with your kids and really being there for them?

Client: Being there for my kids, of course.

> At the end of the session, the therapist gave the card to the client. He asked her to (a) write five more positive self-judgments on the "good self" side, and five more negatives on the "bad self" side; (b) carry the card around in her purse for a week; and (c) pull it out several times a day, read both sides, then put it back in her purse again. During the following session, the client reported she had been much better at defusing from self-judgments (positive and negative) and had developed a greater sense of self-acceptance.

Self-Acceptance vs. Self-Esteem

From an ACT perspective, self-acceptance is far more empowering than self-esteem. In most models of psychology, self-acceptance is taught as a thinking process—that is, telling yourself things like *I accept myself as a fallible human being; we all make mistakes.* While this can undoubtedly be useful, in ACT, the emphasis is on developing self-acceptance through mindfulness rather than self-talk. Self-acceptance develops naturally when we repeatedly defuse from self-judgments (both positive and negative) and thoughts comparing us to others.

A more profound experience of self-acceptance happens when we enter the psychological space of self-as-context and when, from that space, we recognize the conceptualized self for what it is: nothing more or less than an incredibly complex construction of thoughts, memories, and images. The figures below illustrates this progression.

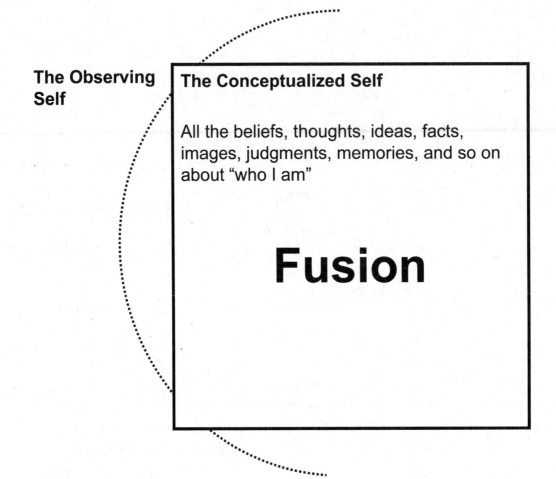

The Observing Self

The Conceptualized Self

All the beliefs, thoughts, ideas, facts, images, judgments, memories, and so on about "who I am"

Fusion

Figure 10.1

In figure 10.1, the person is fused with (attached to) the conceptualized self. And whether this conceptualized self is positive or negative, fusion with it is likely to be problematic. Fusion with a positive self can easily lead to arrogance, narcissism, intolerance of others, and refusal to acknowledge negative feedback; fusion with a negative self can lead to depression, anxiety, feelings of worthlessness, and so on. In either case, lack of self-awareness and psychological inflexibility result.

For example, consider what impact it might have on a manager if he is fused with "I work hard and I don't tolerate fools gladly." Or suppose a police officer is absolutely fused with "I am an officer of the law"—he bases his whole self-worth on this identity, and then one day he becomes permanently disabled and unable to work. He will then struggle to accept and adapt to this significant life change, and his conceptualized self may now contain elements such as "Without my job, I am nobody."

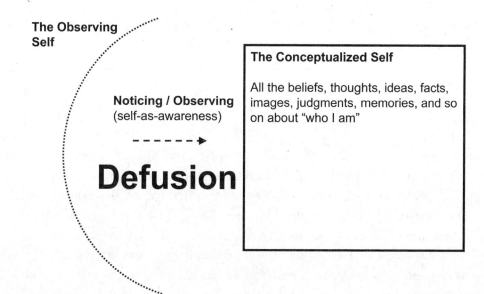

Figure 10.2

In figure 10.2, the person is defusing from thoughts that make up her conceptualized self. Those thoughts then have less influence; they still come up, but they "take up less space." She is no longer clinging to her self-description/self-image/self-concept; instead she "holds it lightly."

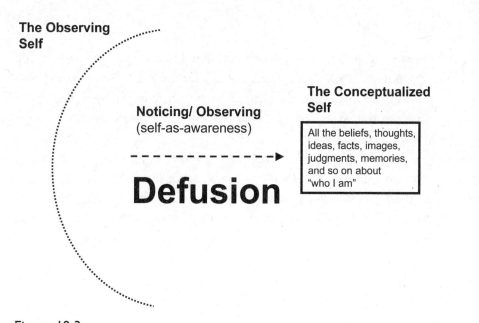

Figure 10.3

In figure 10.3, the person is in the psychological space of self-as-context; from this perspective, there is maximum defusion. The conceptualized self is recognized as a construction of thoughts and not "the essence of who I am."

Who Am I?

At times, when you've taken someone through a self-as-context experience, a client will ask, "Well, who am I then?" It's easy to get bogged down in deep, philosophical questions at this point, and for our purposes in ACT, we don't wish to do that. We're coaches and therapists, not philosophers, gurus, or meditation teachers. So I usually reply along these lines: "'Who am I?' is a big question. There are many different senses of self. In our society, we tend to focus on two main senses of self: the physical self—our body—and the thinking self, more commonly known as 'the mind.' What we're aiming to do here is recognize a third sense of self. The 'observing self' can observe both our thinking self and our physical self, but it is distinct from them. You are comprised of all three of these selves, but whereas the thinking self and the physical self change continuously, the observing self doesn't. It's like a safe place inside you that's always there—a place from where you can observe what's happening in the mind or the body without being harmed."

IS THIS THE SOUL?

At times, clients may ask if this is the soul. My response is simple: "That's not a word I would personally use, but you can call it whatever you like. Whatever words you use to describe it, this is the part of you that notices all those words."

THERAPY VS. MYSTICISM

If you were to "stay in the space" of self-as-context for a prolonged period, you would have the "mystical experience": there is no individual self, "everything is one." We are *not* trying to create mystical experiences in ACT; it is not some religious or spiritual path to enlightenment. With prolonged mindfulness practice, we can "stay in the space" of self-as-context for longer periods, but from an ACT perspective, that's not actually necessary.

In practice, most people get only brief "glimpses" of this space, and then they quickly get "pulled out of it" by their thoughts. However, that's more than enough to serve our purposes. We simply want people to experience that there's a powerful psychological resource within us, a resource that is readily accessible, a place from which to observe and make room for our painful thoughts and feelings. Furthermore, it is a psychological space that frees us to make conscious choices about what we do. How so? Because from this perspective, we can "clearly see" that our thoughts and feelings are transient events that don't define who we are or control our actions.

A TECHNICAL POINT

In the scripts of some ACT exercises, you may read comments like this: "The observing self is there your whole life—from the moment you're born, until the moment you die." For the purposes of coaching or therapy, it's fine to talk this way, however please keep in mind, it's not technically accurate. RFT (relational frame theory; the theory of language and cognition on which ACT rests) explains how we develop this transcendent sense of self, typically around age four, through a process called "deictic framing." This is just one of the many fascinating things you will learn about if you should choose to delve further into RFT.

HOMEWORK AND THE NEXT SESSION

There are two ideas for homework already in this chapter: the first involves contacting self-as-context, and the other involves defusing from the conceptualized self. And, of course, we can make the Good Self/Bad Self Exercise more specific: it could be good mother/bad mother, good therapist/bad therapist, or even good cop/bad cop.

Here's another simple option: we suggest that our client continue with any previous mindfulness practice and we add the instruction, "From now on, as you're doing that, from time to time check in and see if you can notice who's noticing."

You could also ask clients to practice mindfulness exercises that are explicitly oriented toward self-as-context. This is more effective if you have recorded the exercises in session, or if your client has a commercial CD (for example, track 5 of my CD *Mindfulness Skills: Volume 1* is a recording of the Continuous You Exercise).

As for the next session, traditionally we would move on to values and committed action. We would continue to bring in self-as-context experientially as needed as an aid to overcoming any psychological barriers (that is, to facilitate defusion or acceptance).

HOMEWORK FOR YOU

- Read all these exercises and metaphors out loud, and practice them as if you were working with clients.

- Pick two or three cases and identify thoughts, beliefs, judgments, and other self-descriptions that comprise the conceptualized self. Consider how you could introduce self-as-context work with these clients—both brief interventions and longer ones.

- Try these exercises on yourself. In particular, pull out an index card and do the Good Self/Bad Self Exercise, and carry the card around with you for a week. If possible, have a friend or colleague take you through the Continuous You Exercise—or record it

self and then listen to it. And if you have an ongoing mindfulness practice, from
to time notice who is noticing.

SUMMARY

The observing self (self-as-context) is implicit in all mindfulness exercises or practices. It is not really a "self" at all: rather it is the locus or perspective or psychological space from which we observe or notice everything else. If "Notice X" is the basic mindfulness instruction, then in self-as-context work, the X we notice is our own awareness or consciousness. Thus self-as-context can be conceptualized as awareness of awareness, or consciousness of consciousness.

Many mindfulness-based models of therapy never make self-as-context explicit; they rely on people to discover "it" for themselves through ongoing mindfulness practice. However, in ACT we like to make self-as-context explicit as it enhances defusion and acceptance, and allows us to experience a transcendent sense of self.

CHAPTER 11

Know What Matters

VALUES IN A NUTSHELL

In Plain Language: Values are statements about what we want to be doing with our life: about what we want to stand for, and how we want to behave on an ongoing basis. They are leading principles that can guide us and motivate us as we move through life.

Aim: To clarify what gives our life a sense of meaning or purpose, and to use our values as an ongoing guide for our actions.

Synonyms: Chosen life directions.

Method: Distinguish values from goals; help clients connect with and clarify their values so they can use them to inspire, motivate, and guide ongoing action.

When to Use: When looking for guidance from within; when motivation for action is lacking; as a precursor to goal setting and action plans; to facilitate acceptance; to add richness, fulfillment, and meaning to life.

GETTING TO VALUES

The whole ACT model is aimed toward one outcome: mindful, values-congruent living or, in lay terms, a rich, full, and meaningful life. It's this outcome that motivates everything we do in ACT: we wouldn't want someone to accept pain, or practice defusion, or expose herself to challenging situations unless it served to make her life richer and fuller. Some ACT protocols do not explicitly work on values until they've first covered defusion, acceptance, present moment, and self-as-context. However, others start with clarifying values up front. There are pros and cons to both approaches.

On one hand, work around values often triggers fusion and avoidance; therefore some clients will be unable or unwilling to explore values in any depth until they first develop defusion and acceptance skills. On the other hand, some clients will not be motivated to do the hard work of therapy unless they first get in touch with their values.

For a sense of the first approach, you may like to read my self-help book, *The Happiness Trap* (Harris, 2007), which takes the reader step-by-step along the more traditional route of creative hopelessness first, followed by mindfulness skills, and then values and action. For a sense of the second approach, you might want to look at *ACT with Love* (Harris, 2007), my self-help book for relationship issues (Harris, 2009).

Personally, wherever possible, I prefer to start therapy or coaching with a focus on values. That's why, in chapter 5, I suggested that we start clarifying values from our very first encounter with the client. So before reading on, please go back to chapter 5 and read again the section entitled A Basic Guide to Taking a History.

Of course, sometimes we'll have a client who initially won't go anywhere near values. If we give him a values worksheet on the first session, he may leave it blank, put a cross through it, scrunch it into a ball, or protest that he "can't think of anything" or it's "a waste of time." A response like this gives us useful information: it alerts us to a significant lack of contact with or clarity about values, and it usually indicates high experiential avoidance. In these cases, we'll generally need to tread slowly and gently, and do plenty of work around defusion and acceptance before we can get to core values.

Practical Tip   Sometimes we may be lucky enough to have a client who responds dramatically to discussions about values and immediately starts making significant changes in her life. If so, we don't need to go digging around trying to find psychological barriers or trying to "sell her" on mindfulness skills. However, in most cases, as she starts acting on her values, psychological barriers will start showing up.

Regardless of what number session we're in, and which parts of the hexaflex we've covered, if we haven't yet explored the client's values, there's a simple way to lead into it: we compassionately and nonjudgmentally point out that we know a lot about what the client doesn't want—but little or nothing about what he *does* want. For example, we could say, "I think I know quite a lot about what your problems are: the painful feelings you struggle with, the painful thoughts you get entangled in, the difficulties you face in different parts of your life, the things other people do that you don't like, and the things that you do that either don't help or just make things worse. In other words, I know a lot about what you *don't* want, what you've had more than enough of. But there's a big gaping hole in my knowledge here. I know very little about what you *do* want—about what sort of person you want to be, what sort of relationships you want to build, and what you want to do with your life to make it richer, fuller, and more meaningful. So that's what I'd like us to look at now. Would that be okay?"

What Values Are—and What They Aren't

When I describe values to my clients, I say something like, "Values are our heart's deepest desires for the way we want to interact with the world, other people, and ourselves. They're what we want to stand for in life, how we want to behave, what sort of person we want to be, what sort of strengths and qualities we want to develop."

As you read a few books on ACT, you'll encounter several different technical definitions of values. Here's the one that I think is most user-friendly: values are "desired global qualities of ongoing action" (Hayes, Bond, Barnes-Holmes, & Austin, 2006, p.16). Let's break that down into three components:

1. **Ongoing action.** Values are about "ongoing action." In other words, values are about how you want to behave or act on an ongoing basis—what you want to keep on doing. For example, your values may include being loving and caring; giving, sharing, and contributing; being a good friend; maintaining health and fitness; being open and honest. In contrast, goals are about what you want to get or have or complete. Thus, if it's not something you can *do* on an ongoing basis, then it's not a value. Happiness is not a value—you can't *do* it. A sense of belonging is not a value—you can't *do* it. Being loved and respected by others is not a value—you can't *do* it. To have a big car, a big house, a great job, a wonderful partner, or a thin body: those are not things you can do—they are goals, not values.

2. **Global qualities.** Values are about "global qualities" of ongoing action. So let's suppose you want to play baseball. Now clearly "playing baseball" is something you can do on an ongoing basis—it is an ongoing action, but it's not a *quality* of action. To clarify this, here are four possible qualities of that ongoing action: playing baseball *skillfully*, playing baseball *clumsily*, playing baseball *energetically*, playing baseball *half-heartedly*.

So what do we mean by a "global" quality? We mean a quality that "unites" many different patterns of action. For example, if your value is "being supportive" to the other players in your team, then there are many different actions you could take with the quality of "supportiveness." And if your value is "being fair," there are many different actions you could take with the quality of "fairness."

So in order to get to your values around playing baseball, I could ask you questions such as: "*How* do you want to play baseball?" "What personal qualities or strengths do you want to model or demonstrate during the game?" "How do you want to behave in your relationships with the other players, both on your team and the opposing team?" These questions may uncover values such as being focused, being competitive, applying yourself fully, being respectful, being cooperative with your teammates, being fair, "giving it your best," challenging yourself, and so on.

Note that these qualities of action are available to you in any moment: even if you become paralyzed from the waist down and unable to ever play baseball again, you can still be focused, competitive, respectful, cooperative, fair; you can still apply yourself fully to whatever you're doing and "give it your best"; you can still act in ways that challenge you.

3. **Desired.** Values are "desired" qualities of ongoing action. They're statements about how you *want* to behave, how you desire to act, what matters to you, and what's important to you. They're not about what you should do or have to do. (In many ACT textbooks, you'll find the word "chosen" rather than the word "desired"; this is to emphasize that you not only desire these qualities in your actions, but you also consciously choose to employ them.)

VALUES VS. GOALS

Useful questions to clarify values include these: "Deep down inside, what's important to you?" "What do you want to stand for in life?" "What sort of personal strengths and qualities do you want to cultivate?" "How do you want to behave in your relationships?"

When clients answer these questions, they'll usually give us goals rather than values. This is hardly surprising. Our society is largely goal focused, not values focused. So we'll need to do some psychoeducation: explain that values are like directions in which we want to move throughout our lives, whereas goals are things that we want to achieve or complete. To help our clients understand this, we often compare values to a compass (Hayes et al., 1999).

THE COMPASS METAPHOR

Therapist: Values are like a compass. A compass gives you direction and keeps you on track when you're traveling. And our values do the same for the journey of life. We use them to choose the direction in which we want to move and to keep us on track as we go. So when you act on a value, it's like heading west. No matter how far west you travel, you never get there; there's always further to go. But goals are like the things you try to achieve on your journey: they're like the sights you want to see or the mountains you want to climb while you keep on traveling west.

We can give clients a couple of examples to clarify the difference. One of my favorite examples is the contrast between "getting married" and "being loving" (Hayes et al, 1999). If you want to be loving and caring, that's a value—it's ongoing; you want to behave that way for the rest of your life. And in any moment you have a choice: you can either act on that value or neglect it. But if you want to get married, that's a goal. It's something that can be completed, achieved, "crossed off the list." And you can achieve the goal of marriage even if you completely neglect your values around being loving and caring. (Of course, your marriage might not last too long.)

Values are far more empowering than goals because they're always available to us. In any moment, we can act on them or neglect them; the choice is ours. Not so for goals. We can't guarantee we'll ever achieve the goal of marriage, but in any moment we can act on our values around being loving and caring. This is possible even if we don't have a partner; we can be loving and caring toward our friends, neighbors, family, pets, pot plants, environment—and, of course, ourselves.

Here's another example I often give: if you want a better job, that's a goal. Once you've got it, it's "mission accomplished." But if you want to be helpful and efficient and productive, those are values: desired qualities of ongoing action. And in any moment, you can act on those values—even if you don't like your job or you don't currently have one.

Here are a few more examples to really hammer this point home: To lose ten pounds of weight is a goal; eating healthily is a value. To go to the gym is a goal; caring for your body is a value. To have a big house is a goal; supporting your family is a value. To get love and respect from others is a goal; to be loving and respectful is a value. To feel less anxious is an "emotional goal"; acting courageously is a value. To feel happy is an emotional goal; being warm, open, and friendly toward others is a value. To stop criticizing your partner is a "dead person's goal" (a dead person will never criticize his partner); being accepting, understanding, and appreciative is a value.

VALUES VS. DESIRES, WANTS, NEEDS, FEELINGS, VIRTUES, MORALS, AND ETHICS

At times, both therapists and clients may confuse values with the things mentioned in the heading above, so let's quickly clarify the differences.

Wants, needs, and desires. We may want or need or desire all sorts of things from other people—love, respect, kindness, and so on. But those are not values because they're not ways that we want to behave on an ongoing basis. Naturally we validate those wants/needs/desires in our clients. And if a client can fulfill those wants/needs/desires in a manner that's workable, then we help her to do so. Likewise, we help her to accept the pain that arises when there's a gap between what she desires and what she's got.

At the same time, we help our clients to recognize that while we do have a lot of control over how we act, we don't have any control over what we get. So it makes sense to focus on what is most within our control. The most empowering response to unmet needs and unfulfilled desires is to accept the pain, connect with our values, and take action.

Feelings. Values are not feelings. Our values will affect how we feel about any given event or situation and how we act in response to it, but they are not feelings. To get to values, we can ask, "What do I want to stand for in the face of this? How do I want to act in response to this event or situation?"

Virtues, morals, and ethics. Values are beyond right or wrong, good or bad. They are simply expressions of what matters to us. Of course, our society judges those values as good and bad, and the "good" ones get called "virtues." Then our society lays down rules about the right way and the wrong way to act on our values, and it tells us that if we don't act the "right way" we are "bad." This gives rise to morals, ethics, and codes of conduct.

So if our clients start talking about right, wrong, good, or bad, we know they have shifted from values into the realm of morals, ethics, or codes of conduct.

Five Key Points about Values

Aside from the distinction between values and goals, there are at least five other key points to draw out in therapy:

1. Values are here and now; goals are in the future.

2. Values never need to be justified.

3. Values often need to be prioritized.

4. Values are best held lightly.

5. Values are freely chosen.

Let's quickly zip through these one by one.

VALUES ARE HERE AND NOW; GOALS ARE IN THE FUTURE.

Values are here and now: in any moment, you can choose to act on them or neglect them. Even if you've totally neglected a core value for years or decades, in this moment right now you can act on it. In contrast, goals are always in the future: a goal is something that you're aiming for, striving for, working toward. And the moment you achieve it, it's no longer a goal.

Because of this, people who lead a very goal-focused life often find that it leads to a sense of chronic lack or frustration. Why? Because they're always looking to the future and continually striving to achieve the next goal under the illusion it will bring lasting happiness or contentment. In the values-focused life, we still have goals, but the emphasis is on living by our values in each moment; this approach leads to a sense of fulfillment and satisfaction as our values are always available. The metaphor of Two Kids in the Car gets this across well (Harris, 2007).

TWO KIDS IN THE CAR METAPHOR

Therapist: Imagine there are two kids in the back of a car, and Mom's driving them to Disneyland. It's a three-hour trip to get there, and one kid's saying, every five minutes, "Are we there yet? Are we there yet? Are we there yet?" Mom's getting annoyed, the kid's frustrated, they're snapping at each other—it's a state of chronic tension. But the other kid's looking out of the window, waving at the other cars, noticing with great interest all the towns and farms and factories that they're driving past. Now both kids reach Disneyland at the same time, and both have a great time when they get there. But only one of these kids has had a rewarding journey. Why? Because he wasn't just focused on the goal; he also valued exploring, traveling, learning about the world outside the car. And on the way home, the first kid keeps saying, "Are we home yet, are we home yet, are we home yet?" Whereas the other one enjoys the ride by looking out the window and appreciating how everything looks so different at night.

> **Practical Tip** Most people think of success as achieving goals. I invite clients to consider a different definition: success is living by our values. With this definition, we can be successful right now even though our goals may be a long way off (and even though we may actually never achieve them).

VALUES NEVER NEED TO BE JUSTIFIED

Values are like our taste in ice cream: we don't need to justify why we like strawberry or chocolate or maple syrup—or whatever our favorite flavor is. Values are simply statements about what's meaningful to us; we never need to justify that.

However, we may need to justify the actions we take. If, for example, you value connecting with nature, you don't have to justify that—but if you move your family from the city to the countryside, you may have a lot of explaining to do. Our assumption in ACT is that destructive behavior—to self or others—is not motivated by values. This is a pragmatic assumption, because what happens if we start from the alternative viewpoint—that your client's destructive behavior reflects who he really wants to be and what he wants to stand for in life? What sort of therapeutic relationship will we build, if that's our attitude?

Therapists sometimes ask, "What if my client has values I ethically oppose, such as wanting to rape or torture others?" The short answer is you aren't obliged to work with any client if doing so compromises your own ethical standards. The longer answer is this: even in forensic populations where our clients have committed awful crimes such as rape, torture, and murder, if we work hard, build a strong rapport, and dig down under layers and layers of thickened, hardened, encrusted fusion and avoidance, then we'll almost always discover core values similar to our own. When these people committed their crimes, it's highly unlikely they were acting mindfully on their values; they were almost certainly acting impulsively or mindlessly, motivated by fusion and avoidance.

VALUES OFTEN NEED TO BE PRIORITIZED

Because all our values are available in each moment, we'll need to prioritize which we act on. For example, we may value being loving and caring toward our parents, but if they're continually hostile and abusive to us, we may cut off all contact with them because our values around self-protection and self-nurture take priority. Our values around being loving and caring haven't disappeared; they've just been prioritized.

Psychologist John Forsyth has a good analogy for this: our values are like a cube. In any position, some faces of the cube are clearly visible, and other faces can't be seen at all. The unseen faces haven't ceased to exist, they're just not visible in this position. And whenever the cube changes position, some faces come to the foreground, while others recede into the background.

VALUES ARE BEST HELD LIGHTLY

In ACT we say, "Pursue your values vigorously, but hold them lightly." We want to be aware of our values and in contact with them, but we don't want to be fused with them. When we fuse with them, our values start to feel oppressive and restrictive, like commandments we have to obey. They turn into rigid rules rather than flexible guides. To use the compass metaphor: when you go on a journey, you don't want to clutch the compass tightly every step of the way—you want to carry it in your backpack, knowing that anytime you need it to steer a course or find your way, you can instantly pull it out and use it.

VALUES ARE FREELY CHOSEN

We consciously choose to bring these desired qualities to our actions. We don't *have to* act in this way; we choose to simply because it matters to us. To highlight this, we may ask clients, "Suppose I waved a magic wand so you could have any values you wanted; what values would you choose?" This is a neat question, because whatever values you'd choose in a magical world, you can act on those very same values right now in this moment; there's no need for a magic wand. This is often a useful intervention for clients who say, "I have no values."

Bringing Values to Life

There are two ways of working with values. One way is in a very dry, theoretical, wordy, conceptual manner: discussing values, analyzing values, theorizing about values—that is, working with them largely at an intellectual level. This isn't particularly satisfying or useful for client or therapist, and usually indicates that both are lost in fusion and avoidance. You can tell when this is happening because your session will be dull, tiring, intellectual, lifeless, and unsatisfying.

The other way of working with values is at the level of "heart and soul." In other words, rather than just talking or thinking about them, you facilitate deep, intimate, experiential contact with values. (No guesses as to which way we work in ACT.)

Effective conversations about values have a sense of openness, vitality, and freedom. When a client truly connects with her values, it brings a sense of liberation and expansiveness; she realizes that even in desperate situations she has choices; that she can open up her life and take it in meaningful directions.

During these conversations, your client will be very much in the present—engaging with you, sharing with you, letting you in. You'll see him "coming to life" in front of your eyes. The session will be alive, engaging, and fulfilling—and often intense emotions will arise, running the full gamut from joy and love to sadness and fear. You'll often experience a profound sense of connection as you get to see deep into the heart of a fellow human being and bear witness to the pain and the love that resides within.

WORKING WITH VALUES

In the transcript that follows, the client is a single, middle-aged woman, struggling to cope with her son's behavior. Her twenty-three-year-old son has a heroin addiction, and every few days he comes home to beg for money. If she doesn't give him the money, he becomes aggressive; he often screams and yell abusively, blames her for screwing up his childhood, accuses her of being cold and uncaring, or insists that she doesn't really love him. This has been going on for over two years. She constantly worries about him, and after his visits she feels hopeless, guilty, and remorseful. She says she knows that giving him money is "wrong" because it "just feeds his habit," but she finds it "too hard to say no."

Client: You know, to be honest, sometimes I think it'd be easier if he would just ... die. (*She bursts out crying.*)

Therapist: (*pause*) I can see you're in a lot of pain right now ... and I wonder if just for a moment we can slow this right down ... and I wonder if you could look at what's happening here from your observing self ... just kind of take a step back and notice what's going on, how you're sitting in the chair, the position of your body ... and notice the feelings showing up inside you ... where they are in your body ... and also notice the thoughts whizzing around in your head. (*pause*) And what's your mind telling you right now?

Client: (*wiping her eyes*) I'm a monster. I mean, what sort of mother am I? How could I think something like that?

Therapist: So your mind's telling you that you're some sort of monster because you have thoughts that life would be easier if your son were dead?

Client: Yeah. I mean, he's my son. He's my son! How can I think like that?

Therapist: (*pause*) Remember we talked about how your mind is like a super-duper problem-solving machine?

Client: Yeah.

Therapist: Well, there's a big problem here, isn't there? I mean, a very big, very painful problem. Right? So quite naturally, the problem-solving machine goes into action. It starts cranking out solutions. And let's face it: one solution to any problematic relationship is to have the other person disappear. So that thought, about your son disappearing, is just your mind doing its job. And you know what? There's no way you can stop it from doing that.

Client:	But maybe David's right. Maybe I don't really love him.
Therapist:	Well, that's an interesting thought. (*pause*) I'll bet your mind loves to torment you with that one.
Clien:	Yeah. All the time.
Therapist:	Can I ask, what're you feeling in your body right now?
Client:	I just feel sick. Really, really sick.
Therapist:	And where do you feel that most intensely in your body?
Client:	Right in here. (She places a hand on her stomach.)
Therapist:	Okay, so just notice that feeling for a moment ... notice where it is ... and what it's doing. (*pause*) What would you call this emotion?
Client:	Oh—it's guilt. I hate it. I feel it all the time.
Therapist:	Okay. So notice that guilt for a moment ... Observe it ... Breathe into it ... Close your eyes if you'd like ... and just breathe into it ... and see if you can, in some way, just open up around it ... give it some room.... And at the same time, I'd like you to tune in to your heart ... Just take a moment to get in touch with what your son means to you ... (*pause*) What does this feeling tell you about your son, about what he means to you?
Client:	(*crying*) I just want him to be happy.
Therapist:	(*pause*) So your mind says, "Maybe I don't really love him." What does your heart say?
Client:	Of course I do.
Therapist:	You said it. I mean, if you didn't care about him, you'd have no guilt, right?
Client:	(*teary but relieved*) Yeah.
Therapist:	So tell me, you really care about David ... so what sort of mom do you want to be to him?
Client:	I just want him to be happy.
Therapist:	Okay. So let's suppose I wave a magic wand and David is happy forever after. Then what sort of mother would you want to be?
Client:	I don't know. I just want to be a good mom.

Therapist: Okay. So if you wanted to earn that title—of being a good mom—how would you be toward David? What sort of qualities would you want to have as a mother?

Client: I don't know.

Therapist: Well, suppose a miracle happens, and David sorts his life out, and a few years from now we interview him on national television, and we ask him, "David, what was your mom like when you were going through the worst of that heroin addiction?" In the ideal world, what would you like him to say?

Client: I guess I'd like to him to say that I was … um … loving … and kind … and … um … supportive.

Therapist: Anything else?

Client: That I was there for him when he needed me.

Therapist: So to be loving, kind, supportive—that's what you want to stand for as a mother?

Client: Yeah.

Therapist: Okay. So just sit with that for a moment. To be loving, kind, supportive: that's what matters to you as a mom.

Client: Yeah. (*She sits upright, nodding her head slowly.*) I want to do what's best for him. I want to do the right thing. And I know that giving him money—that's not it.

Therapist: Okay. (*pause*) So next time your son comes over, it seems like you have a choice to make. On the one hand, you can let your mind bully you—push you around and tell you what to do. And you know exactly what your mind's going to tell you—that you have to give him the money, and if you don't, you're a bad mother, and saying no is so stressful and painful, it's easier to just give him the money, and then he'll leave you alone. That's one choice. On the other hand, you could choose to let your mind say whatever it likes, but instead of buying into it, you can be the sort of mother you really want to be—loving, kind, supportive, and doing what's best for David in the long run. Which will you choose?

Client: Well, I—I want to be loving and supportive. I want to help him.

Therapist: So if you were truly acting on those values instead of being pushed around by the "can't say no" story, then how would you respond to David's requests for money?

Client: (smiles thinly) I'd say no.

Therapist: You'd say no?

Client: (nods) Uh-huh.

Therapist: What are you feeling right now, as you say that?

Client: I'm really nervous. I'm shaking.

Therapist: I can see that, and I'm sure I'd feel the same way if I were in your shoes. So the question is are you willing to make room for these feelings of nervousness and shakiness if that's what it takes to be the sort of mom you truly want to be?

Client: Yes.

Giving her son money to "feed his habit" was actually inconsistent with this client's core values. The action was motivated by avoidance (trying to get rid of guilt and anxiety) and fusion (with thoughts like "It's too hard to say no," "I can't stand to see him like this," or "I'm a bad mother if I don't help him"), not by values. After the intervention above, the conversation turned to the many different ways in which she could act on her values: how she could be loving, kind, supportive to David in other ways without giving him money (or things he could sell for cash).

You can see in that transcript the overlap and interplay between defusion, acceptance, and values. We call this "dancing around the hexaflex"—moving flexibly and fluidly from one process to another as required.

Practical Tip   Clients will often give you values such as "I want to be a good Mom/Dad" or "I want to be a good friend." This is a good starting point, but it's a bit vague and nonspecific. It's generally useful to explore further, with questions such as: "So what are the qualities of a good Mom/Dad/friend?" or "If you wanted to earn that title—good Mom/Dad/friend—how would you behave toward your children/friends?"

TECHNIQUES FOR CLARIFYING AND CONTACTING VALUES

In this chapter, we're going to cover a lot of techniques. But remember, they're only a means to an end: to help our clients connect with their own humanity, to find their own sense of meaning and purpose in life. So while applying these techniques, we always need to be mindful: attuned to our client and watchful for those qualities of vitality, openness, and liberation.

Figure 11.1 below summarizes many common values clarification techniques. Please read through them all to get a sense of the many different ways we can do this work.

WHAT MATTERS?
What do you really want? What matters to you in the big picture? What do you want to stand for? Is there anything in your life right now that gives you a sense of meaning, purpose, vitality?

THE SWEET SPOT
Vividly recall a rich, "sweet" memory and get in touch with the emotions. What is meaningful about this memory?

DISAPPROVAL
What do you disapprove of, or dislike, in the actions of others? How would you act differently, if you were in their shoes?

MISSING OUT
What important areas of life have you given up or missed out on for lack of willingness?

FORMS AND WORKSHEETS
Valued Living Questionnaire
Bull's Eye
Life Compass
Valued Actions Inventory
List of Common Values

CHILDHOOD DREAMS
As a child, what sort of life did you imagine for the future?

ARTISTIC METHODS
Paint, draw, or sculpt your values.

LIKES
What do you like to do?

ROLE MODELS
Who do you look up to? Who inspires you? What personal strengths or qualities do they have that you admire?

MIND-READING MACHINE
Imagine I place a mind-reading machine on your head, and I tune it into the mind of someone very important to you, so you can now hear their every thought. As you tune in, they're thinking about YOU--about what you stand for, what your strengths are, what you mean to them, and the role you play in their life. In the IDEAL world, where you have lived your life as the person you want to be, what would you hear them thinking?

Clarifying Values

MAGIC WAND
a. I wave this magic wand and you have the total approval of everyone on the planet--no matter what you do, they love, respect, and admire you--whether you become a surgeon or a serial killer. What would you then do with your life? How would you treat others?

b. I wave this magic wand, and all these painful thoughts, feelings, and memories no longer have any impact on you. What would you do with your life? What would you start, stop, do more of, or less of? How would you behave differently? If we watched you on a video, what would we see and hear that would show us magic had happened?

SPEECHES
Imagine your eightieth birthday (or twenty-first or fiftieth or retirement party, and so on). Two or three people make speeches about what you stand for, what you mean to them, the role you played in their life. In the IDEAL world, where you have lived your life as the person you want to be, what would you hear them saying?

LIFE AND DEATH
a. Imagine your own funeral: imagine what you would like to hear people saying about you.
b. Act out your own funeral--psychodrama style
c. Write your obituary or fill in a blank tombstone.
d. Imagine you somehow know you only have twenty-four hours to live, but you can't tell anyone: who would you visit, and what would you do?

WEALTH
You inherit a fortune. What would you do with it? Who would be there to share those activities or appreciate the things you buy? How would you act toward your new life?

EXPLORING YOUR PAIN
a. Pain As Your Ally: What does this pain tell you about what really matters, what you truly care about?
b. Pain As Your Teacher: How can this pain help you to grow or learn or develop new skills and strengths? How can it help you better relate to others?
c. From Worrying to Caring: What do your fears, worries and anxieties show you that you care about? What do they remind you is very important?

CHARACTER STRENGTHS
What personal strengths and qualities do you already have? Which new ones would you like to develop? How would you like to apply them?

IF ... THEN ...
If you achieved that goal, then how would you change as a result? What would you do differently from there on? How you would behave differently with friends, family, colleagues, customers, and others?

Figure 11.1 **Common Values Clarification Techniques**

As you can see, there are techniques galore available to you, and many of them involve asking questions. And if we ask these questions dryly and intellectually, we'll get dry, intellectual responses. So take your time with these questions; don't rush them. Ask your client to consider deeply, to take her time. We could say, "Can you sit with this question for a while? Really reflect on it and see what comes up. Take your time with it. There's no hurry." We could also invite her to close her eyes and contemplate. If an answer seems superficial, we could say, "I could be wrong about this, but my impression is we're only just scratching the surface here. See if you can go deeper—really explore this. Tune into your heart. Deep down, what really matters to you?"

Most of these techniques are far more powerful when we deliver them as an experiential exercise as opposed to just having a conversation. For example, we can start off with a short mindfulness exercise, such as Mindfulness of the Breath, and then ask our client to close his eyes and silently reflect upon the question or imagine the scene. The transcript below, which includes the Imagine Your Eightieth Birthday Exercise, illustrates this.

IMAGINE YOUR EIGHTIETH BIRTHDAY

Therapist: So I'm going to ask you to imagine your eightieth birthday and to imagine that three different people stand up to make speeches about you. And keep in mind, this is a fantasy—an imaginary exercise—so it doesn't have to follow the rules of logic and science. You can be eighty, but your friends may look exactly as they do today. And you can have people there who are already dead, or who'll be dead by the time you're eighty. And if you want to have children one day, then you can have your children there. Also keep in mind, you aren't trying to realistically predict the future. You're creating a fantasy—if magic could happen so that all your dreams come true—then what would your eightieth birthday look like? So if your mind starts interfering and saying things like, *People don't mean what they say at these events* or *No, that person would never say that about me,* then just say "Thanks, mind" and come back to the exercise. Okay?

Client: Okay.

Therapist: Okay. So I invite you to get into a comfortable position, and either close your eyes or fix them on a spot … and for the next few breaths, focus on emptying your lungs … pushing all the air out … and allowing them to fill by themselves … Notice the breath flowing in and flowing out … in through the nostrils … down into the lungs …. and back out … Notice how, once the lungs are empty, they automatically refill … And now, allowing your breath to find its own natural rate and rhythm … no need to keep controlling it … I'd like you to do an exercise in imagination … to create a fantasy of your ideal eightieth birthday … not to try and realistically predict it but to fantasize how it would be in the ideal world, if magic could happen and all your dreams came true … So it's your eightieth birthday, and everyone who truly matters to you … friends, family, partner, parents, children, colleagues … anyone and everyone whom you truly care about, even if they're no longer alive, is gathered there in your honor … This might be a small intimate affair in a family home or a huge affair in a classy restaurant … it's your imagination, so create it the way you want it … Now imagine that one person whom you really care about—friend, child, partner, parent, you choose—stands up to make a speech about you … a short speech, no more than three or four sentences … and they talk about what you stand for in life … what you mean to them … and the role that you have played in their life … and imagine them saying whatever it is deep in your heart you would most love to hear them say. (*Pause 40 to 50 seconds.*)

The therapist now repeats this for two other people—always allowing the client to choose who will speak—and each time allowing forty to fifty seconds of silence for reflection.

Therapist: Most people find that this exercise brings up a whole range of feelings, some warm and loving, and some very painful. So take a moment to notice what you're feeling … and consider what these feelings tell you … about what truly matters to you … what sort of person you want to be … and what if, anything, you're currently neglecting. (*Pause 30 seconds.*) And now, bringing the exercise to an end … and notice your breathing … and notice your body in the chair … and notice the sounds you can hear … and open your eyes and notice what you can see … and take a stretch … and notice yourself stretching … and welcome back!

Afterward we debrief the exercise in detail: What happened? What did people say about you? What does this tell you about what matters to you, what you want to stand for, and what sort of person you want to be?

We can also inquire about fusion and avoidance: How did your mind try to interfere with the exercise? Did you get hooked at any point? How did you unhook yourself? What feelings showed up for you? Did you make room for them or struggle? Did you avoid doing the exercise?

FORMS AND WORKSHEETS

All the forms and worksheets mentioned in the Forms and Worksheets box in figure 11.1 above are downloadable at no cost from www.actmadesimple.com. To get a sense of how these forms work, please stop reading, download a copy of each, and fill them in for yourself. Hopefully you already did the Life Compass and the Bull's Eye back in chapter 5; if not, please do them now.

Both these forms are quick, simple tools for rapidly gathering some information about your client's (or your own) values. You can fill them in collaboratively during a session or give them out as homework. The Bull's Eye is particularly useful as a quick assessment tool on the very first session. You can also ask your client to quickly fill one in during the check-in at the start of each session; it's a simple guide for tracking how therapy is progressing.

The Life Compass is also very useful because (a) it gives a visual overview of the client's life; (b) it identifies core values that cut through many different domains of life; and (c) if your client feels overwhelmed by all the changes he wants to make, you can ask him to "just pick one box to start with."

Problems in Clarifying Values

As a general rule, it's easier to do values work with high-functioning/worried-well/coaching clients than with lower-functioning clients or those with high levels of experiential avoidance. This is because the more someone's life is driven by experiential avoidance, the more he becomes disconnected from his values. Obvious examples include many clients with borderline personality disorder or chronic addictions to alcohol or narcotics. Often these clients have repeatedly hurt, abused, or neglected their body, their friends, their families, their partners, and so on. This is the sad consequence of long-standing unworkable behavior that is driven by fusion and avoidance. Not surprisingly, it gives rise to a lot of emotional pain. To connect with neglected values, therefore, means to connect with all that pain.

So if clients repeatedly resist, avoid, or put up blocks to values—"I don't know," "Nothing matters," "I don't have any values," "I don't see the point," "I don't deserve to have a life," "This is so corny"—that usually indicates experiential avoidance and necessitates work with acceptance and defusion. Of course sometimes the client simply has no idea what "values" are; if she has led a deprived or impoverished life, "values" may seem like something from another planet. Thus in one program for ACT with borderline personality disorder, they actually give the clients a list of thirty common values and ask them to check the ones that personally resonate (Brann et al., 2007–09).

WORKING FROM GOALS TO VALUES: USEFUL QUESTIONS

When we ask a client about values, she will commonly give us goals. He may describe the partner, job, or body he wants to have, or the things he wants to get from others such as love or friendship or forgiveness. Or she may say she wants fame, wealth, status, respect, or success. Or he may give us an emotional goal: to feel happy or to have more self-confidence. Or she may give us a dead person's goal: to not use heroin, to not have panic attacks, to not lose her temper, to not feel self-conscious. So to get to the values underlying a goal, we can ask any or all of the following questions (preface them with this phrase, "If this goal were achieved …"):

- What would you do differently?

- How would you act differently?

- How would you behave differently in your relationships, work life, social life, family life, and so on?

- What personal qualities or strengths would it demonstrate?

- What would it show that you stand for?

- What would it enable you to do that is meaningful and that matters in the big picture?

For example, if you had self-esteem, or you felt happy, or you had a sense of belonging, or you had a big car/great body/fantastic job, then how would you act differently? What would you do differently? How would you behave differently?

If clients give us a negative goal—something that they don't want—we can often quickly transform it into a positive one by asking "What do you want instead?" For example, if the client says, "I want to stop fighting with my mom," we can ask, "So what would you like to do instead? How would you like to be when you spend time with her?"

If clients give you a positive goal, additional useful questions to elicit underlying values include "What's that in the service of?" "What's important/ meaningful about that?" "What is it that matters about achieving that goal?" "What's important about that?" "What would having that enable you to do?" For example, the values underlying a holiday may be about being adventurous, nurturing mental health, or spending quality time with the family, and so on.

Practical Tip   As long as you're not coming across like the Spanish Inquisition, it's okay to keep asking questions. Clients rarely get to core values after only one or two questions. If you're concerned, you could say, "My mind's telling me that you're going to get annoyed with all these questions. I keep asking because we're trying to get to something of fundamental importance here, and my sense is, so far, we're just scratching the surface. So is it okay if we keep going with this a bit longer?"

PLEASING OTHERS

Some clients are so focused on gaining approval from others or doing what they've been told to do by their parents, religion, or culture that they disconnect from their own core values. To help reconnect them, here's a useful question: "Suppose I were to wave a magic wand so that you automatically had the approval of everybody whose opinion matters to you; so that whatever you did, they totally approved of it, whether you became a saint or a serial killer. Once this wand has been waved, you'd never have to impress anyone or please anyone ever again—whatever you do, they'd be delighted. Then—what would you do with your life? And how would you act in your relationships?"

WHEN THE GOAL IS TO CHANGE OTHERS

If a client says, "I want my wife/husband/mother/boss/colleague to be more cheerful/cooperative/ friendly/loving/respectful," and so on—or "less abusive/lazy" and so on, we may ask, "Let's assume I have a magic wand, and I can instantly change this person to fit your ideal. If you did have that ideal relationship, how would you act differently? What personal qualities or strengths would you like to develop or bring into that relationship? What sort of friend/relative/colleague would you like to be? How would you ideally treat the other person?"

After this, we may consider how the client can influence the behavior of others by acting on his own values. We would emphasize that we can't control others; we can merely influence them. And the more we take control of our own actions, the more effectively we'll be able to influence others.

HOMEWORK AND NEXT SESSION

Homework can involve writing about values, thinking about values, meditating on values, discussing values with loved ones, or filling in the forms and worksheets named in figure 11.1. A simple homework assignment is this: "Between now and next session, would you be willing to do two things? One, notice when you're acting on your values, and two, notice what it's like to do so, what difference it makes."

In the next session, we might do more work around values or move on to goal setting and taking action. And if fusion and avoidance get in the way of clarifying values, then we'd dance across the hexaflex to defusion and acceptance.

From time to time, we'll encounter a high-functioning client who's already doing all the things that matter—going to work, looking after the kids, keeping fit, and so on—but is deeply unfulfilled. Often her lack of fulfillment is because, although she's doing what matters, she's not psychologically present. Instead she's caught up in her head: lost in thoughts about all the things on her "to do" list, or immersed in an ongoing commentary about what's not good enough, or consumed by worrying, ruminating, or daydreaming. With these clients, we would work on "being present."

HOMEWORK FOR YOU

For this chapter, there's no homework for you. Nah, I'm just kidding! There's actually lots of it. If you haven't yet completed all the aforementioned values forms, please download them and do so.

- Read all the values interventions out loud, as if taking your clients through them.

- Think of other questions you might ask. Are there any other exercises you know, or ideas you have, about ways to get clients in touch with values?

- Pick two or three clients and identify what values they've lost touch with. Consider what exercises you could do to help reconnect them with their values.

- Reflect on your own values as a therapist: What matters to you, deep in your heart, about doing this work? What do you want to stand for as a therapist? What personal strengths and qualities do you want to bring into the therapy room?

- Over the next week, notice when you're in touch with your values—and what that's like. What difference does it make in your life?

SUMMARY

Technically values are desired qualities of ongoing action. Poetically they're our heart's deepest desires for how we want spend our brief time on this planet. Metaphorically they're like a compass: they give us direction and keep us on track. Helping our clients to get in touch with their values can be difficult; we often encounter all sorts of misconceptions and misunderstandings, most commonly around the difference between values and goals. Furthermore, we'll frequently come up against barriers in the form of fusion and avoidance. Thus we'll often be dancing back and forth between values, defusion, and acceptance. However, with patience and persistence, we can usually help our clients get in touch with their hearts—and when we see that happen, it's truly magical.

CHAPTER 12

Do What It Takes

COMMITTED ACTION IN A NUTSHELL

In Plain Language: *Committed action* means taking larger and larger patterns of effective action, guided and motivated by values. It also means flexible action: readily adapting to the challenges of the situation, and either persisting with or changing behavior as required; doing what it takes to live by our values.

Aim: To translate values into ongoing, evolving patterns of action. To establish the pattern of repeatedly returning to our values, no matter how many times we lose touch with them.

Synonyms: None.

Method: Use values to set goals, and break those goals down into specific actions. Ask the client to commit to this action. Identify barriers to action, and overcome them using the other five core ACT processes.

When to Use: Whenever a client needs help with translating values into workable action. This includes learning any new skills necessary for values-congruent living.

GETTING TO COMMITTED ACTION

Committed action happens in every session. Turning up for therapy is committed action; doing a mindfulness exercise or discussing a painful topic is committed action; doing ACT homework is committed action. However, committed action doesn't usually take center stage until we have clarified values.

Almost always, as we move from values to goals to taking action, we'll encounter psychological barriers. So if we've already covered some or all of the four mindfulness processes—defusion, acceptance, contacting the present moment, self-as-context—we can now use them for overcoming these barriers. And if we haven't yet covered these components of the hexaflex, then we can now move on to them.

Under the heading of committed action, we can incorporate any and all traditional behavioral interventions—skills training, exposure and desensitization, behavioral activation for depression, and so on. So, for example, we may teach crisis coping, problem solving, self-soothing, assertiveness, communication, or conflict resolution skills. As long as these skills are in the service of mindful valued living (and they aren't emotional control strategies, such as distraction techniques), then they can be considered a part of ACT.

Committed Action: Step by Step

Basically there are four steps to committed action:

1. Choose a domain of life that is high priority for change.

2. Choose the values to pursue in this domain.

3. Develop goals, guided by those values.

4. Take action mindfully.

Our ultimate aim is to generalize this approach into larger and larger patterns of committed values-guided action, creating a domino effect that spills over into all domains of life. Setting Values-Based Goals (below) is a worksheet to help you with the first three steps: picking a life domain, clarifying values, and setting goals. Please read through it now.

SETTING VALUES-BASED GOALS

Three Steps to Setting Values-Based Goals

Step 1: The domain of life I choose to work on is (circle one or two, but no more): work, health, education, social, parenting, intimate partner, family, spiritual, community, environment, leisure, personal growth.

Step 2: The values underlying my goals (in this domain of life) are:

When it comes to setting goals, make sure you set a SMART goal:

- **S***pecific: Specify the actions you will take—when and where you will do so, and who or what is involved. For example, this is a vague or nonspecific goal: "I will spend more time with my kids." This is a specific goal: "I will take the kids to the park on Saturday afternoon to play baseball." Make your goal specific enough so that you can easily tell whether or not you've achieved it.*
- **M***eaningful: If this goal is genuinely guided by your values as opposed to following a rigid rule, trying to please others, or trying to avoid some pain, then it will be personally meaningful. If it lacks a sense of meaning or purpose, check in and see if it's really guided by your values.*
- **A***daptive: Does the goal help you to head in a direction that, as far as you can predict, is likely to improve, enrich, or enhance your quality of life?*
- **R***ealistic: The goal should be realistically achievable. Take into account your health, competing demands on your time, financial status, and whether you have the skills to achieve it.*
- **T***ime-framed: To increase the specificity of your goal, set a day, date, and time for it. If this isn't possible, set as accurate a time frame as you possibly can.*

Step 3: My values-based goals are ...

- **an immediate goal** (something small, simple, and easy that I can do in the next twenty-four hours):

- **short-term goal(s)** (things I can do over the next few days and weeks):

- **medium-term goal(s)** (things I can do over the next few weeks and months):

- **long-term goal(s)** (things I can do over the next few months and years):

SMART GOALS, LIVE-PERSON'S GOALS

Note the SMART acronym for goal setting (which is a bit different from some other versions.) Goals need to be:

S = Specific

M = Meaningful

A = Adaptive

R = Realistic

T = Time-framed

(Also make sure to avoid emotional goals and dead-person's goals.)

Of course, we can do all this goal setting conversationally if we (or our client) don't like forms. However, writing it down in session makes it more tangible and gives our client a valuable reminder to take away. We may well find that during this work, our client starts to fuse with unhelpful thoughts about it all being too hard, hopeless, pointless, or doomed to failure. This provides an excellent opportunity for defusion, as you'll see in this transcript:

Client: *(frowning at the worksheet)* This is a waste of time. *(She puts her pen down.)* I've done this before. I write goals down, but I never follow through on them.

Therapist: So you're having the thought that this is going to be just like all the other times?

Client: It's not just a thought. It's true.

Therapist: Well, I could try to debate with you here—try to convince you that the thought's not true. Or I could try to motivate and inspire you. Or I could lecture you on how important this is. Or tell you not to think that way. Or tell you to think positively. Do you think any of those things would be useful?

Client: *(chuckles)* No.

Therapist: So let's just take a look at this from the observing self. Just take a step back and notice what your thinking self is telling you.

Client: *(She pauses, observing her thoughts.)* Just the same as before. This isn't going to work. It's a waste of time.

Therapist: So if you let those thoughts tell you what to do, will that take you closer to the life you want to live—or further away?

Client: Further away.

Therapist:	So what're you going to do here? Let those thoughts bully you around and tell you what you can and can't do? Or do something that's likely to make your life work?
Client:	Hmm. When you put it that way … *(She picks up the pen and starts writing.)*
Therapist:	Now as you keep writing, just notice what your mind's doing. Notice all the ways it tries to get you to stop.
Client:	*(She stops writing again and, smiles.)* It's saying this is a complete waste of time.
Therapist:	Good stuff! Now see if you can get your mind to have a full-on temper tantrum—you know, the full works: screaming, shouting, stamping its feet!
Client:	*(smiling, continuing to write)* Oh yeah … It's having a complete meltdown now. A real doozy.

Practical Tip   You can reinforce defusion by offering your client a range of alternative responses to a problematic thought: "I can debate with you whether it's true or false, tell you not to think that way, lecture you, tell you to think positively, give you advice, reassure you. Do you think that would stop your mind from having these thoughts?" Your client will almost always say no, and then you can move on to any defusion technique your client has previously embraced, for example, "So why not let Radio Doom and Gloom keep broadcasting and invest your energy in doing something that truly matters to you?"

PUBLIC COMMITMENTS

People are far more likely to follow through on public commitments than private ones. So we usually ask the client to say out loud exactly what he's committing to. As many people feel awkward making public commitments, I like to give a rationale, something along these lines:

Therapist:	What I'm about to ask you may seem a bit odd, but research shows that when people make public commitments, they're far more likely to keep them. So, if you're willing to, I'd like you to say out loud exactly what it is you're committing to—and as you say it, just notice any thoughts and feelings that arise.
Client:	You mean, tell you what I've written?
Therapist:	Yes, please. Say it out loud, like you really mean it. And notice what shows up in your mind and your body.
Client:	I commit to taking the kids to the park on Saturday afternoon to play baseball.
Therapist:	Great. You looked a bit uncomfortable as you said that. What feelings showed up?

Client:	My stomach. It knotted up.
Therapist:	And did your mind have anything unhelpful to say?
Client:	You bet. I'm too busy with work. I don't have time. It's a hassle. Leave it till next month.
Therapist:	So are you willing to make room for those thoughts and feelings in order to do what matters?
Client:	Yes.

When clients speak their commitments out aloud, they commonly experience uncomfortable thoughts and feelings. It's useful to inquire about their private experiences and ensure that they're willing to make room for them.

THE TINIEST STEP?

A very useful question, once you've identified a life domain and some core values, is this: "What's the smallest, tiniest, simplest, easiest step you can take in the next twenty-four hours that will take you a little bit further in that direction?"

Learning to take small steps is important. When clients get too focused on big long-term goals, they're pulled out of living in the present; they get sucked into the mindset of "I'll be happy once I've achieved that goal." And, of course, they may never achieve it, or it may take much longer than they expected, or it may not make them happy even if they do achieve it.

So I like to remind clients of the famous saying from the *Tao Te Ching*: "The journey of a thousand miles begins with one step." Living our values is a never-ending journey; it continues until the moment of our final breath. And every little step we take, no matter how tiny, is a valid and meaningful part of that journey. (I also like to quote Aesop: "Little by little does the trick.")

To show you how values, goals, and actions come together, let's consider Sarah—a thirty-eight-year-old nurse, single for four years since her divorce. Sarah very much wanted to find a new partner, get married, and have children, and she was worried that she would soon be too old to conceive. Of course getting married and having kids are goals—they can be crossed off the list, achieved, done!—not values. So using the worksheet above, Sarah identified two life domains as priority: "intimate partner" and "parenting." We then looked at her values in each domain.

Initially Sarah said what she wanted was to be loved and cherished. Now these are common desires that almost everyone has, but they are not values; values are about how we want to behave, not what we want to get. With further exploration (and plenty of work around accepting the intense sadness that arose), Sarah identified her values in the domain of "intimate partner" as connecting, being caring, being loving, being supportive, being nurturing, being playful, being present, being emotionally intimate, and being sexually active. Under "parenting" her values were almost identical (except for "being sexually active").

Sarah recognized that "marriage and kids" were not realistic as immediate goals (next twenty-four hours) or short-term goals (next few days and weeks), so she wrote them down as medium- or long-term goals.

Next she looked at short-term goals. In the domain of "intimate partner," she set goals to (a) join a dating agency and go on some blind dates, and (b) attend some mixed-sex Latin dancing classes. In the domain of "parenting," her goals were to (a) take her teenage niece out for a day trip and (b) visit a couple of friends who had young children.

In terms of immediate goals, Sarah was stumped. Here's how the session went:

Therapist: You've identified quite a few important values here. Which seems the most important?

Sarah: Um. I think, more than anything else, connecting and being intimate.

Therapist: Okay, so what's a small, simple, easy thing you could do in the next twenty-four hours, in line with those values?

Sarah: I don't know.

Therapist: No idea?

Client: No.

Therapist: Well, the key here is to think outside the box. If connection matters to you, there are hundreds of different ways to do it; you can connect with animals, plants, people, your body, your religion. And the same for being intimate—there are all sorts of different ways you can do that, including being intimate with yourself.

Sarah: I never thought about it that way.

After some discussion along these lines, Sarah identified an immediate goal of having a long, hot, soothing bath: this was a way of being intimate with herself and connecting with her body.

IMPOSSIBLE GOALS

At times, clients will have impossible goals. For example, Alex was a forty-two-year-old former social worker on long-term disability benefits. He was referred with a fifteen-year history of chronic PTSD, major depression, and chronic pain syndrome. His problems had started fifteen years earlier when he had been horrifically assaulted, resulting in severe back and neck injuries that required multiple operations to deal with those injuries.

Prior to the assault, Alex had been a passionate amateur football player; now he could barely get around with a cane. When we first started work on values and goals, Alex kept talking about how he wanted to play football again, even though many surgeons had told him it was impossible. I said to him, "Well, here's the thing, Alex. It's not my place to tell you what's possible and what's not. But can we agree that today, right now, in the next twenty-four hours, playing football is not possible?"

Alex agreed with that, so we then explored his values underlying the goal of playing football again. Initially he came up with the following: winning against other teams, getting respect, having a social life. None of these are values: they're not desired qualities of ongoing action. So I asked him, "Suppose I wave a magic wand so you instantly achieve all these goals: you play football again, you win all your games, you get lots of respect, and you have a great social life. Then, how would you act differently … toward yourself and your body and other people? As a player, what sort of personal qualities would you like to have? How would you like to behave toward the people you socialize with?"

With further exploration along these lines, we were able to get to some core values: being active, taking care of his health, contributing to a team, being sociable, being competitive, being a "good friend," connecting with others. I then pointed out there were many different ways he could act on these values, even though he couldn't currently play football. To which Alex protested, "But that's not the same."

Consider for a moment, before reading on: How would you have responded to Alex's comment?

What we're dealing with here is a reality gap: a large gap between current reality and desired reality. And the bigger that gap, the more painful the feelings that will arise. So naturally we need to validate and normalize those feelings, to compassionately acknowledge how painful they are, and to help our client to accept them.

Therefore my response to Alex was this:

Therapist: Absolutely. It's not the same. It's not the same thing at all. Not even close. And when there's a huge gap between what you want and what you've got, that hurts. I can see how upset you are right now, and I can only begin to imagine how much you're suffering. (*pause*) And in my experience, when people are hurting the way that you are right now, it's because they're in touch with something really important; something that matters. (*pause*) So suppose I could give you a choice here. One option is that you learn how to make room for these painful feelings and how to drop the struggle with them so you can put your energy into doing something that's important, something that truly matters to you, deep in your heart—so you can stand for something in the face of this painful reality. The other option is to get all bogged down in these painful feelings and just kind of give up trying, and put your life on hold. Which option do you want to choose?

At that point, Alex experienced a huge wave of sadness, resentment, and fear, so we worked on acceptance, defusion, and self-compassion. Alex learned to accept the painful feelings related to his losses, and to defuse from the thoughts that kept dragging him into bitterness and hopelessness—"I can never have the life I want," "It's not fair," "There's no point going on."

After a couple more sessions, we returned to Alex's values and started setting small realistic goals. For example, two of his core values were "contribution" and "being sociable." Instead of a sports team, Alex started contributing to a health team: the nurses at his local "old folks'" home. He started going in on a voluntary basis to socialize with the elderly residents. He would make them cups of tea, chat about the news, and even play chess with them (which was acting on his value of being competitive). He found this very satisfying, even though it was a million miles from playing football.

So, to summarize, here's what to do when a goal is impossible or a long way off:

1. Validate the pain arising from the reality gap.

2. Respond to the pain with acceptance and defusion.

3. Find the values underlying the goal.

4. Set new goals based on those underlying values.

Barriers to Action—and How to Deal with Them

If clarifying values and setting goals were enough to ensure valued living, the task of ACT therapists would be a lot easier. Unfortunately, when it comes to making positive life changes, we commonly encounter psychological barriers. The most common of these are summarized by the acronym FEAR:

F = Fusion

E = Excessive goals

A = Avoidance of discomfort

R = Remoteness from values

Let's take a quick look at each of these barriers.

F is for fusion. When we set out to make change, it's normal for our mind to throw up "negative" thoughts: *I'm too busy, I can't do it, I'll fail, It's too hard,* and so on. This isn't a problem if we defuse from them, but if we fuse with those thoughts, they can prevent us from moving forward.

E is for excessive goals. If our goals exceed our resources, we'll either give up or fail. Necessary resources could include skills, time, money, and physical health.

A is for avoidance of discomfort. Change usually gives rise to uncomfortable feelings—most commonly anxiety. If we're not willing to accept this discomfort, we won't move forward (that is, we stay in our "comfort zone").

R is for remoteness from values. Why are we bothering to put in all this hard effort? If we lose touch with the values underlying this goal—if it doesn't seem meaningful or important—then we readily lose motivation. "Remoteness from values" commonly presents in four ways: (1) clients can't or won't access their values; (2) they confuse rules and morals with values; (3) they pay lip service to values but don't truly connect with them; and/or (4) they give you the values of their religion, culture, or parents rather than their own.

(By the way: the above version of the FEAR acronym is different to the one you'll find in other ACT textbooks; I changed it to make it more comprehensive.)

So how do we address these barriers? Well, the antidote to FEAR is DARE:

D = Defusion

A = Acceptance of discomfort

R = Realistic goals

E = Embracing values

So let's take a look at what's involved in order to DARE.

D is for defusion. We identify the thoughts that hold us back and we defuse from them.

A is for acceptance of discomfort. We make room for our painful thoughts and feelings, not because we like them or want them, but so that we can do what matters.

R is for realistic goals. If we lack the necessary resources, we have two options. Option 1: Create a new goal to acquire the necessary resources. If we lack necessary skills, our new goal is to learn them. If we lack money, our new goal may be to borrow it or save it up. If we lack physical health, our new goal is to improve it. And if we lack time, our new goal is to rearrange our schedule (which may require us to give up other activities). Option 2: If it's not possible to get the required resources, then we accept the limitations of reality and change our goal to adapt in the best way possible.

E is for embracing values. If we're lacking in motivation, let's reflect for a moment on why we're doing this. What's important or meaningful about this action? Does it truly matter? If so, why?

If we write these acronyms on a business card for our clients to carry around in a purse or wallet, we provide them with a concrete way to help them to identify their barriers and respond effectively. These acronyms also help us decide what to do in therapy. If our client gets stuck, we figure out the barriers using FEAR, and then we target them with DARE.

Note that both of these acronyms can account for external barriers. If there's an external barrier to action, then we'll be dealing with the E of FEAR: our goal exceeds our resources. And we respond with the R of DARE: we set a realistic new goal, either to overcome the barrier (assuming that's both possible and workable) or to accept it and adapt to it.

REASON-GIVING

We're all very good at coming up with reasons for why we can't or shouldn't do things that take us out of our comfort zone. And if we fuse with these thoughts, they'll hold us back. There are many ways we can defuse from reason-giving (as with any other category of thinking). One simple way is to name it and anticipate it, as we see in this transcript.

Therapist: You know our mind is pretty amazing. It's not only a problem-solving machine and a judgment factory, it's also a reason-giving machine. As soon as we have to face any sort of challenge and step out of our comfort zone, our mind will manufacture a whole list of reasons not to do it: *I'm too tired. It's too hard. I'll fail. It's too expensive. It'll take too long. I'm too depressed. I don't have enough confidence. I'm too anxious. Others wouldn't approve. I don't deserve it. It's not the right time. I shouldn't have to do this. It'll all go wrong.* [*Modify these reasons so they're directly relevant to your client's issue.*] The machine never stops—it keeps on churning out reason after reason after reason. Your mind, my mind, everybody's mind produces these sorts of thoughts. That's just what minds do. And this is only a problem if we let these thoughts bully us around—if we let them dictate what we can and can't do. But if we treat them the same way as all our other unhelpful thoughts—see them for what they are, hold them lightly, unhook ourselves—then they can't stop us from doing what truly matters. So what sort of reasons is your mind giving you right now as to why you can't or shouldn't do what we've been talking about? [*Elicit as many reasons as possible.*] Okay, so as far as I can see, these are all perfectly valid reasons not to take action. So now I invite you to take a good honest look at the situation and consider this question: if you don't take any action here—if you just stop trying, give up, stay put, do more of the same—will that enrich and enhance your life in the long run? [*Elicit an answer; usually the answer will be no.*] So then, are you willing to take action, even though your mind can and will give you all sorts of perfectly valid reasons not to do it?

If your client says "yes," you can now use all manner of defusion techniques. You can silently name the process: "Aha! Here's reason-giving!" You can say to yourself, "I'm having the thought that I can't do this because I'm too tired." You can say to yourself, "Thanks, mind. Good reason-giving." You can sing the reasons, write them on cards, observe them dispassionately, treat them as a special broadcast from Radio Doom and Gloom, and so on.

If your client says no, you can say—very slowly, gently, and compassionately:

Therapist: Well, here's the thing. If you're waiting till the day your mind stops giving you reasons, you'll probably be waiting forever because that's what minds do. They give you reasons not to take action. So just imagine coming back to see me in ten years' time ... and you tell me that nothing has changed in your life ... nothing ... that the last ten years have been just more of the same. You've been waiting ten years for the day your mind stopped giving reasons … and nothing has changed. (*pause*) Is that the future you truly want?"

Your client is almost certain to now say no, in which case you once again can ask:

Therapist: So are you willing to take action, even though your mind can give you all sorts of perfectly valid reasons not to do so?

One last strategy to consider is something I call "the kidnap question":

Therapist: Okay, so you've just given me six or seven perfectly valid reasons not to do this. Now, if you're willing to, I'd like you to imagine something. Imagine that the person you love most on this planet was kidnapped. And the deal is, unless you take this action we've been talking about, you'll never see this person again. Would you take this action, even though your mind can give you all sorts of perfectly valid reasons not to do it?" [*Elicit an answer; your client is bound to say yes.*] Okay. So at the moment, it's like this: the rich, meaningful life that you would ideally like to have has been kidnapped, and you'll never get to see that life unless you take action. Are you willing to take this action, even though your mind gives you all sorts of reasons not to do it?

THE WILLINGNESS AND ACTION PLAN

We can reduce the impact of psychological barriers by anticipating them. A simple way to do this is to use the Willingness and Action Plan below. (It's also downloadable free from www.act madesimple.com.)

Part 1 of the form specifies values, goals, and actions. Part 2 asks clients to predict their own psychological barriers. Being forewarned is forearmed, and it increases the chances that they'll respond with acceptance and defusion. (Be sure to ask your client to include as much reason-giving as possible in the section on thoughts.) Part 3 breaks the goal down into small doable steps, and also includes a section for any useful self-talk—for example, "The journey of a thousand miles begins with one step" or "It's okay to make mistakes."

Once this form is completed, ask your client to read parts 1 and 2 out loud in session as a public commitment. Again, you can do all this conversationally without using forms, but a written record acts as a powerful reminder. You could also print out a few copies and give them to your client for ongoing use.

BREAKING COMMITMENTS

Everyone breaks commitments at times. This is part of being human. Often our client will be quick to raise the issue of failure: "What if I fail?" "I've tried doing this before, but I never stick to it." If our client doesn't raise this issue, then we'll need to raise it ourselves. Here's an example:

Therapist: It's a given that from time to time you'll break a commitment. That's called being a real human, not a fictitious superhero. It's unrealistic to expect that we'll always live by our values and follow through on our commitments. What is realistic is to get better at it. We can get better at staying on track, faster at catching ourselves when we go offtrack, and better at getting back on track again. And when we do go offtrack, what helps is being kind and accepting toward ourselves: we accept the painful thoughts and feelings, then reconnect with our values, and get moving again. What doesn't help is beating ourselves up. I mean, if beating yourself up was a good way to change your behavior, wouldn't you be perfect by now?

It's also useful to talk to clients about the two main commitment patterns:

The Two Commitment Patterns:

- **Pattern 1:** Make a commitment, break a commitment, give up.

- **Pattern 2:** Make a commitment, break a commitment, lick your wounds, pick yourself up, learn from the experience, get back on track, make another commitment.

The first pattern leads to getting stuck. The second leads to continued growth. You can ask clients to identify their pattern—and if it's pattern 1, ask them to honestly assess it in terms of workability.

Basically we want our client to build bigger and bigger patterns of valued action, extending into every area of her life. And in the process, we want her to become her own ACT therapist: identifying her own FEAR and responding with DARE.

Practical Tip   There are two very common pitfalls for therapists in this stage of the work. The first is being too pushy. If we try to harangue, coerce, or push our clients into action, it will probably backfire. The second is being too wishy-washy. If we don't actively encourage our client to set specific goals, make a public commitment, and confront her psychological barriers, then she may well not follow through.

HOMEWORK AND THE NEXT SESSION

For homework, your client takes the action that he committed to in the session. It's important to anticipate possible barriers and discuss effective responses. The FEAR/DARE acronyms are very useful, and you can accentuate their effectiveness with the worksheet From FEAR to DARE below.

THE WILLINGNESS AND ACTION PLAN

1. My goal is to (be specific):

   The values underlying my goal are:

   The actions I will take to achieve that goal are (be specific):

2. The thoughts/memories, feelings, sensations, urges I'm willing to make room for in order to achieve this goal are:

   - Thoughts/memories:

   - Feelings:

   - Sensations:

   - Urges:

3. It would be useful to tell myself that:

4. If necessary, I can break this goal down into smaller steps.
   The smallest, easiest step I can begin with is:

   The time, day, and date when I will take that first step are:

FROM FEAR TO DARE

From FEAR to DARE: Part 1

Let's assume you have clarified your values and set yourself a goal, but you haven't followed through on it. What stopped you? The FEAR acronym covers most of the common barriers:

F = Fusion (stuff your mind tells you that will hold you back if you get caught up in it)

E = Excessive goals (your goal is too big, or you lack the skills, time, money, health, or other resources)

A = Avoidance of discomfort (unwillingness to make room for the discomfort this challenge brings)

R = Remoteness from values (losing touch with—or forgetting—what's important or meaningful about this)

So now, in as few words as possible, write down everything that has stopped you from following through:

Now go back and label each answer with one or two of the letters F, E, A, or R, whichever best describe(s) this barrier:

- Was it F = fusion with a story (for example, I'll fail, it's too hard, I'll do it later, I'm too weak, I can't do it, or others)?

- Was it E = excessive goal (you lacked the time, money, health, facilities, skills, or support necessary; or it was just too big and you got overwhelmed)?

- Was it A = avoidance of discomfort (you were unwilling to make room for the anxiety, frustration, fear of failure, or other uncomfortable thoughts and feelings)?

- Was it R = remoteness from your values (you forgot or lost touch with the values underlying this goal)?

The antidote to FEAR is DARE.

D = Defusion

A = Acceptance of discomfort

R = Realistic goals

E = Embracing values

Go through your barriers, one by one, and work out how you can deal with them, using DARE. On the next page, you'll find some suggestions to help you.

This worksheet has been reformatted to fit the layout of this book. Rather than photocopying it, we recommend you use the original version, downloadable from www.actmadesimple.com

From FEAR to DARE: Part 2
Defusion Strategies

- Name the story.
- Thank your mind.
- Acknowledge "Here's reason-giving" or "Here's judging."
- Name the demon/monster/passenger.
- Recognize this is Radio Doom and Gloom broadcasting.
- Simply let the thoughts come and go like passing cars.

Acceptance Strategies

- Name the feeling.
- Observe the feeling like a curious scientist.
- Rate the feeling on a scale of 1 to 10.
- Commit to allowing the feeling.
- Breathe into the feeling.
- Make room for the feeling.
- Give the feeling a shape and color.

Realistic Goal Setting

- If you lack skills, set new goals around learning them.
- If your goal is too big, break it down into small chunks.
- If you lack resources, brainstorm how you can get them.
- If you lack time, what are you willing to give up in order to make time?
- If the goal is truly impossible—for example, due to health or financial issues, or external barriers over which you have no direct influence, then set a different goal.

Embracing Values

- Connect with what matters to you about this goal.
- Is this goal truly meaningful?
- Is this goal aligned with your values?
- Is this goal truly important?
- Does this goal move your life forward in the direction in which you wish to go?

Using these ideas (and others of your own or of your therapist/coach), write down how you can respond to the barriers you listed above:

Finally, ask yourself these questions:

- *Am I willing to make room for the difficult thoughts and feelings that show up without getting caught up in them or struggling with them?*
- *Am I willing to take effective action in order to do what, deep in my heart, matters?*

If your answer is yes, go ahead and give it a go.

If your answer is no, consider these three questions:

1. Does this really and truly matter to you?
2. If it does, then what is the cost to you of avoiding it or putting it off?
3. Would you rather have the life-draining pain of staying stuck or the life-enhancing pain of moving forward?

This worksheet has been reformatted to fit the layout of this book. Rather than photocopying it, we recommend you use the original version, downloadable from www.actmadesimple.com

In the next session, we review how things turned out. Did the client follow through on her goals? If so, what was that like? What difference did it make in her life? And what's the next step in this valued direction? If he didn't follow through on his goals, we explore what stopped him and use FEAR/DARE to get him moving again.

HOMEWORK FOR YOU

- Pick two or three cases where your client is stuck, and identify their probable barriers using FEAR. Then write down some ideas about how you can use DARE to get them moving again. As usual, read the transcripts in this chapter out loud, as if you were talking to a client. (And modify my language to suit your own style.)

- Download copies of the worksheets in this chapter (from www.actmadesimple.com) and fill them in for yourself. Identify where you're getting stuck in important areas of your life and clarify what you can do to get moving again. Think of one small step you can take in a valued direction, and make a public commitment (for example, to a friend, colleague, or your partner) to follow through on it.

- If you follow through on your commitment, do it mindfully and notice what difference it makes in your life. If you don't follow through on it, identify what stopped you, in terms of FEAR.

SUMMARY

Committed action means doing what it takes to live congruently with our values. Some of our clients will have very few psychological barriers to action; simply helping them to get in touch with their values and asking about values-congruent goals will be enough to get them moving. However, most of our clients will have at least some barriers in the form of FEAR: fusion, excessive goals, avoidance of discomfort, and remoteness from values. The way through those barriers is DARE: defusion, acceptance of discomfort, realistic goals, and embracing values.

Committed action does not mean striving for perfection and pressuring ourselves to achieve all our goals. It means a commitment to valued living: the commitment to return again and again to our values, no matter how many times we lose touch with them.

CHAPTER 13

Getting Unstuck

WORKABILITY: OUR BEST FRIEND

Here's my guarantee to you. As you start working with ACT, both you and your clients will get stuck. Repeatedly. I guarantee this will happen or your money back! Fortunately ACT provides us with an incredibly powerful tool for getting unstuck: workability. Kirk Strosahl, one of the pioneers of ACT, says it this way: "When we're doing ACT, workability is our best friend." From a stance of workability, we never need to judge, criticize, or attack a client's self-defeating behaviors, nor do we need to convince or persuade her to stop. Instead we ask her to look honestly and openly at her current behavior and its long-term effects on her life, and to assess whether her actions are helping her to grow as a human being and live a vital, meaningful life—or not. We may ask questions such as these: "Is what you're doing working in the long run to make your life richer and fuller?" "Is this taking you closer to the life you really want?" "Is this helping you to be the person you want to be?"

However, we need to be very careful here: it's easy for us to start "bullying" our clients. Bullying means that we have already decided what will work for the client and what won't work (Strosahl, 2004). When we fuse with our own ideas about what is best or right for our client, we start imposing our own agenda. Our client may then start saying the things we want to hear in order to appease us. If this happens, the exercise is empty because the client is not genuinely taking responsibility for his own life. Strosahl warns us: "In order to use the workability strategy, you have to be relentlessly pragmatic and non-judgmental and to truly mean it. This is not a game, a trick or a form of therapeutic manipulation" (Strosahl, 2004, p. 226). Keeping this in mind, let's look now at some of the many ways workability can help us out.

Helping Us with Creative Hopelessness

Workability enables us to do "mini" creative hopelessness interventions at any time in any session. Whatever the problematic behavior is, we can always ask, "So when you do that, what effect does it have on your life in the long run?" This is more effective if we first normalize the behavior: "It's completely natural that you would do this, given your past life experience. Lots of people would do the very same thing under similar circumstances. The question is, if you keep on doing it, will it make your life richer and fuller—or will it do the opposite?"

Practical Tip   When talking of workability, we don't have to use the terms "rich, full, and meaningful life" or "living by your values." There are many ways to communicate the concept of mindful, valued living. We can talk of vitality, a life worth living, a life that grabs you, a better life, being the person you want to be, doing what's important/meaningful, doing what matters to you, doing what you care about, enhancing or enriching life, thriving, flourishing, and so on.

Helping Us with Defusion

Workability enables rapid defusion, and it's particularly useful when a client insists that a thought is true. We can say, "I won't argue with you over whether it's true or not. What I'd like you to do is to take a good look at what happens when you get all caught up in this thought." Then we can ask, "If you give this thought all your attention and let it dictate what you do, what happens to your life in the long run?" or "Does getting caught up in this thought help you to be the person you want to be? Does it help you to do the things you want to do?"

This is particularly useful when our client starts insisting change is impossible. For example, a client with an addiction may say, "I know this won't work for me. I've tried before. I've got no control over it." We can respond, "Okay, so your mind says, *This won't work. I've got no control.* Fair enough. That's the sort of stuff that minds say. I won't argue with that. I just want you to consider something. If we go along with that—if we let your mind dictate what happens in this room—then where do we go from here? Do we stop the session and give up?" We could then go on to say, "I fully expect your mind will keep telling you that this therapy won't work and you have no control. I don't know any way, other than major brain surgery, to stop that from happening. So can we let your mind say whatever it wants and give this a go anyway?"

This strategy is also very useful when clients insist that nasty negative self-judgments are true—for example, "But it's true. I am fat/ugly/stupid/a loser." We can say, "When your mind says this stuff to you, does it help if you get all caught up in it or hold on to it? Does buying into these thoughts—giving them all your attention, allowing them to dictate what you do—does that make your life richer, fuller, and more meaningful? If not, how about we practice learning to let them come and go without holding on to them?"

Helping Us with Clients Who Are Making Progress

If what the client is doing is "workable," then we can reinforce this behavior by increasing awareness around it. For example, we may ask questions such as these: "What's it like when you act in this way? What happens to your life? What happens to your sense of vitality? How could you do more of this?" It can also be useful to ask, "How did you do that? How did you make that happen? What did you do differently? What did you have to make room for? Did your mind try to interfere—and if so, how did you respond? What does this tell you about what works in your life?"

Helping Us to Catch Ourselves

Because we're fallible human beings, it's inevitable that at times we'll try to persuade, convince, debate, or argue with our clients. And when we respond in this way, we aren't doing ACT. So whenever I catch myself doing this, I promptly apologize. I say, "I'm really sorry. I just realized I've been trying to convince you here, and that's not what I want this to be about. This is not a place for me to try to impose my beliefs on you and tell you what to do with your life. It's a place for us to work together, to discover what works in your life. So can we please just rewind to before I started debating with you? Let's just bring this back to your life and your experience rather than my beliefs. And the question I'd like you to consider is this: regardless of what anyone else thinks (including me), if you keep doing what you're doing, is it working in the long run to make your life better? If it is, then by all means keep doing it, and let's focus on something else. But if it's not, how about we take a good honest look at it—except this time we'll do that without me trying to convince you of anything?"

Helping Us to Find Our Footing

When we're "lost" in a session or wondering where to go to next in therapy, we can always come back to workability. We can ask, "On a scale of 0 to 10, how well is your life working? If 10 means that the way you're spending each day gives you a real sense of vitality and fulfillment and 0 means that the way you're spending each day makes life seem pointless, meaningless, and not worth living at all, where are you on that scale?"

If a client scores highly, then let's talk about when to end therapy. If a client scores low—for example, 3 or 4—we could ask, "What would have to happen to get to a 5? What's getting in the way of that?" His answer will either give us information about further goals or reveal something about psychological barriers.

Helping Us with "I Don't Know!"

At times, we'll ask clients important questions and they'll answer, "I don't know." For example, this often happens early on with values work. If we suspect that the function of "I don't know" is to avoid the discomfort that discussing values often elicits, then we can bring in workability in a variety of different ways: "How is it working for you so far, going through life not knowing what matters to you?" "If we stop the conversation right there, with your very first answer of 'I don't know,' then where would that leave you?" "If it could make a real difference in your life, would you be willing to spend some time on this? Would you be willing to stick with the question and explore it even though no answer immediately comes to mind?" From here, we can dance into any number of values interventions—from formal worksheets to imagining your eightieth birthday. Alternatively, we can move into acceptance and defusion interventions in order to deal with the painful thoughts and feelings we've elicited.

Helping Us with "I've Got No Choice!"

Often our most challenging clients will tell us they have no choice or no control over their actions. They will insist that when strong urges show up—to commit suicide, drink alcohol, take drugs, and so on—they have no choice but to "give in." Other clients may insist that they're powerless or hopeless or incapable of making change, or they may say things such as, "Whenever I try to improve my life, it always goes wrong; I always fail or get hurt." We would first validate how much they have suffered: "Clearly this issue has created a lot of pain and difficulty for you. And you've tried hard, and so far nothing has worked." Then we would say, "And now you have a choice to make. One choice is to hold on tightly to *I have no choice, I have no control, There's nothing I can do*—and just give up trying, and carry on living the way you are. The other choice is to take action that moves you in a valued direction, even though you're having the thought that it's pointless and hopeless. Which of these two choices is guaranteed to keep you stuck and stop your life from improving? Which of these two choices stands the best chance of improving your life?"

Helping Us with "But It Works!"

Some clients will insist that their self-defeating behavior works for them in the long run. Here are two classic examples: "Worrying helps me prepare for the worst" and "I like getting stoned. It's the only way I can relax." We need to validate that, yes, there are indeed some real benefits to these strategies, and at the same time, there are other ways to obtain those benefits that would be far more workable. I use a metaphor about a rickety bicycle to convey this.

THE RICKETY BICYCLE METAPHOR

Therapist: You can cycle from New York to Mexico on a rickety old bicycle with bad suspension and a worn-out seat, and it will eventually get you there. But what condition will you be in by the time you arrive? There are many more effective ways to make that journey: cars, buses, trains, planes. When you (*Name the client's issue here: for example, get stoned, do all this worrying*), that's like riding a rickety bicycle. Would you like to learn an alternative that will get you to your destination in much better condition?

After using the Rickety Bicycle Metaphor, we then teach the necessary skills (or we help the client access resources for learning them). For example, if our client wants to "prepare for the worst," we can teach him strategic planning and problem solving. If our client wants to relax and marijuana is the only way she knows to do so, we can teach her relaxation skills (while being clear they are not the same as mindfulness skills).

OVERCOMING RESISTANCE

Resistance is a state, not a trait. In the right context, anyone would be resistant to therapy. Suppose you were being treated by a "witch doctor" in some third world country. If he told you there was an evil spirit in your body and the only way to get rid of it was to eat a live squid, would you be resistant?

Resistance in therapy generally boils down to a few key factors: treatment mismatch, secondary gains, the therapeutic relationship, and FEAR. Let's take a look at each of these now.

Treatment Mismatch

Did you adequately consent with your client? Did you explain what ACT involves? Was he expecting an "easy ride"? Did she just want someone to listen to her without expecting to do much work? Was he expecting something very different, such as long-term psychoanalysis? Not everybody is open to ACT, and we may need to refer clients on or work with a different model. This issue is largely avoided by giving adequate information when obtaining informed consent (see chapter 5).

Secondary Gains

Are there benefits for the client (whether conscious or unconscious) if she "stays stuck," such as proceeds from a legal settlement, or care and attention from others while she's in the sick role? To address the issue of secondary gains, we need to compassionately bring it into the client's awareness and nonjudgmentally explore it. We may need to do a cost-benefit analysis, framed in terms of workability—for example, we might say, "It seems that staying stuck works in the short run to gain benefits X, Y, and Z, but does it work in the long run to make life rich and full?" or "I'm willing to be wrong about this, but here's how I see it. If you don't make any changes here, there are some genuine short-term benefits for you—such as A, B, and C. What I'd like you to do is weigh these benefits up against the long-term costs of staying stuck."

Therapeutic Relationship

A strong therapeutic relationship is essential for effective therapy. Is there room for improvement here? Check in with yourself: Have you fused with unhelpful beliefs, judgments, or assumptions about this client? Are you moving too fast or too slow? Are you being too pushy or too passive? Too serious or too playful? Do you need to validate his experience more or show more compassion? Do you need to be more present, open, and accepting? Do you need to provide more rationale for the client as to why you're encouraging her to make these changes or practice these skills? Are you yourself fused and avoidant in session: skating around important issues instead of approaching them or getting lost in your own internal dialogue? In chapter 14, we will explore the therapeutic relationship in more detail; suffice it to say for now, the best way to build and strengthen the therapeutic relationship is for us to embody ACT during our sessions.

FEAR

In the last chapter, we discussed FEAR: fusion, excessive goals, avoidance of discomfort, and remoteness from values. All these factors can play a major role in resistance. The key is to identify them and then target them with DARE: defusion, acceptance of discomfort, realistic goals, and embracing values.

Resistance Is Fertile

When we encounter resistance in our clients—or perhaps it's better to describe it as "avoidance of making changes"—most of us tend to get frustrated or irritated, or we doubt our own abilities, blame the client, or blame ourselves. While this is normal, it isn't particularly helpful. A better alternative is simply to apply ACT to this issue itself. (I often say that ACT reframes your entire life because every problem you encounter becomes an opportunity to get better at ACT.)

In other words, whenever a client seems stuck, our first step is to look mindfully at what's happening, look at the situation with openness and curiosity, and notice the thoughts and feelings showing up. We might say something like, "Why don't we just take a step back and notice what's happening here?" Then nonjudgmentally explore the FEAR factors that are (almost certainly) involved.

Practical Tip Psychological flexibility is the capacity to be present, open up, and do what matters. So if your client starts to close off or shut down while the session is focused on opening up (defusion and acceptance) or on doing what matters (values and committed action), then your best option is to focus on being present. Ask your client to notice what's happening; to notice her thoughts and feelings; and to come back to the room and get present with you. Fusion and avoidance tend to "wither and fade" when we're fully in the present moment.

ACCEPTANCE OF BEING STUCK

There will be times that no matter what we try, our client will remain stuck. Haven't you ever experienced this in your own life? Despite all your wisdom, knowledge, resourcefulness, and experience, you somehow found yourself stuck: you were unwilling or unable to take the action that would really make a difference in your life? At these times, our default is to beat ourselves up, which clearly doesn't help. Beating ourselves up for getting stuck is about as useful as rubbing salt into fresh wounds. A more life-enhancing response is to turn these painful situations into opportunities to develop self-acceptance and self-compassion.

We can ask our clients questions like these: "Can you accept yourself as a human being even though you are temporarily stuck?" and "Can you be kind and caring toward yourself instead of beating yourself up?" Section 7 of the Acceptance of Emotions Exercise (see chapter 8) is a lovely exercise to practice here for developing self-compassion.

And notice the paradox: if we can use these situations to develop self-acceptance and self-compassion, then we're still growing and developing useful life skills even though we may be "stuck" on this particular issue.

HOMEWORK FOR YOU

- Play around with the concept of workability. Keep it in the back of your mind and use it as a resource for innovation in your work. Play around with different ways of talking about it.

- Start looking at your own behavior through the lens of workability and notice what effect that has. In particular, look at what you do in your closest relationships. Instead of getting caught up in right/wrong or should/shouldn't (as most of us do at times), start looking in a defused and accepting way at how workable your behavior is and whether there's any way you can improve on it.

■ Think of one or two clients who seem stuck or resistant. Identify the factors that may be contributing to their resistance and brainstorm ways that you might respond.

Practical Tip Whenever our clients seem stuck, resistant, or unmotivated, look for FEAR factors and respond with DARE. If a search for FEAR factors doesn't reveal the barriers, then consider treatment mismatch, secondary gains, or the therapeutic relationship.

SUMMARY

The whole ACT model rests on the concept of workability. Again and again, we ask our clients to assess whether their actions are giving them meaning, fulfillment, and vitality—or struggle and suffering? When we rely on workability for motivation, we never have to coerce, persuade, or convince our clients to change; we simply open their eyes to the consequences of their actions and allow them to choose their own direction. And sometimes, despite our best efforts to help them get moving, our clients will stay stuck—in which case, we can at least provide them with a safe, compassionate space in which they can rest.

CHAPTER 14

I and Thou

THE THERAPEUTIC RELATIONSHIP

In just about every model of therapy or coaching, the therapeutic relationship is considered important—and rightly so. In ACT, we especially emphasize this relationship. As a therapist or coach, we aim to embody the entire ACT model in session: to be mindful, nonjudgmental, respectful, compassionate, centered, open, receptive, engaged, warm, and genuine. We regard the client as an equal: a fellow human being who, just like us, gets caught up in his mind and ends up struggling with life. This attitude is very much summarized by the Two Mountains Metaphor (see chapter 5).

Being Mindful

ACT is a very active therapy that places much less emphasis on supportive listening than most other models. However, even a few minutes of truly mindful, genuinely compassionate listening can be incredibly powerful—far more so than an entire hour of disengaged listening.

One of the greatest gifts we can give other humans is to make them the center of our attention in an atmosphere of complete acceptance, openness, and compassion. So we listen to our clients carefully, kindly, genuinely—with an open heart and an open mind. We listen compassionately to their struggles. We notice and validate their pain—and acknowledge how they've suffered. We ask them to be willingly vulnerable. And we create a compassionate, nonjudgmental space where this is possible. Through this mindful, caring interaction, a strong, trusting, and open relationship is forged.

In each and every session, we have the opportunity to bear witness to the pain and suffering of our client in a manner that perhaps no one else has ever done. We take the time to listen completely, carefully, and open-mindedly; to notice our client's body language and facial expressions; to respond genuinely and empathetically; and to validate her experience in the process. If we catch ourselves "tuning out," not paying full attention, getting caught up in our thoughts, then the moment we realize it, we can gently acknowledge it and bring our attention back to our fellow human being. In this way, every session becomes a mindfulness practice in and of itself.

Asking Permission

"Is it okay if … ?" "Could I ask you to … ?" "Would you be willing to … ?"—these are all useful ways to ask the client's permission. This is simply showing respect. It's a key ingredient for building and maintaining rapport, especially when we're asking our clients to do exercises that are likely to bring up painful thoughts and feelings. The more painful the experience is likely to be, the more essential it is to know we have genuine permission—and not just an automatic yes response.

At times, it's also useful to say, "You don't have to do this. I wouldn't want you to go along with it just because I've suggested it." It's important, too, to make sure the client understands the rationale behind the exercise. If he doesn't, then take the time to explain it.

Saying "I'm Sorry"

When we screw up, make a mistake, offend, upset, or invalidate a client, then the moment we realize it, let's take action: acknowledge it, admit it, and give a genuine, heartfelt apology. We're modeling something very useful each time we do this; in many intimate relationships, there's a notable paucity of apologizing!

At times, even the most experienced of ACT therapists will find themselves lecturing, coercing, convincing, debating with, or trying to persuade their clients. When we're doing this, we aren't doing ACT. So the moment we catch ourselves doing this, it's useful to acknowledge it and to apologize. I say something like, "I'm really sorry. I've just realized what I've been doing here. I've been trying to convince you of something. You didn't come here so that I could force my belief systems on you. Can we please rewind here—go back to the point before I started trying to convince you—and start again from there?"

Being Playful

Playfulness, irreverence, and humor can play an important part in enhancing rapport. This often comes into its own when working with defusion. When laughter arises spontaneously in session, it's generally a good sign. On the other hand, watch out for insensitivity and invalidation. When someone is sharing a heartbreaking story of pain and suffering, playfulness would be inappropriate. And if our client's in terrible distress, we certainly wouldn't be using zany defusion techniques.

Practicing Self-Disclosure

While we don't have to self-disclose, ACT advocates that we do so if and when it's likely to be beneficial to the client in the service of normalization, validation, promoting self-acceptance, or enhancing the therapeutic relationship.

The ACT stance is that therapy involves an intimate relationship. However, intimacy is a two-way street; it requires openness from both parties. If the therapist is a "blank slate" and the client knows nothing of her inner world—nothing about what she values or cares about, or what she truly feels and thinks—then clearly they do not have an intimate relationship. When our clients come into therapy, they're in a vulnerable position, which makes for a very unequal relationship. However, if we as therapists deliberately and openly share our own values and vulnerabilities, that helps to establish a powerful bond with our clients.

Obviously that doesn't mean we "dump on them" or say, "Hey, you think you've got problems—listen to mine!" We use self-disclosure judiciously—when it's likely to normalize and validate a client's experience, deepen the therapeutic alliance, or model something useful. Here are some forms of self-disclosure that could be helpful in the right context.

"I have to confess, that's thrown me …" When your client has said something that has thrown you, stunned you, knocked you off your feet, it's often useful to admit it. You may then like to suggest a couple of minutes of mindful breathing or similar exercise so you can both center yourselves.

"I feel disconnected from you" or **"I feel as if you're not fully present right now."** If you sense your client dissociating, disconnecting, withdrawing, detaching, or wandering off inside her own mind, it's often helpful to draw attention to it—and to highlight what happens to your relationship with the client during these moments.

"I'm noticing a couple of different thoughts here …" At times, my mind suggests several different directions I could take the session in—all of them valid. It's often useful to share these thoughts and gauge the client's response. At other times, my mind makes several different judgments about the same situation. Again, in the right context, this can be useful to share.

"I'm noticing I feel a bit …" In the right context, it can be very useful to share emotional reactions.

Confronting Problematic Behaviors

From time to time, we all have clients who behave "problematically" during the session—for example, they may endlessly rehash the same old story or continually blame everyone else for their problems in life without ever looking at their own role. When this happens, most of us have a tendency to grit our teeth and try and put up with it rather than openly address it.

Why do we do this? Usually because we either fuse with thoughts like "It would be rude of me to interrupt" or "If I say something about it, she'll get upset with me"—or we experience feelings of anxiety that we're not willing to make room for. At these times, it's very useful to explicitly model ACT. We could say something like, "I'm noticing something happening here, and I want to bring it to your attention. My mind's telling me you're going to be upset or offended by what I say, and I'm noticing quite a lot of anxiety in my body, and a strong urge just to sit here and not say anything. However, I'm committed to helping you create the best life you can possibly have. And if I sit here and say nothing, then I'll be neglecting those values. So I'm going to do what matters here, even though my heart is racing—I'm going to tell you what I'm noticing."

Notice how, in doing this, we have explicitly modeled five of the six core ACT processes: defusion, acceptance, values, action, and contacting the present; self-as-context is implicit but not explicit. And by now, we'll have our client's full attention! Then, with an attitude of openness and curiosity, defused from any judgments or criticisms, we describe the behavior we're noticing and point to the fact that it's preventing useful work in the session. From there, we may explore the function of the behavior—"Can I ask what you're hoping to achieve by doing X?"—or whether it plays out in other relationships and, if so, what are the consequences. We may also inquire about the client's thoughts and feelings in response to our observation—and do some work around acceptance and defusion if necessary.

Declaring Our Values

In the homework section at the end of chapter 11, I asked you to reflect on your values as a therapist. If you haven't done so, please go back and reflect on those questions. When we go into a session consciously guided and motivated by our core values, we'll do a different sort of therapy than when we're on automatic pilot or fused with thoughts like *Here we go again; another day, another dollar!* or *This is going to be a tough one.*

ACT advocates that we declare our values to our clients. For example, "I want you to know, I'm in this room working with you for one sole purpose: to help you create a better life, a life that you feel is worth living" or "I'm committed to helping you turn your life around and take it in a direction that adds meaning, purpose, and fulfillment." When said genuinely, this is a powerful message that unites therapist and client in a common—and incredibly worthwhile—cause.

Slowing Down and Leaning In

"Slow down and lean in" is a phrase I picked up from a workshop with psychologist Robyn Walser. When we get stressed or anxious in response to what's happening in session, most of us tend to speed up—talk more, talk louder, give advice, start lecturing, and so on—or we lean back —disengage, tune out, withdraw. Obviously this isn't helpful for the therapeutic relationship. So aim to do the opposite: slow down and lean in! Notice your thoughts and feelings, notice your tendency to speed up and lean out, connect with your values, and then lean in (literally) and slow down. Talk less, talk slower, and pause frequently.

Sitting with It

A major challenge for most ACT therapists is letting go of the need to fix the client's problems. And yet, the more we take on the role of problem fixer, the more we disempower our client. In ACT, we help clients cultivate enough psychological flexibility to effectively contact their own problem-solving resources—and if problem-solving skills are lacking, we'll teach them. However, there are all sorts of problems in life that can't be "solved" or "fixed"—the loss of a loved one, the pain of rejection or failure, the heartache of loneliness, the inevitability of aging, infirmity, and illness. In such situations, we help clients develop the ability to step out of problem-solving mode altogether and into the psychological space of mindfulness and acceptance. This is useful whenever (a) problems cannot be solved, or (b) when problem-solving attempts create even bigger problems.

Therefore, we need to learn the ability to "sit with it": to let the situation be as it is and allow our client to have his thoughts and feelings without rushing in to "rescue" him. This means that very often we'll need to make room for our own feelings of anxiety, our own impatience, and our own urges to rush in, fix it, solve it, or say the right thing.

Of course, that's not the same as allowing the client to wallow in her suffering; rather we aim to create a space of acceptance and defusion—a space within which both client and therapist can be present with their thoughts and feelings without fighting them, without being swept away by them, and without needing to take any immediate action. This is, if you like, "a breathing space." (No wonder so many mindfulness practices from different traditions are centered around the breath.) From a space of mindfulness, we can then make a wise choice by taking the entire situation into account, connecting with our values, and engaging in conscious action. At times, to help myself along with this, I may say to the client, "I'm feeling a strong urge right now to try and fix this for you. My mind's telling me all sorts of things to say to you—bits of advice, things you could do, blah, blah, blah. The challenge for both of us here is to see if we can just sit with this stuff—just make some room for all these thoughts and feelings and urges showing up—without rushing in to try and fix it."

(Of course, if there are practical skills that clients would benefit from learning—skills that will help them to solve those problems in their lives that *can* be solved through overt action—then ACT advocates that we either teach clients those skills or point them in the right direction to learn them.)

Defusing from Our Own Judgments

Of course we all aim to be nonjudgmental, and we may achieve that—for a while. But sooner or later, judgments will happen. Our mind is a well-oiled judgment machine; it won't stop judging for long. So, when our judgments about our clients do pop up, the challenge is to recognize them and defuse from them, and to let them come and go without getting caught up in them. If we realize a judgment has hooked us, we can silently say, *Aha! A judgment!*, then gently refocus on our client.

Revealing Yourself as a Novice

When it comes to doing ACT, do you ever feel your heart racing or your stomach knotting? Do you ever have thoughts like *I don't know if I can do this* or *What if my client "freaks out"?* Or maybe you think, *I'll fumble my words, I'll screw it up, This is too hard,* or *I'll do it wrong.* If so, good. This shows you that you're a normal human being. Normal humans typically feel anxious whenever they move out of their comfort zone. However, if you start fusing with ideas that you've got to do this stuff perfectly right from the word go or else your clients will react negatively, you're going to make life very hard for yourself. So if you're a total ACT newbie, I'd encourage you to take the pressure off yourself by simply admitting it. You could say something like, "Can I be totally honest with you? I'm a bit nervous about telling you this; my mind's telling me that you might lose some respect for me. The truth is I'm still a bit of a newcomer to this ACT stuff. I really like the model, I've found it very helpful in my life, and obviously I think it's going to be useful for you or I wouldn't recommend it. However, because I'm relatively new to it, from time to time I might stumble or get a bit tongue-tied. And for some of the longer exercises, I may even need to pull out a book and use the scripts to read from. Would you be okay with that?"

Obviously you don't *have* to disclose this (and whatever you do, don't say any part of it that isn't true), but many therapists find it gives them permission to be imperfect or to read from a script if desired. Furthermore, you're modeling openness, willingness, and self-acceptance, and your self-disclosure helps to establish a more intimate therapeutic relationship.

APPLY ACT TO YOURSELF

Hopefully you can see that everything in this chapter follows quite naturally from applying ACT to yourself as a therapist or coach. And obviously this holds true for every relationship in your life: the more you act from a space of mindfulness and values, the healthier your relationships will be. So why leave ACT for the therapy room? Why not spend some time now reflecting on your most meaningful relationships and think about how ACT principles can enrich and enhance them? And then put it into practice and see how it works. You may be surprised!

CHAPTER 15

The Therapist's Journey

FROM CHUNKY AND CLUNKY TO FLUID AND FLEXIBLE

When therapists are new to ACT, we tend to slice the model up and center each session around a major "chunk" of it—much as I've done in chapters 6 to 12 of this book. For example, we might do a session with a major focus on defusion, then another centered around acceptance, and another with an emphasis on the observing self, and so on. Typically as we become familiar with the model and realize how the six core processes all interconnect and complement each other, our therapy becomes less "chunky" and more "blended." We learn to "dance around the hexaflex," working explicitly with several processes in each session (and implicitly with all processes). Our therapy becomes more fluid, more flexible, more creative. We start to modify and adapt tools, techniques, and metaphors, creating new ones of our own (or borrowing them from our clients).

Hopefully you've already started to appreciate the interconnectedness of this model. To get a better sense of it, spend some time studying the ACT hexaflex diagram (see chapter 1) and identify how each of the six components interacts with all the others. Also, as you reread this book or move on to other ACT textbooks, notice how virtually every intervention contains several overlapping core processes. For example, suppose you ask a client, "Can you just sit with this feeling for a moment? Just notice where it's most intense. Then take a step back and look at it from the observing self." Here you have three processes in one brief intervention: present moment, self-as-context, and acceptance. (If you look more closely, you'll see that values, committed action, and defusion are also involved in this exercise, but they are less obvious. Can you spot them? First, in ACT, acceptance is always in the service of valued living, so this exercise is in some way linked to the client's values. Second, doing the exercise is, in itself, a committed action. Third, as we fully contact our experience in the present moment, there is always some defusion that happens.)

The journey from "chunky, clunky" ACT to "fluid, flexible" ACT requires time, practice, patience, persistence, and reflection. We'll screw up again and again. We'll get it wrong. Our minds will beat us up for being lousy therapists. But if we each bring an attitude of openness and curiosity to our mistakes—What did I do that was ineffective? What did I miss? What did I fuse with? What could I do differently next time?—we can learn valuable lessons from them. (And we may like to recall the words of Sir Winston Churchill: "Success is the ability to go from failure to failure without loss of enthusiasm.")

WHAT CAN WE BRING IN FROM PREVIOUS TRAINING?

One of the beautiful things about doing ACT is that it enables us to bring in a vast wealth of experience and knowledge from our previous training in other models. Look once more at the diagram in figure 15.1:

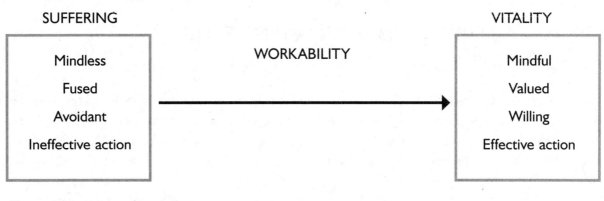

Figure 15.1

You can basically use anything from any other model that helps the client move in the direction of workability. Take a few moments to think about your previous training and how you can fruitfully use it. What do you know that can help clients to:

■ clarify their values and connect with a sense of meaning or purpose?

■ be present, conscious, aware, open, connected to their experience, centered, or grounded?

■ set goals and break them down into actions?

■ increase self-awareness around the short-term and long-term effects of their behavior?

■ be aware of and accept their thoughts and feelings?

- be aware of their thoughts, detach from their thoughts, let go of their thoughts, or see their thoughts just as thoughts?

- connect with a transcendent sense of self such as "the silent witness," "the observing self," "metacognitive awareness," "pure consciousness," or "the 'I' that notices"?

- be compassionate and accepting toward themselves or others?

- make effective behavioral changes, or learn new life-enhancing skills?

- make life as rich, full and meaningful as possible?

Hopefully you can see that there's a wealth of knowledge you already have that you can bring to your ACT work. What you need to be wary of is bringing in theories or techniques intended primarily to avoid or get rid of unwanted private experiences; these simply do not fit into the ACT model. Examples include the challenging and disputing of cognitions, visualizations to dissolve unwanted feelings, thought stopping, and distraction techniques.

Ask yourself these questions: What is the purpose of this technique? Is its aim to attack, suppress, avoid, reduce, or get rid of an unwanted private experience? If so, it's not ACT-consistent. Of course, that doesn't mean you can't use it in therapy; it just means (a) that it's not ACT, and (b) if you're doing ACT and also trying to incorporate this technique, you risk sending conflicting messages and undermining acceptance.

WHERE TO NEXT?

ACT is a big model. While you can certainly start using it straight away and immediately get positive results in your work, most therapists find that it takes at least a year of devoted practice, reading, and learning to get a good handle on both ACT theory and practice and to implement it fluidly and flexibly. So take your time—enjoy the journey, don't rush it. Remember Aesop's famous words: "Little by little does the trick."

In terms of further learning, I recommend that as soon as possible you attend an experiential ACT workshop. Reading books, listening to CDs, and watching DVDs are valuable, but they can't compare to actually attending live training and applying these six core processes to yourself. In appendix 2 of this book, I'll talk about where you can find training and supervision, and I'll also recommend a variety of books, CDs, and DVDs that can take you into ACT in more depth.

PARTING WORDS

The hardest part of writing this book was choosing what to leave out. There is so much more I'd like to share with you, but if I did, this book would be ten times the size it is now! So with great reluctance, I'll leave you now with a few parting words.

Be yourself

If you try to do ACT interventions by parroting them word for word from books, there's a good chance they'll come out stilted or artificial. Modify and adapt; use your own words and your own style; be creative and innovative if you wish to. VERY IMPORTANT: if anything I suggest in this book doesn't suit you, either modify it or leave it out. If you read a few ACT books, and/or attend a few different workshops/demonstrations, you'll see wildly different ways of doing ACT as well as a vast array of different styles and techniques. That is because ACT is a process-based model, not a technique-based model. So the way that you do ACT with your clients will inevitably be different than the way that others do it. (Isn't it great we can all be individuals?)

At the same time, make sure you attune and adapt to your clients' needs. For example, your style may be to do brief therapy, but there's no virtue in moving quickly if your client is not ready for it or feels invalidated by it. Likewise, there's no virtue in moving slowly or "hanging back" when your client is ready and eager for change and willing to do what's necessary.

Practice, Practice, Practice

Whoever said "Practice makes perfect" was lying! But practice does lead to improvement. So if you haven't done any of the homework in this book, please take a look at what's stopping you. Have you fused with thoughts such as *Too hard, Too busy, Do it later*? Or are you trying to avoid the inevitable feelings of anxiety that come when you take risks, face challenges, or try out new behaviors? Have a look at your barriers in terms of FEAR—and respond with DARE. Remember, the more you apply ACT in your own life to deal with your own issues, the more naturally it will come to you in the therapy or coaching room.

Make Mistakes

I've said it before and I'll say it again: you will make mistakes and screw up. This is an inevitable part of learning. So when it happens, practice ACT on yourself. Thank your mind for the "lousy therapist" story or the "too hard" story. Breathe into your frustration, anxiety, disappointment, and make room for it. Have compassion for yourself.

Then reflect on what you've done and learn from it so that you and others can benefit from the experience.

Come Back to Your Values

And again and again, come back to your values. Connect with why you moved into this profession in the first place: your desire to help others, your desire to make a difference, your desire to make the world a better place. And take the time to appreciate the privilege of our work: the unique opportunity we have to see deeply into the hearts and souls of others, and to help them connect with those healing places inside themselves.

Case Conceptualization Made Simple

This is a very basic guide to case conceptualization. (There are far more sophisticated tools available; this one is designed to get you "up and running" quickly.) You can download this sheet from www .actmadesimple.com, and I encourage you to print out twenty copies and use one for each of your next twenty sessions. I guarantee that doing so will give you a big boost in terms of understanding and applying this model.

A QUICK GUIDE TO ACT CASE CONCEPTUALIZATION

1. What valued direction does the client want to move in?
   (What domain of life and what values seem most important to this client? Does she have any values-congruent goals?)

2. What stands in the client's way?
   (Identify the barriers to valued living: fusion, avoidance, and unworkable action.)

   a. What is he fusing with?
      (Identify problematic fusion, including reasons, rules, judgments, past, future, and self-description.)

   b. What is she avoiding?
      (Identify thoughts, feelings, memories, urges, sensations, and emotions that this client is trying to avoid or get rid of.)

c. What unworkable actions is he taking?
   (What is the client doing that makes his life worse or keeps him stuck?)

You can use the diagram below to help you plan your next session. Write down any metaphors, exercises, questions, techniques, or worksheets that you could use in the next session to help your client make a workable shift.

APPENDIX 2

Resources

There are now a wealth of resources for ongoing learning and training in ACT. Here are a few ideas to get you started.

SECTION A: RESOURCES BY DR. RUSS HARRIS

Books

Harris, Russ, *ACT with Love* (Oakland, CA: New Harbinger, 2009)
   ACT with Love is an inspiring and empowering self-help book that applies the principles of ACT to common relationship issues, and details how to move from conflict, struggle, and disconnection to forgiveness, acceptance, intimacy, and genuine loving. It also functions as a step-by-step clinical guide for therapists wishing to use ACT for relationship problems, and is linked to its own resource-packed website: www.act-with-love.com.

Harris, Russ, *The Happiness Trap* (Wollombi, NSW, Australia: Exisle Publishing, 2007)
   The Happiness Trap translates ACT into simple everyday language and practical user-friendly exercises. It is a self-help book written for everyone and anyone, applicable to everything from work stress to major depression. It's widely used by ACT therapists and their clients all around the world, and is currently translated into twelve different languages. A website—www.thehappinesstrap.com—offers many free resources to use with the book.

CDs and MP3s

Mindfulness Skills: Volume 1 & *Mindfulness Skills: Volume 2*

Available as either CDs or downloadable MP3 files, these volumes cover a wide range of mindfulness exercises for use by you or with your clients. You can order them via www.actmadesimple.com (or if you live in Australia, via www.actmindfully.com.au).

Online Resources

This book is linked to the ACT Made Simple website a www.actmadesimple.com. On this site, you'll find many free resources, including downloadable copies of all the handouts in this book. You'll also find some valuable online training in the form of E-courses and webinars.

Workshops

Russ runs ACT training workshops around the world. For details of Australian workshops, visit www.actmindfully.com.au. For workshops in other countries, you'll find information on www.act madesimple.com.

Newsletter

The *Happiness Trap Newsletter* is a regular, free, e-mail newsletter, packed with useful information, tools, and tips relating to ACT. You can register for it under the main menu at any of the websites mentioned above.

SECTION B: GENERAL RESOURCES

ACT Textbooks and Self-Help Books

A wide range of ACT textbooks and self-help books now exists with the majority of them published by New Harbinger. Visit the New Harbinger website at www.newharbinger.com, or go to www.amazon.com (or some other large website that sells a wide range of books) and do a search for titles on "acceptance and commitment therapy." These textbooks are all very good, and they cover the application of ACT to a wide range of issues and conditions, from chronic pain and PTSD to depression and anxiety disorders. These three books stand out as particularly relevant to new ACT practitioners:

Hayes, Steven C., Kirk Strosahl, and Kelly Wilson, *Acceptance and Commitment Therapy: An Experiential Approach to Behavior Change* (New York: Guilford Press, 1999)

This is the ground-breaking theoretical and philosophical text that first introduced ACT to the world, and you'll find it widely cited in every other textbook on ACT.

Luoma, Jason B., Steven C. Hayes, and Robyn D. Walser, *Learning ACT* (Oakland, CA: New Harbinger, 2007).

This step-by-step, skills-training manual for ACT therapists lives up to its description as "the most comprehensive guide to utilizing ACT in your clinical practice."

Ramnerö, Jonas, and Niklas Törneke, *The ABCs of Human Behavior: Behavioral Principles for the Practicing Clinician* (Oakland, CA: New Harbinger, 2008)

This is an excellent book on the science, theory, and philosophy underlying ACT: functional contextualism, applied behavioral analysis, and relational frame theory (RFT).

DVDs

You can also buy DVDs showing how to do ACT with clients: the series is collectively known as *ACT In Action* by Steven C. Hayes (Oakland, CA: New Harbinger, 2008).

Professional Organization: ACBS: Association for Contextual Behavioral Science

Membership in ACBS includes the following:

- Opportunities to participate in the online ACT and/or RFT communities, where you can share ideas and receive advice from ACT therapists and/or RFT researchers all around the world.

- Extensive resources for clinicians, including articles, videos, podcasts, handouts, protocols, papers, and even PowerPoint presentations on ACT/RFT.

- Opportunity to list yourself as an ACT therapist on the official worldwide ACT website.

- Help in finding an ACT therapist or a supervisor, or an ACT workshop near you.

- And much more …

Consider joining ACBS, which the parent organization of ACT and RFT. ACBS membership operates on a system called "voluntary dues." That means you pay whatever you think it's worth. (There is a minimum fee of $1 to join.) If you're not sure you want to join, take a look at what ACBS has to offer at www.contextualpsychology.org.

RFT Tutorial

If you want to learn about RFT, the post-Skinnerian behavioral theory of language and cognition that underlies ACT, then a good starting point is the free online tutorial available at www.contextual psychology.org/rft _ tutorial.

References

Bach, P., & Hayes, S. C. (2002). The use of acceptance and commitment therapy to prevent the rehospitalization of psychotic patients: A randomized controlled trial. *Journal of Consulting & Clinical Psychology, 70,* 1129–1139.

Bach, P., & Moran, D. J. (2008). *ACT in Practice.* Oakland, CA: New Harbinger.

Bond, F. W., & Bunce, D. (2000). Mediators of change in emotion-focused and problem-focused worksite stress management interventions. *Journal of Occupational Health Psychology, 5*(1), 156–163.

Brann, P., Gopold, M., Guymer, E., Morton, J., & Snowdon, S. (2007–09). Forty-session acceptance and commitment therapy group for public-sector mental health service clients with four or more criteria of borderline personality disorder. A program of Spectrum: The Borderline Personality Disorder Service for Victoria (Melbourne, Victoria, Australia).

Branstetter, A. D., Wilson, K. G., Hildebrandt, M., & Mutch, D. (2004, November). Improving psychological adjustment among cancer patients: ACT and CBT. Paper presented at the meeting of the Association for Advancement of Behavior Therapy, New Orleans, LA.

Brown, R. A., Palm, K. M., Strong, D. R., Lejuez, C. W., Kahler, C. W., Zvolensky, M. J., et al., (2008). Distress tolerance treatment for early-lapse smokers: Rationale, program description, and preliminary findings. *Behavior Modification, 32*(3), 302–332.

Dahl, J., Wilson, K. G., & Nilsson, A. (2004). Acceptance and commitment therapy and the treatment of persons at risk for long-term disability resulting from stress and pain symptoms: A preliminary randomized trial. *Behavior Therapy, 35*(4), 785–801.

Dalrymple, K. L., & Herbert, J. D. (2007). Acceptance and commitment therapy for generalized social anxiety disorder: A pilot study. *Behavior Modification, 31,* 543–568.

Eifert, G., & Forsyth, J. P. (2005). *Acceptance and commitment therapy for anxiety disorders.* Oakland, CA: New Harbinger.

Feldner, M., Zvolensky, M., Eifert, G., & Spira, A. (2003). Emotional avoidance: An experimental test of individual differences and response suppression using biological challenge. *Behaviour Research and Therapy, 41*(4), 403–411.

Frankl, V. (1959). *Man's search for meaning.* New York: Simon & Schuster.

Gaudiano, B. A., & Herbert, J. D. (2006). Acute treatment of inpatients with psychotic symptoms using acceptance and commitment therapy: Pilot results. *Behaviour Research and Therapy, 44*(3), 415–437.

Gifford, E. V., Kohlenberg, B. S., Hayes, S. C., Antonuccio, D. O., Piasecki, M. M., Rasmussen-Hall, M. L., et al. (2004). Acceptance theory–based treatment for smoking cessation: An initial trial of acceptance and commitment therapy. *Behavior Therapy, 35,* 689–706.

Gratz, K. L., & Gunderson, J. G. (2006). Preliminary data on an acceptance-based emotion regulation group intervention for deliberate self-harm among women with borderline personality disorder. *Behavior Therapy, 37*(1), 25–35.

Gregg, J. A., Callaghan, G. M., Hayes, S. C., & Glenn-Lawson, J. L. (2007). Improving diabetes self-management through acceptance, mindfulness, and values: A randomized controlled trial. *Journal of Consulting and Clinical Psychology, 75*(2), 336–343.

Harris, R. (2006). Exercise from Russ Harris's Introductory ACT Workshop handout.

Harris, R. (2007). *The happiness trap: Stop struggling, start living.* Wollombi, NSW, Australia: Exisle Publishing.

Harris, R. (2008a). ACT in a Nutshell. E-course from www.thehappinesstrap.com.

Harris, R. (2008b). An Interview with Steven Hayes. *The Happiness Trap Newsletter,* November 2008.

Harris, R. (2009). *ACT with Love.* Oakland, CA: New Harbinger.

Hayes, S. C., Barnes-Holmes, D., & Roche, B. (Eds.). (2001). *Relational frame theory: A post-Skinnerian account of human language and cognition.* New York: Kluwer Academic/ Plenum Publishers.

Hayes, S. C., Bissett, R., Roget, N., Padilla, M., Kohlenberg, B. S., Fisher, G., et al. (2004). The impact of acceptance and commitment training and multicultural training on the stigmatizing attitudes and professional burnout of substance abuse counselors. *Behavior Therapy 35*(4), 821–835.

Hayes, S. C., Bond, F. W., Barnes-Holmes, D., & Austin, J. (2006). *Acceptance and mindfulness at work.* New York: The Haworth Press.

Hayes, S. [C.], Masuda, A., Bissett, R., Luoma, J., & Guerrero, L. F. (2004). DBT, FAP, and ACT: How empirically oriented are the new behavior therapy technologies? *Behavior Therapy, 35,* 35–54.

Hayes, S. C., Strosahl, K. D., & Wilson, K. G. (1999). *Acceptance and commitment therapy: An experiential approach to behavior change.* New York: Guilford Press.

Hayes, S. C., Wilson, K. W., Gifford, E. V., Follette, V. M., & Strosahl, K. (1996). Experiential avoidance and behavioral disorders: A functional dimensional approach to diagnosis and treatment. *Journal of Consulting and Clinical Psychology, 64*(6), 1152–1168.

Kabat-Zinn, J. (1990). *Full catastrophe living.* New York: Dell Publishing.

Lindsley, O. R. (1968). Training parents and teachers to precisely manage children's behavior. Paper presented at the C. S. Mott Foundation Children's Health Center, Flint, MI.

Lundgren, T., Dahl, J., Yardi, N., & Melin, J. (2008). Acceptance and commitment therapy and yoga for drug refractory epilepsy: A randomized controlled trial. *Epilepsy and Behavior, 13*(1), 102–108.

Mandela, N.(1994). *Long walk to freedom.* London: Time Warner Book Group.

Ossman, W. A., Wilson, K. G., Storaasli, R. D., & McNeill, J. W. (2006). A preliminary investigation of the use of acceptance and commitment therapy in group treatment for social phobia. *International Journal of Psychology and Psychological Therapy, 6,* 397-416.

Ramnerö, J., and N. Törneke. (2008). *The ABCs of human behavior: Behavioral principles for the practicing clinician.* Oakland, CA: New Harbinger.

Robinson, P. (2008). Integrating acceptance and commitment therapy into primary pediatric care. In L. A. Greco & S. C. Hayes (Eds.), Acceptance and mindfulness treatments for children and adolescents (pp. 237–261). Oakland, CA: New Harbinger.

Strosahl, K. D. (2004). ACT with the multi-problem client. In Steven C. Hayes & Kirk D. Strosahl (Eds.), *A practical guide to acceptance and commitment therapy* (pp. 209–244). Oakland, CA: New Harbinger.

Strosahl, K. D. (2005, July). Workshop on ACT as a brief therapy. Presented at the ACT Summer Institute, Philadelphia, PA.

Strosahl, K. D., Hayes, S. C., Wilson, K. G., & Gifford, E.V. (2004). An ACT primer. In Steven C. Hayes and Kirk D. Strosahl (Eds.), *A practical guide to acceptance and commitment therapy* (pp. 31–58). Oakland, CA: New Harbinger.

Tapper, K., Shaw, C., Ilsley, J., Hill, A. J., Bond, F. W., & Moore, L. (2009). Exploratory randomised controlled trial of a mindfulness-based weight loss intervention for women. *Appetite, 52,* 396–404.

Titchener, E. B. (1916). *A textbook of psychology.* New York: MacMillan.

Twohig, M. P., Hayes, S. C., & Masuda, A. (2006). Increasing willingness to experience obsessions: Acceptance and commitment therapy as a treatment for obsessive-compulsive disorder. *Behavior Therapy, 37*(1), 3–13.

Walser, R. D., & Westrup, D. (2007). *Acceptance and commitment therapy for the treatment of post-traumatic stress disorder and trauma-related problems.* Oakland, CA: New Harbinger.

Wegner, D. M., Erber, R., & Zanakos, S. (1993). Ironic processes in the mental control of mood and mood-related thought. *Journal of Personality & Social Psychology, 65*(6), 1093–1104.

Wenzlaff, R. M., & Wegner, D. M. (2000). Thought suppression. *Annual Review of Psychology, 51,* 59–91.

Zettle, R. D. (2003). Acceptance and commitment therapy vs. systematic desensitization in treatment of mathematics anxiety. *The Psychological Record, 53*(2), 197–215.

Zettle, R. D. (2007). *ACT for depression.* Oakland, CA: New Harbinger.

Russ Harris is an internationally acclaimed acceptance and commitment therapy (ACT) trainer and author of the ACT-based self-help book, *The Happiness Trap,* now published in over fifteen languages and twenty countries. He is widely renowned for his ability to train therapists in ACT in a way that is clear, accessible, and fun. ·

Foreword writer **Steven C. Hayes, Ph.D.,** is University of Nevada Foundation Professor of Psychology at the University of Nevada, Reno. He is the author of dozens of books and scientific articles, including the successful ACT workbook *Get Out of Your Mind and into Your Life.*

Index

E

F

G

H

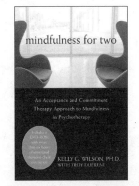

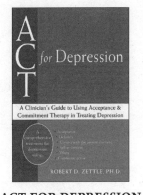